100 *Places in Cuba*
Every Woman Should Go

100 Places in Cuba
Every Woman Should Go

CONNER GORRY

TRAVELERS' TALES
AN IMPRINT OF SOLAS HOUSE, INC.
PALO ALTO

Travelers' Tales and Solas House are trademarks of Solas House, Inc.,
Palo Alto, California. travelerstales.com | solashouse.com

Art Direction: Kimberly Nelson
Cover Design: Kimberly Nelson
Cover Photo: Mariele O'Reilly
Interior Design and Page Layout: Howie Severson/Fortuitous Publishing
Interior Photos: Patricia Harris
Author Photo: Jack Kenny

Image credits: pg. 58: http://laventana.casa.cult.cu/media/zinnia/images
/textoroberto.jpg; pg. 87: Ice Boy Tell; pg. 149: Kirua; pg. 166: Wilder
Mendez / Lezumbalaberenjena at en.wikipedia; pg. 202: John M. Kennedy T.
(restoration work based on public domain old sources); pg. 215: Axelode

Library of Congress Cataloging-in-Publication Data is available upon request

ISBN 978-1-60952-129-5 (paperback)
ISBN 978-1-60952-130-1 (ebook)
ISBN 978-1-60952-167-7 (hard cover)

First Edition
Printed in the United States
10 9 8 7 6 5 4 3 2 1

For Sandra Gorry, world traveler and
Mom Extraordinaire, who encouraged me from
a very young age to "live your dreams."

*Cubans—all of them, male or female, young or old,
rich or poor, have so much charm, that one can be
lenient about their faults. Yes, charm is the national
industry, all right. To be simpático is as natural
and as necessary to a Cuban as breathing.*

—Consuelo Hermer and Marjorie May
*Havana Mañana: A Guide to Cuba
and the Cubans* (1941)

Table of Contents

SECTION II
MUSIC, ARTS, & LETTERS

SECTION III
POPULAR IN THE PROVINCES

SECTION IV
TRAVEL WITH NIÑOS & NIÑAS—OF ALL AGES

SECTION VII
BEST BEACHES

SECTION VIII
FESTIVALS, FIESTAS, & EVENTS

Introduction

Cuba is like licorice or reggaetón: you love it or hate it. Sound extreme? Maybe, but not to those who know the island—a place fueled by melodrama and gossip (what I call the national sport), plus burning hot passions from baseball and tattoos to illicit trysts and ice cream. For such a lively, colorful country, the Cuban palette skews heavily towards black and white when it comes to outlook and opinions. Descended from globetrotting Spaniards, swashbuckling pirates, and strong, brave African slaves, with some Chinese, Haitians, and French thrown in for good measure, Cubans are among the most resilient, rhythmic, humorous, and yes, extreme people I've met in my travels. This "in-your-face, take-it-or-leave-it" attitude is refreshing in our passive/aggressive, PC world—invigorating even—but can be frustrating to the point of tears as well, believe me. Sometimes I'm loving *and* hating this place at the same time.

My Spanish was pretty shoddy when I arrived in Havana on a hotter-than-Hades afternoon in 1993 to volunteer along-side Cubans in the countryside, and I didn't speak a word of Cuban—a Spanish vernacular unto itself. Slowly, like a five-year old learning the alphabet and butchering basic rules of grammar, I started to drop the final letters of words and incorporate the Spanglish peculiar to this island, which has been occupied militarily, culturally, and politically to some degree by the USA

for centuries. Take language, for instance. Here, laundry deter-
gent is called "Fa," for Fab, the brand favored by Cuban housewives before the Revolution; a double in baseball is a "two base"
(pronounced "tu bay"); and a beer is universally called a "lager."
Facebook, meanwhile, which is taking the island by storm, is
known as "Feisbu." Another peculiarity of the Cuban idiom
is the liberal use of terms and phrases that traveled with the
1.3 million slaves forced to these shores from Nigeria, Angola,
Benin, Sierra Leone, Ghana, and elsewhere; by 1841, almost 45
percent of the island's population were enslaved blacks, complemented by another 10 percent of free blacks. A day won't pass
without you hearing "*Asere! Qué bolá?!*" in the streets, a phrase
with African roots. The equivalent of "Hey man! What's up?,"
Cubans went wild when President Obama threw it out during his
historic visit to the island in March 2016.

It's not only the local lingo that can drive you *loco*. The two
currency system is maddening at first but becomes second nature
after a little practice—and is a great way to jump into daily life
here; when you see a pineapple costs $10, that's *moneda nacional*,
also known as MN, *pesos cubanos*, and CUP (four interchange-
able names for one currency; talk about confusing!). The other
money, the so-called hard currency, is the Convertible Cuban
Peso and has even more monikers: CUC, "kooks," *divisa, fula,
caña*. Many people, yours truly included, still refer to CUCs as
dollars—a holdover from when USD was the hard currency used
here. Plans to unify the CUC and CUP, announced more than
six years ago, have yet to be realized and seem a long way off given
Cuba's perennial economic crisis. Until the ship can be righted
and the currencies united, that 10 CUP pineapple costs about
35 cents CUC at the official exchange rate.

Transportation is another realm fraught with frustration since schedules for local bus departures and routes are non-existent, long-distance bus tickets must be bought in person and often sell out, train travel is only for hardy folk with time to burn, and planes on domestic routes are often grounded or re-routed due to mechanical problems. Nevertheless, when you approach a Cuba trip with good will and humor, remain open to serendipity—a very real and useful travel tool here—and embrace the classic axiom, "It's the journey, not the destination," you're sure to have transformative, perhaps even transcendental experiences.

Two recent encounters drove this home and to the heart. On a brilliant sunny Havana day, a young woman walked up to me and two Cuban friends outside the arrivals area of José Martí International Airport. Traveling solo and carrying one small knapsack and a body full of tattoos, Olivia asked if we'd be willing to share a taxi into the city center. Traveling alone, light, and on a budget, willing to approach strangers with a question and offer: Olivia was my kind of traveler. We said we would take her ourselves, but had arrived by motorcycle with sidecar and were full up. *Sin problema*, we told the young woman from New Orleans who had only a single hour of Cuba experience under her belt, no map or Spanish, and nowhere to stay: we'd help her figure it out. While my friend Ana got on her cell and rang up her casa particular contacts, José approached a fellow in a mint sky blue 1956 Chevrolet, asking if he was looking for a fare. Within 15 minutes, Olivia had a cheap, cool ride directly to an affordable, centrally located home where the English-speaking hosts awaited her with a frosty lager. We ran into her later that week and she told us she was having the trip of a lifetime; her story may have turned out differently were it not for her moxie.

Shortly thereafter I met Jim, Blake, Kevin, and Jeff, four bros from New York who came to Havana on a quick whim of a trip. On Day 2, Kevin tumbled into the sea after slipping on the moss-slickened rocks at the Morro-Cabaña. He surfaced quickly, holding his iPhone above the water as his friends fished him out. They made their way back to their casa and began hunting for raw rice in which to plunge the phone overnight in an effort to salvage it—a trick that works, I've found. Night had fallen by this time; they didn't know where to buy rice and no stores (let alone bodegas, where most Cubans get their rice) were open. The quartet popped into a restaurant and in broken Spanish asked one of the waiters if he would sell them some rice. A diner overheard their conversation, rose from the table where he was sharing dinner with his family, took the guys to his home, gave them some rice (refusing payment, of course), and invited them back the next day for some coffee and conversation. They were thrilled and so was I: here were four dudes whose Cuba trip could have been filled with a classic car tour, mojitos, *jineteras* looking for tricks on the Malecón, and getting sick on Cohibas. Instead, they embraced serendipity, solidarity, and the spirit of experiential travel. I don't know if they ever got the iPhone working, but I know they made indelible travel memories.

For female travelers, Cuba can be a jumble of contradictions vacillating between machismo and chivalry, honesty and grift, hordes of admirers and moments of loneliness. Solo travelers, especially, can have a hard time meeting other like-minded foreigners since connection opportunities are few and far between: the hostel concept is virtually unknown and there are no "expat" bars or hangouts like you find elsewhere. While there are Wi-Fi parks across the island where you can befriend other foreigners, many visitors prefer to embrace the off-line culture still prevalent in Cuba—especially since Donald Trump became US President. Then there's what Rebecca Solnit calls "Manistan" in her book *Men Explain Things to Me* and I call "Macholandia"—a republic unto itself where men are all-knowing and too sexy for their own bad selves. As one expat friend recently observed: "There's entirely too much testosterone on this island." This machismo often manifests itself in sexual innuendo, regardless of age difference, race, size, origin or sexual orientation: he's 80 and you're 25? He'll make a stab at it. You say you're gay? He'll say you've never had the right man. Old travel tricks are likewise ineffective: wearing a wedding ring—or even traveling with your actual husband!—won't deter Cuban men from open propositions, brazen come-ons, and practicing the local custom of *piropos*. Loosely translated as "flirty compliments," these run the gamut from creative to gross, fall-on-the-floor hilarious to seriously disrespectful. One of my all-time favorites was when a man pedaled by on a Flying Pigeon (1 million of these Chinese bikes were imported during the economic crash of the 1990s known as the Special Period) saying: "Your name must be Alice because looking at you sends me to Wonderland." On the flip-side, I was walking Toby in the park last week when a guy said to me: "*Ay mami*, put that leash and collar around my neck, let me be your dog!" Less endearing and not at all appealing. If you don't speak Spanish, *piropos* are easier to pay no mind, but many times it's just a sexually charged hissing sound—much harder to ignore. If your hackles jump at every *piropo* thrown your way, it can get oppressive.

Given this scenario, it can come as a surprise at how empowered Cuban women and girls are. In some ways, the history of Cuba reads like a feminist tract, partly explaining this seeming contradiction. Machete-wielding women known as *mambisas* galloped into battle during the Second (and definitive) War of Independence, gaining fame for their valor and determination. Women played a definitive role throughout the Revolution as well, though you wouldn't necessarily know it from the image of bearded guerrillas descending victoriously from the mountains projected by the international media. As Julia Sweig states in *Cuba: What Everyone Needs to Know*, "Behind the macho bravado that captured Cuba and the world's attention were a host of extraordinarily brave and talented women who made survival and success possible." Indeed, there were history-makers like Melba Hernández and Haydeé Santamaría, the only women who fought in the attack on the Moncada Barracks, the seminal event in the nascent revolution; Celia Sánchez, who took to the Sierra Maestra, rifle in hand, alongside Fidel, Che, Raúl, and the rest; and Vilma Espín, who organized forces in the city—she would go on to marry Raúl Castro and lead the charge on policy changes related to gender parity and rights until her death in 2007. Nevertheless, the binary gender paradigm is still deeply rooted here—cooking, cleaning, and child rearing are mostly the purview of women, while men play sports, fix cars, and take out the garbage. Never mind that women make up 69 percent of the professional workforce, more than 60 percent of scientists with advanced degrees are women, and the emerging private sector is full of entrepreneurial females: restaurateurs, designers, and yes, even bike mechanics and metal workers. Like most things in Cuba, or anywhere for that matter, you take the good with the bad and this island, the biggest in the Caribbean, has much more of the former than the latter. Importantly: from the cities to the countryside, Cuba is a very safe travel destination overall, no matter your gender.

This island, too often falsely characterized as "stuck in time" or "preserved in amber," is in constant evolution and these days, changing fast. There are many reasons for this rapid transformation, some more evident than others, such as the arrival of (for Cubans) new technologies including cell phones, internet and Wi-Fi, and digital television. Another major factor is the ongoing economic reform package known as the *Lineamientos*. Set in motion in 2010, these far-reaching reforms permit Cubans to buy and sell their homes and cars legally for the first time since 1959; relaxed travel restrictions for Cubans including doing away with the exit permit previously required and allowing residents to remain off-island for two years; and made it possible to open private businesses. This has injected new energy into daily life and spurred creativity and productivity in a land where blinking Christmas lights used to be the height of marketing and it was impossible to find food after 11 P.M. Today, there are 24-hour restaurants, Cubans of means bar hop until daybreak, private galleries host frequent openings, public transport options are varied, and you can have your iPhone repaired while copying the latest Netflix and FX series onto your hard drive. This is a breath of fresh air for Cubans with the resources to launch and patronize these businesses but a nasty taunt for the two out of three people who work for the state, the majority of whom earn the average monthly salary of \$29CUC—and can only dream of owning a smart phone or cutting into a steak.

The other dramatic change affecting lives across the island is tourism. In 2017, international arrivals broke records, with more than 4 million visitors choosing Cuba for their foreign vacation. This has deposited over 3 billion dollars in government coffers, with revenues going to national programs including the universal health and education systems, infrastructure upkeep, and massive development projects like the new port and industrial zone at Mariel. Nevertheless, the country has been caught unprepared, with the sudden influx of visitors causing shortages of hotel rooms and transport; onerous lines at immigration, baggage claim, and money changers at airports (Havana is particularly bad); and a distortion of the local economy. Known as the "inverted pyramid," where a taxi driver, guide, casa owner, or anyone working in tourism makes more than a neuro-surgeon, lawyer, or engineer, it's something talked about all the time—from the street to the highest levels of government. Throughout my 1,800-plus mile road trip exploring the 100 places in this book, Cubans were incredibly vocal about the problems created by tourism and how it's affecting their daily lives. In Trinidad, where every other house rents to foreigners and makes sure they have a bountiful breakfast, Rogelio told me: "A pineapple costs 25 pesos here—when you can find them. Before I got three for that price." He went on to lament how the vegetable market was stripped bare last time he went to buy produce to feed his family. On the other side of the island, Alicia from seaside Yumurí explained what's happening in her hometown: "We've always lived off whatever we could catch—octopus, lobster, and fish. But tourists can pay more and fresh fish now costs 35 pesos a pound; on my fixed income, I can't afford it."

The upshot? The tourism boom is creating a 1 percent in Cuba, a layer of the (relatively) super rich, while triggering a brain drain from the state to the private sector. In whatever context, this is unsustainable. Then there's the environmental impact of 4 million visitors drinking bottled water, using air conditioning with abandon (most Cubans don't have AC in their homes), and arriving on cruise ships or staying in all-inclusive resorts—two modes of travel with debatable benefits for the host country and proven disadvantages for the environment. Obviously, this is a two-way street and for the most part,

Cubans are not environmentally conscious (you will see beer cans tossed from car windows during your visit), all of which argues for meaningful exchange and mutual learning between visitors and locals to help sustain the beauty of this unique country. All these issues form part of the national dialogue in today's Cuba. According to Cuban journalist and historian Graziella Pogolotti, "For a country like ours, lacking in great mining wealth, tourism is a source of income of indisputable importance. The challenge is to devise strategies that enhance the possibilities of development in favor of the nation, culturally and humanly, because in the virtues of our people lies the soul of the nation." Maintaining the health of that soul tops the agenda moving forward. For now, Alicia's resigned smile while she explains astronomic fish prices, Rogelio tickling his two-year old granddaughter as he dreams of an affordable pineapple, Olivia walking Havana on a shoestring budget, eyes and heart wide open, and Kevin and company sharing stories in the home of a Cuban gentleman, are helping buoy the "soul of the nation." Every tourism-dependent economy faces similarly complex challenges and I certainly don't have any facile solutions for how to resolve them (especially given the internal, very Cuban contradictions exacerbating them), but I do know that raising awareness is a first step. By picking up this book, you're embarking on a journey of discovery, of places to go in Cuba, of course, but also an exploration of what makes this place tick, the currents flowing beneath the surface, and the vulnerabilities faced by a nation emerging into a new era.

The election of US President Trump also ushered Cuba into a new era—or thrust it back into an older one predating the Obama thaw between the United States and its island neighbor to the south. For travelers holding US residency or citizenship reading this, it's important to note that there have been no "substantive changes to the legal categories of travel," according to expert embargo lawyer Lindsay Frank during a Havana press conference in January 2018. And what's more, during the 2017 Madrid Travel Show, Cuba was elected as the safest country in the world to travel.

Neither licorice nor reggaetón excites my senses, but Cuba does—every day. I hope it does the same for you, whether you're reading this from your favorite armchair or Varadero lounge chair, on a porch in Viñales or riding the bus to Baracoa.

CONNER GORRY
HAVANA

I

Havana Good Time

1

El Prado

SINCE 1772, THIS BREEZY BOULEVARD lined with marble benches and antique iron streetlamps has been a destination for *habaneros* looking to escape overcrowded conditions in Habana Vieja and Centro Habana—the two neighborhoods bifurcated by the Prado—for an evening stroll, a lunchtime tryst or to conduct a bit of informal business. It's reminiscent of a European boulevard with good reason—Madrid's Prado and Barcelona's Ramblas were used as blueprints for Havana's famous promenade. Over the years, various additions and renovations beautified this popular public space but it

wasn't until renowned landscape architect Jean-Claude Nicolas Forestier lent his vision to the Prado, adding the bronze lions guarding its entrance near Parque Central and the sorely-needed shade trees, that it achieved the elegance it exudes today. Forestier had a heavy hand in shaping modern Havana, having designed parts of the University of Havana, Parque Almendares and other iconic spots around town. Along with the Malecón (where the boulevard leads), there is no better place to watch the pulse and swirl of the city and its inhabitants than the Prado.

The pastime provides free and ripe opportunity to meet and greet—until it's closed to the public, something which occurred when Karl Lagerfeld and the House of Chanel presented their cruise wear collection along the Prado in 2016. After centuries of being a place of respite and recreation for *habaneros*, suddenly it was off limits. While it provided work for some Cubans and those living right on the boulevard rented space on their balconies for $10CUC a head, not everyone was on board (pun intended!) with the program. This came right on the heels of the *Fast and Furious 8* filming in Havana where people were kept from walking their streets and accessing their homes during the shoot. In his 2017 book *Cuba-US Relations: Obama and Beyond*, Cubanologist Arnold August categorizes these two events (and many more) as "hipster imperialism," a phenomenon that brings the global entertainment economy in conflict with Cuban values—in this case, access to public places. Rubbing salt into the wound is the fact that Cubans are huge movie buffs and *fashionistas*; they wanted to see all the wonderful clothing and perhaps snap a selfie with Vin Diesel. Still, the Hollywood/Parisian road show came and went and the Prado quickly returned to its normal rhythm.

On weekends, the entire promenade is flanked with artists selling their work, creating new ones and giving classes to local kids in painting, drawing, ceramics, and photography. On Saturdays, a semblance of Cuba's system of trading houses is in full swing. Before buying and selling of homes was legalized in 2011, the only way for an individual to acquire a different home was to trade theirs with someone else. Known as the *"permuta,"* it was a long, laborious process (two years looking and finagling was not uncommon) with much jumping through hoops to find an available, appropriate house, pay some money under the table to cover the difference ("legitimate but not legal" as my professor friend says) and process the transfer of title and other paperwork.

※

Se Permuta, a full-length comedy by notable Cuban director Juan Carlos Tabío, is full of social commentary and insight.

※

Things have changed mightily since then—Havana is now peppered with real estate agencies sporting banks of computers and agents ready to pull up multiple listings across all neighborhoods with detailed descriptions and full-color photos. But the *permuta* system still works; you can see the old school action on the stretch of the Prado near Hotel Sevilla.

2 Las Plazas of Habana Vieja

SPANISH CONQUISTADORES WERE LUKEWARM ON the crocodile-shaped island that Columbus stumbled upon in 1492, foiled in their attempts to find the motherlodes of gold, the apocryphal El Dorado, which drove many a conquistador to ruin. They gave short shrift to the Antilles' biggest island as a result, preferring to run roughshod over Hispaniola and Mexico, where the streets were supposedly paved with precious metals. Early explorers even failed to agree on what to call the island: before settling on Cuba, a bastardization of an indigenous name upon which experts can't agree, it was known as Juana, Fernandina, San Diego, and Ave Maria Alfa y Omega. Where to settle Cuba's capital was also an improvised, uncertain affair, skipping from Santiago de Cuba to Batabanó, before San Cristóbal de la Habana was founded in 1519. Swampy, and prone to mosquito swarms and flooding, Havana wasn't the ideal spot, but boasted a deep, navigable bay which proved highly attractive to Spanish sugar barons who berthed their galleons to offload slaves and packed the holds with sugar, getting filthy rich in the process. The geographical location, of course, was also perfect for pirates. The boom you hear each night at 9 p.m. sharp is the *cañonazo* (the cannon shot), a holdover from those days when the bay was closed to all boat traffic, a giant chain strung across the entry.

Habana Vieja, the colonial city that sprung up and spread like herpes in a whorehouse—quickly, virally, indiscriminately—is now a UNESCO World Heritage Site and Cuba's #1 tourist destination. People from all over the world come to ogle its spectacular colonial palaces, walk its cobblestone streets, and explore its beautiful (and not so) nooks and crannies. Managing a visit to Habana Vieja can be a bear—there are too many tourists for the too narrow streets, often trailed by aggressive hustlers (*jineteros* in local lingo) and what real life looks like is best appreciated off the beaten track and away from the carefully restored sections. The three best tips I have for folks wanting to experience this part of town with minimum hassle is: don't book your accommodation here (it's dead at night and you'll be besieged by hustlers as soon as you step out the door); hail a bici-taxi for a cheap, backstreet tour; and spend a morning hopping from one beautiful plaza to another.

✻

Cuba has seven cultural and two natural sites
on the UNESCO World Heritage list. Check it
out: whc.unesco.org/en/statesparties/cu.

✻

My favorite of all is Plaza Vieja, a wide-open square lined with colonnaded buildings hiding interesting sites. There's a luthier workshop, Fototeca (the national photo gallery), Cuba's only camera obscura providing live, 360° views of the neighborhood—sheets flapping on the line, dogs wagging their tails—and various places to appreciate the best in Cuban contemporary art, including the Centro de Desarrollo de las Artes Visuales, a fine art gallery housed in a beautiful colonial mansion. For good people watching and refreshments, there's a microbrewery on one corner of the plaza and a cafe on another—the whole bean coffee here makes a special gift or souvenir; both places have outside tables. Heading northeast, you hit Plaza de San Francisco de Asis, nicknamed "pigeon plaza" by Cubans who like to come here and whip the birds into a feeding frenzy around the central fountain. Anchoring this irregularly shaped plaza is the Lonja de Comercio, a luxurious office building housing international press bureaus, joint ventures, and apartments like you might find in Manhattan. Looking up is always a good way to pull back the veil on Havana's charms: across the plaza is the Basilica de San Francisco de Asis, built in 1719 and adorned with one of the highest bell towers—it flirts with 125 feet—in the hemisphere. Once the house of worship for the city's elite, these days the Basilica is a classical concert hall and headquarters of Ars Longa, the national baroque orchestra. International musicians are often invited to play here and if you get the chance to attend a performance among the gilded angels and the fabulous *trompe l'oeil* backdrop, grab it. Guarding the entrance here is a statue of the Caballero de Paris, a brilliant, but tormented fellow who wandered the streets of Habana Vieja reciting prose and poetry, dying in poverty but immortalized in bronze. Stroking his beard and making a wish is a Havana tradition long observed, which is why it shines so brightly.

A few blocks north is the Plaza de Armas. Originally established in 1582, it's the oldest square in Cuba. Among its quirky attributes is the only wooden street in Havana (in front of the Museo de la Ciudad), the antique book bazaar ringing the central park, and the statue of La Giraldilla, the symbol of Havana crowning the ornate roof of the Castillo de la Real Fuerza (and emblazoned on every bottle of Havana Club rum); this is the hemisphere's oldest colonial fort. On the northeast corner of this plaza is El Templete, a neo-classical pantheon celebrating the place where Havana was founded in 1519. In reality, the ceiba tree—an important symbol to Cubans the world over—spreading its crown over El Templete is what actually marks the spot of the first mass in Havana and the founding of the city. But like much in Cuba, even this symbolic tree is a trick: city authorities have cut down and replanted ceibas here repeatedly, as recently as 2016 when the previous tree was confirmed to be termite-infested (the metaphor was not lost on locals). No matter for superstitious Cubans married to their traditions: every November 16, people stand in line for hours to take three turns around the tree, intoning wishes for health, wealth, or a visa. Finally, two blocks northeast of here is the Plaza de la Catedral, site of Havana's baroque cathedral, built between 1748 and 1787. It's prettiest at night, when the crowds slip away and the unequal towers and facade are softly lit. At other times, it's clogged with tourists snapping photos of Cuban women smoking cigars so tourists will snap photos of them (for a fee) and people making their way to El Bodeguita del Medio for an overpriced, watered-down mojito. For me, the most interesting places to visit around this plaza are the Taller Experimental de Gráfica (see Chapter 19) in a small alley off the southwestern corner where Cuban printmakers are hard at work creating under bright lights, the air thick with the smell of ink and sweat, and the Centro Wilfredo Lam (headquarters of the Bienal de la Habana; see Chapter 8), a contemporary art gallery named for and featuring Cuba's most celebrated artist. Known in art circles as a "tropical surrealist," Lam is the quintessential Cuban mongrel—an exotic mix of Chinese, African, and Criollo (those of Spanish descent born in Cuba). I'm surprised there isn't a cocktail named after him. Having one of the best galleries in the city bearing his name is honor enough.

3 La Loma del Ángel

LA HABANA VIEJA—LITERALLY OLD HAVANA, the first permanent settlement in the city, dating from 1519—is the number one tourist attraction in the country, though I predict its status will be challenged by Fidel Castro's grave in Santa Ifigenia cemetery in Santiago de Cuba (see Chapter 71). Wandering the cobblestone streets linking colonial plazas, each one more picturesque than the last, is a lesson in history; branch off and out of the painstakingly restored areas (what Cuban's call "Disneyland" for obvious reasons) and into the 'hood, however, and an entirely different world unfolds. Here, laundry hangs listlessly from balconies held up by wooden scaffolding, chunks of mortar crash to the sidewalk too often, shirtless men crowd tables under streetlamps shouting as they slap down dominos, and exhausted housewives haul buckets of water to third floor apartments via a rope and pulley system. In this part of town, running water is only available every other day, few people have air conditioning, and the daily struggle is defined by how families are going to put food on the table. In short, Habana Vieja is a tale of two cities. For insight into the historical context that has resulted in the grand contradictions evident today—luxurious colonial palaces next to falling down tenements; well-heeled Cubans and tourists sidestepping mounds of household garbage; the sound of lobster sizzling on the grill mixing with the knife sharpener's peal—the area known as La Loma del Ángel, behind the Iglesia del Santo Ángel Custodio (1847), is a good place to start.

Just a handful of years ago, this pocket neighborhood exemplified the dichotomy of modern-day Havana, with boarded up state stores and bakeries cheek-by-jowl with new colonizers including moneyed artists and designers, huge potholes in streets running alongside freshly painted homes, and nary a tourist in sight. Some people would venture to the church where José Martí was baptized and where the first (and to date, still most famous) novel exploring interracial dynamics, *Cecilia Valdés* (1882) is set, but few ventured beyond.

*

Cecilia Valdes by Cirilo Villaverde is the story of a
beautiful mulatta and her star-crossed romance
with a young white man of means, who
unbeknownst to either, is her half-brother.

*

Today, the little hillside neighborhood of La Loma del Ángel is a tourist attraction. The cobblestone streets are completely repaired and closed to traffic, little sidewalk cafés with chic umbrellas serve crepes and fruit salads, there are no lack of artists' studios where visitors can browse and buy, and the cultural events organized by Papito and ArteCorte (see Chapter 42, Playgrounds, for other initiatives by this socially responsible business) are a spontaneous carnival. Just a few blocks outside of this enclave is where the real Habana Vieja lives.

4 El Capitolio

AS THE BEST-PRESERVED HISTORICAL CITY in the Americas, Habana Vieja is chock full of gorgeous buildings inside and out. Dating from the 16th century through the early 20th, some are in disrepair or falling down, more are downright crumbling, while many others gleam. Others still seem to be undergoing perpetual renovation. File under this last category the Capitol building. Anyone from the United States will feel an eerie déjà-vu beholding the Capitolio—it was modeled on the US Capitol and looks like a carbon copy, albeit flanked by palm trees, its marble plazas a beehive of activity with skateboarding kids, peanut sellers and photographers. Before construction began on this monumental public work, this was a military parade ground, a bullfighting ring, a botanical garden, and train station—the city's first.

As soon as the first shovel hit the dirt, the Capitolio project was beset with problems, from the cost ($20 million US, all told), to accidents and delays—ground was broken in 1912, but the building wasn't finished until 1929. According to Claudia Lightfoot in her exquisitely researched book *Cities of the Imagination: Havana*, "a large slice of the $20 million disappeared in graft and straightforward theft....one politician's house, now the Museo Napoleónico in Vedado, was supposedly entirely built from materials filched from the site." Patterns set in motion a century ago still hold strong: the refurbishment of the Museo de la Música (a building of eclectic styles dating from 1902) has been ongoing for more than a decade and many neighbors have improved their living spaces with materials from the construction site. The Capitolio itself has been undergoing renovations since 2012 (who knows in that time how many resources have been "detoured," as Cubans say) and was opened to visitors as this book went to print. Insiders tell me it's spectacular and that the time to see it is now while the renovation is fresh and accessible to the public—word on the street is that this building, long the headquarters of the Ministry of Science,

Technology, and the Environment, will once again house the Parliament once the renovation is finally finished.

Everything about the Capitolio is over-the-top extravagant, from the grand marble staircase guiding people inside to its 300-foot high dome. The Statue of the Republic guarding the entrance hallway is enormous, weighing 49 tons and covered entirely in 22-carat gold leaf. It's almost 65 feet tall and if the statistics are credible, it's among the largest indoor statues in the world. If there was any doubt about Cubans' propensity for flaunting their wealth and gains, no matter how ill-gotten, the Capitolio dispels it—quickly. No expense was spared in the construction and decor here. Says Cuban historian Ciro Bianchi, the diamond embedded in the floor (known as Kilometer 0— from this point all distances in Cuba are measured), is from the crown of the last Russian czar. What Bianchi doesn't mention is that the diamond was stolen under mysterious circumstances—further providing evidence for the Cuban grift and graft stereotype that's so pervasive. Ironically, the two statues flanking the stairway entrance are entitled "Labor" and "Virtue." The czar's diamond eventually graced the desk of President Grau. Today, the real gem is kept in a bank vault—or so they say. The Salon de los Pasos Perdidos (the Room of the Lost Steps, so called because the cavernous hall plays acoustic tricks on visitors, their footsteps being swallowed in their wake), with its arched, gilded ceiling and geometric marble floors, is breathtaking. I admit I'm a sucker for libraries—my first job out of university was at the San Francisco Public Library and I've had a romantic interlude or two in some closed stacks—but the one here will make even the hardest of heart swoon. It can all be a bit overwhelming and give you a stiff neck admiring all the friezes and finery; when you need a break, head to the tranquil interior garden, a hidden oasis few know about.

5

Gran Teatro de la Habana Alicia Alonso

PEOPLE TALK ABOUT "DOWNTOWN" HAVANA, which is a misnomer; asking a local how to get to downtown or the "city center" is met with a question mark written across their face. Havana turns on different axes, so "center" or "downtown" depends on your perspective. There's Vedado, which for many young Cubans, is the center of all the action; there's Habana Vieja, where tourists spend the most time (and money) and where Havana was founded 500 years ago, so technically could be considered downtown; and what about Centro Habana? Sure, central figures in the name of the city's grittiest and liveliest of neighborhoods, but even Cubans can't agree precisely where it ends and Habana Vieja begins. But there's a center-of-the-Cuban-universe feeling provided by sitting on a shady bench in Parque Central, taking in the 1950s cars honking the *Godfather* theme, eavesdropping on the fellas debating the latest in baseball (known as the *"esquina caliente,"* the hot corner, this is a park highlight), and sneaking sidelong glances at the "Rastafarians"—in quotes because dreadlocks do not a rasta make. The center of the park is anchored by an iconic statue of "the Cuban apostle," José Martí and directly across the street is one of the jewels in Havana's architectural crown: the Gran Teatro de la Habana.

This theater has been the headquarters of the Ballet Nacional de Cuba since 1959, taking a brief (for Cuba) recess during renovations concluded in 2014. Upon re-opening, it was renamed the Gran Teatro de la Habana Alicia Alonso, but people still call it simply, the Gran Teatro or the Lorca—shorthand for the Sala García Lorca, the 1500-seat theater where main events are held. The building facade is a poem cast in stone, marble and bronze, exquisitely lit at night, with soaring sculptures representing Theatre, Music, Education, and Charity. Its majesty can be a bit overwhelming and stands as testament to the roots and power of Spanish wealth and influence in Cuba: inaugurated in 1915 after a major overhaul, this was once the Palacio del Centro Gallego, the social club and welcome wagon for transplanted Spaniards. Prior to the Spanish renovation, this space housed the Teatro Tacón, which opened in 1838 with a performance of Verdi's opera *Aida*; since then, the list of luminaries who have tread the boards here is long, including Andres Segovia, Ernesto Lecuona, Eliades Ochoa, and of course, Alicia Alonso.

The renovations put a completely new face on the theater, which was in dire need. The facade was scrubbed clean of decades of Havana filth, the ceiling frescoes restored, new seats were installed and the floors now sparkle; the grand ballroom upstairs sits empty, but it's easy to imagine the Spanish upper crust waltzing around the marble dance floor, peeking at eligible bachelors behind a flirty wave of a fan. There are some interesting sculptures up here and photography opportunities galore, thanks to the wall of windows wrapping around the corner. There are daily tours with a lethargic docent short on facts, but getting access to the renovated spaces and the art gallery upstairs make it worth the $5CUC. The theater re-do included the inauguration of an attached restaurant—Café Intermezzo and the theater's La Cava is a wonderful place to get a post-performance glass of wine. During intermission, your best bet is to slip into the back bar accessible through a side door inside the theater, a local secret. After dance performances, the ballerinas often have a beer here.

6 *Asociación Yoruba de Cuba*

ONE OF CUBA'S DISTINGUISHING CULTURAL features is the omni-presence of Afro-Cuban religions and their adherents: offer-ings to the saints can be found strewn around town, and the hypnotic thumping of drums used to invoke the deities heard for blocks. Born out of necessity (like much in Cuba), slaves were prevented from practicing their religion, but were permitted to keep and play their drums. In order to continue worship-ping their saints or *orishas* without incurring even more mental and physical abuse from their overlords and other authorities, they masked their native beliefs by overlaying these *orishas* with saints from the Catholic canon. Similar syncretic systems exist in Brazil (*candomblé*) and Haiti (*vodou*).

One of the most striking manifestations of the practice of Yoruba, Santería, Ifá, and other faiths falling under the rubric of Afro-Cuban religions, are initiates clad in white from head to toe—down to their parasols, Bic lighters, and iPhones. You'll see children as young as two years old dressed as initiates. The rites for initiation are strict and last a year. Technically. Cubans are born rule breakers so many tend to view the rules and rites as suggestions rather than dictums. You will also see people already initiated wearing the beaded necklaces in the colors of their saints (white and red, the colors of Changó, and blue and white, those of Yemayá, are common). Several Havana sites are regular spots for making offerings and supplications to the *ori-shas*, including the Bosque de la Habana in Parque Almendares, La Puntilla in Miramar, and along the coast at 1ra and 36A, also in Miramar. Folks walking around town toting chickens or baby goats are on their way to make their offerings.

According to Cuba's syncretized nomenclature, Saint Barbara is Yemayá, while Saint Lazarus is Babalú Ayé. The best place to learn about how this all works is the Asociación Yoruba de Cuba, a museum and cultural center dedicated to Afro-Cuban religions. There are altars to each *orisha* explaining a bit of the creation myths behind each, with which Catholic saint they are related, and what offerings they prefer and why. You can hire a guide (likely only Spanish-speaking) at the museum and they have regular *tambores*, drum ceremonies, where it's not uncommon for a practitioner to

fall into trance and start speaking in tongues. A visit to this museum gives a great overview of the religions and is complemented well by a visit to the black Virgin housed in the Iglesia de Nuestra Señora in Regla. You can have your shells read here and buy flowers to offer to the virgin, who represents Yemayá in the Afro-Cuban canon. Another opportunity to see the mixture of beliefs as they play out in the Cuban context is to join the pilgrimage to El Rincón each December 17th, Saint Lazarus day. On the *orishas'* holy days—June 29 (Oggun), September 7 (Yemayá), 8 (Oshun), and 24 (Obatalá)—there are ceremonies, known as *toques del santo* all over town. The syncopated drumming is hypnotic and runs all night long on these days; you can only enter if you are specifically invited. If you receive an invitation, take it.

7 *Barrio Chino (Chinatown)*

WEALTHY LANDOWNERS—GROWING COFFEE, tobacco, and sugar, primarily—saw the writing on the wall and had already begun supplementing slave labor with cheap workers from abroad when the trade was officially abolished in 1867. The first wave was Maya from the Yucatán, followed by a huge influx of Chinese—some 130,000 arrived on Cuban shores in the 20-year period between 1853 and 1874. This so-called "coolie trade" was hardly more humane than the slave trade from Africa it replaced, and Chinese laborers were treated like chattel on the sugar plantations, but over time, a unique miscegenation emerged that today reaches beyond Cuba's borders. If you've ever eaten at a Chinese-Cuban restaurant (New York and Miami are full of them), it's a result of this centuries-old mixture. Slowly but surely, Chinese immigrants assimilated into Cuban society, mingling with freed blacks and Creoles (those of Spanish heritage born in Cuba) creating a new ethnic mix. Anyone with eyes even slightly almond-shaped is nicknamed "*chino*" here, something that fiercely irks foreigners of other Asian origins when the 100th Cuban yells out "*Hola chino!*"

The Chinese in Cuba retained their traditions and culture to the extent that you'll see groups of elders practicing Tai Chi in parks, kids taking martial arts classes in school yards, and big, multi-colored dragons snaking through the crowd at the annual May Day parade. In recent years, strengthened ties between

Cuba and China have led to a wave of Chinese specialists working on engineering, mining, and other projects and thousands of Chinese students matriculating at Cuban universities.

The first stop for getting a glimpse at Cuba's Chinese community is Barrio Chino—Chinatown. In the preface to *Barrio Chino de la Habana: Imagen del Tiempo*, by Italian photographer Giuseppe Lo Bartolo, Cuban writer Jaime Saruski gets right to the point: "forget everything by way of comparisons with other Chinese communities such as that of Vancouver, South East Asia, of Latin America and the Chinatowns of San Francisco and New York. If you don't, you will lose yourself in a labyrinth of questions without answers." In other words: manage expectations, keep an open mind, and you'll be pleasantly surprised.

The official entrance to Havana's Chinatown is at the intersection of Dragones and Galeano streets and is heralded with a spectacular green and red gate, which belies how small the neighborhood is (many Chinese Cubans left in the 1960s, once the socialist bent of the revolution was confirmed). Indeed, most activity swirls around the "Cuchillo," literally the "knife," an alley jammed with Chinese-Cuban restaurants employing aggressive barkers waving menus in the face of all passersby. But brave the gauntlet and meander around the adjacent streets where there are Chinese associations and social clubs, the Chinese newspaper *Kwong Wah Po*, and elders playing Mah Jong instead of dominoes. Another anomaly of the Chinese community in Havana is the Cementerio Chino, a dedicated cemetery for the Chinese community where the mausoleums are mini-pagodas and the epitaphs are in Chinese. It was restored recently and makes for a great photo session. If you're craving good, authentic Chinese food while in Havana, a former resident of Shanghai swears by Tin Hao, far from Chinatown, at San Lázaro and Hospital streets.

8 Women-Owned Businesses Worth Patronizing

I HAVE BIASES—WE ALL DO, those who claim they don't are in denial. My personal bias (one of them anyway) is to recommend and patronize women-owned businesses whenever possible. My default for spending my hard-earned money extends to any business owned by society's more vulnerable, including women and people of color, as well as any business pursuing an ethical, sustainable, and environmental agenda. While ethical and sustainable businesses are slow to take in Cuba's sluggish economy where the bottom line is top priority and Cubans of color are under-represented in the entrepreneurial class, women are a primal force in the private sector; according to the latest statistics, 32 percent of private workers are women. The creativity and drive of Cuban women is evident everywhere you look—at home, work, in the street, and at play. If you've ever shared a meal cooked by a Cuban mom, you know they are magicians, inventing a delicious spread on a shoestring budget with minimal ingredients. When combined with a high-quality product or service, this thrift and savvy is what sets Cuban businesswomen apart.

Two places making their mark on the new economy are Clandestina and Pisco Labis, in Habana Vieja. For wholly original, handmade Cuban clothes, crafts, home accessories, and more, these boutiques are obligatory. Clandestina, with its motto "99% Cuban Designs" (according to the owners, 99 percent is more marketable and memorable than 100 percent), gained overnight fame after President Obama bought t-shirts for his daughters there. At $30CUC each, it's not a place many Cubans can afford to shop, but for unique souvenirs, it's worth making a special trip. Pisco Labis, meanwhile, is a cool collective of more than a dozen Cuban craftspeople where upcycled wine bottles are made into chandeliers, old jeans are transformed into fashionable A-line dresses, and candle stubs are repurposed into scented pillars. There's a relaxed vibe here, allowing you to browse the two floors of merchandise at your leisure.

On the gastronomic side, Café Bahia, a block from the Cira García Hospital in Playa, is a guaranteed good meal no matter if you opt for the ceviche, fish of the day, or shrimp tacos. The maritime theme is simple, yet elegant and the outdoor deck shaded with a sail is a lovely perch to enjoy an ice cold lemonade or Cristal. Another simple place that excels at what they do is the Burner Brothers pastry shop (Calle C #719). Rather than two brothers, it's actually a brother-sister team, with mom pitching in; Tony and Sandra taught themselves to bake, burning many of their first batches in the process (hence the name). Here you can try Havana's best brownie, chocolate chip or oatmeal raisin cookies, mini-cheesecakes, blue cheese tarts, and other inventive delicacies. I won't temper my assessment of Dulce's Nancy with any wishy-washy language: there is simply no better cake to be had in the city than those that come from Nancy's kitchen tucked away in a lush garden festooned with orchids. There's no storefront, you just have to know she's there, baking her heart out (Hidalgo #8 between Calle 2 and 4, accessed off the Plaza de la Revolución); tell her Conner sent you.

If you want to shed calories after so many sweets, there's no better way than a bicycle tour with Vélo Cuba, a women-owned and operated bike shop. They have multi-lingual guides, rent bikes and do repairs. When you're ready to be pampered, O2 Club tucked into a privileged corner of Nuevo Vedado, offers a full menu of manicures, facials, and massages provided in clean, modern facilities. Twin sisters Omara and Odalys (O2, get it?) founded this space in 2012 as a straight ahead spa; it has since grown into a multi-service center for health and well-being with courses, a café, and beautiful garden.

✳ www.O2habana.com

9

Gran Hotel
Manzana Kempinski

ONCE UPON A TIME THERE was a Spanish millionaire named Don Antonio Gómez-Mena who made a fortune in sugar and set to spending it. Gómez-Mena bought four sugar mills, a yeast factory, a distillery, and invested in real estate in and around Havana, consolidating his wealth. His most outrageous purchase was the Manzana de Gómez, a property covering a square block in the heart of Havana bounded by Zulueta, Monserrate, Neptuno, and O'Reilly streets. Construction began in 1890, but only the first floor was complete when Gómez-Mena bought the centrally located building; the other four floors went up between 1916 and 1918 when global sugar prices skyrocketed during World War I. Cuba's sugar class was suddenly flush with cash, earning the nickname "fat cows"; this period in the island's history is universally known as the time of the "*vacas gordas*." Tourists flocked to the Manzana de Gómez to shop in its elegant arcaded mall and send hand-tinted postcards of the building to the folks back home. Eventually the boom went bust, politics intervened, a revolution was launched and won and the Manzana de Gómez slid into neglect and disrepair. Anyone who wanders the streets of Havana will find the city's seedy side, and Manzana de Gómez in the 1990s, when I first visited, was a dark and grimy place, the columns caked with centuries of urban grit, the passages shadowy in feel and deed. The stores of the commercial center were as bare and abandoned as the people who drifted inside just for a look, hungry for a simple change of scene.

Then rumors started circulating a handful of years ago that the Manzana de Gómez was slated for a major overhaul. This was good news, if true: the Manzana de Gómez sits at the intersection of urban blight and nouveau riche bling, with luxury hotels and fabulously restored buildings renting to foreigners alongside overcrowded one-room homes and well-worn laundry drooping from balconies verging on collapse. The rumors proved right: scaffolding went up, heavy machinery lumbered to the site, and construction and restoration began on the historic building. News drifted out that it was being transformed into a luxury hotel, with first-class, first-world boutiques on the ground floor and prices to match. It was the first construction site I've ever seen in Havana working two shifts—the stadium lights beaming rays into the dark streets seemed to say: "This is a serious endeavor, a new era in Havana construction where we'll finish on time, within budget, and to specifications." The press reported on the progress, while locals from the overcrowded homes with droopy laundry salvaged the windows and sashes, fittings and bricks from the guts of the building unceremoniously dumped on the curb. Then new rumblings and rumors hit the street that hundreds of workers from India were contracted to "speed up construction," according to national press reports. Cubans were affronted, yet understanding. As my friend Alberto said: "How can we import labor with so many people needing jobs? Then again, this way construction will actually get done, with less theft and slacking."

It was in this environment that European luxury hotel chain Kempinski Hotels opened the Gran Hotel Manzana Kempinski to guests in May 2017. It was a revelation—like nothing we have ever seen on the island. It fairly shimmered, backlit in the Havana twilight. The restored, enlarged building gleamed and the commercial arcade was floor-to-ceiling windows and every corner was Swiss-clean. Forget that Montblanc and Versace are selling $3000 pens and $2000 handbags in the swanky shops. Forget that neighbors from those one-room homes are quickly shuffled away from wealthy tourists lingering at the hotel entrance. Forget that the most talented, award-winning Cuban scientist could never afford to book a room. Forget all these contradictions and take my advice: stay here if you've got the money, honey because this place is simply incredible (and no, I'm not getting paid to write this!). Every detail is over-the-top elegant, from the fresh white cala lilies that are so abundant, you can smell them from the glass elevator, to the in-room espresso machines. Flat screen TVs, high-tech bathroom glass that frosts at the flick of a switch, luxurious king-sized beds in a chic color scheme and (wait for it!) free Wi-Fi, await once you slip your card in the door. This is real, European-standard luxury, heretofore unknown in Havana.

❋ www.kempinski.com/en/havana/gran-hotel
-kempinski-la-habana

Sure, there are other "five star" hotels in the vicinity, but the Gran Hotel Manzana Kempinski knows no competition. Hands-on, detail-oriented General Manager Xavier Destribats explained the strategy to me: "This is Kempinski's first property in the Americas, it's our flagship, and we worked very closely with City Historian Eusebio Leal to honor the history and charm of Havana." Destribats points to the courtyard between the hotel and the Museo de Bellas Artes, which will soon be landscaped to create a public green space, the restored plaza and fountain nearby, and the long section of Habana Vieja's original wall dating from the 1600s that has been restored and preserved in the hotel museum. The overall layout emphasizes privacy and luxury, with several patios, balconies, and lobbies, planted and exquisitely furnished, that are ideal for a business meeting or tryst. The views of the Bacardí building, an art deco jewel, from the spa sundeck and the bird's eye view of the Floridita from the Bar Daiquirí are a location scout's wet dream. The Jacuzzis, saunas, private massage rooms, and salon in the spa are Palm Desert quality (day passes available) and there's a gym so well-equipped you'll feel guilty not using it.

Even if you can't afford a night here, splash out with drinks and dinner on the 6th floor where you'll be treated to Havana's money shot: uninterrupted views of the Museo de Bellas Artes, the Gran Teatro, Parque Central, and the Hotel Inglaterra. Unfortunately, the neon blue infinity pool here is only open to guests.

10

The Mighty Malecón

YOU'VE SEEN IT IN photos—at daybreak, at sunset, with waves breaching the sea wall and gushing into the avenue. Probably you've seen it in movies, too—the now classic *Buena Vista Social Club* and more recent *Fast & Furious 8* jump to mind. A Google search on "Havana's seawall" results in dozen of pages and hundreds, if not thousands, of images of what has become the iconic symbol of Cuba, figuring large on travel websites, in music videos and fashion magazines, and on the cover of guide-books. It's to Havana what the Eiffel Tower is to Paris and the Empire State Building is to New York. Yet ask a Parisian the last time they visited the Eiffel Tower or a New  Yorker the last time they went to the observation deck of the Empire State Building and the answer may be "never" or "the last time my relatives were in town." While it's logical that emblematic sites are co-opted for marketing hot travel destinations, the difference with the Malecón is that Cubans hang out, have parties, make music, fish, swim, and contemplate life there all the time (the other difference from the aforementioned sites is that the Malecón is free). As I type this, I guarantee a kid is doing a back flip into the waters below and a guy is baiting his hook somewhere along the eight miles of Havana's seawall. Sometimes referred to as "the city's sofa" because folks settle in so comfortably here on blistering summer nights, the Malecón holds such power over the Cuban psyche it is the first place emigres visit upon returning to the patria and the last place they go before moving overseas. This isn't hyperbole: I've attended two going away parties on the Malecón in the past month.

So why such mystique around what is, when all is said and done, just a wall? What would drive Martha Gellhorn, former resident and wife of Ernest Hemingway, to grow weak in the knees after four decades away to write: "The first morning in Havana, I stood by the Malecón, feeling very weepy with homesickness for this city?" Why are there hundreds of people clustered together on the wall at the base of Vedado's La Rampa every single night and still hundreds more spread out like birds on a wire east toward Habana Vieja and west toward Miramar? I've thought a lot about this because the Malecón's allure has infected me too: when I'm away from Havana for a spell or sinking into that expat state of blue that comes on unexpectedly when you live long-term in a foreign country, I go to the seawall, kick off my shoes and lay back. The salty sea breeze and negative air ions are panacea for body and soul, that much is clear. And though there are parts that get crowded—especially in densely-populated sections of Vedado and Centro Habana—it's one of the few places in Havana where Cubans can secure some privacy.

Havana hosts nearly 20 percent of the country's population according to official statistics. But with 70 percent of the national economy based here, the figure is certainly higher since folks pour in from the drought-stricken, struggle-ridden provinces every day (despite laws controlling internal migration to the capital). On average, one building collapses in the city almost every day and existing housing stock, woefully inadequate and insufficient, is rapidly being converted into rental accommodation for tourists. All of these factors have created a housing crisis, what authorities categorize as one of the country's biggest problems; it's not uncommon for four generations to share a two-bedroom apartment, like my neighbors, or to squeeze half a dozen people into one-room *solares* (inner-city tenements, sometimes with shared kitchen and bathroom). On the Malecón, Cubans living in overcrowded and dilapidated housing can get away from a nagging mother-in-law, bickering parents, or their four mold-festering walls. Lovers can secret themselves (or not, a YouTube search will yield many videos of Cubans caught *en flagrante*) in darker sections for conjugal fun. Marriage proposals and first kisses, plans to flee and plots to swindle: it is all going down on the Malecón. There's another simple, practical factor to the Malecon's magnetism: temperatures are always cooler along the seawall. In a city where summer temperatures often top 100°F accompanied by stifling 100 percent humidity, and air conditioning is a luxury reserved for tourists and the well-to-do, spending an hour or two people watching with a few cold beers by the sea is pure survival tactic. As you may imagine, Cubans are proprietary about their patrimony, especially when it comes to the Malecón; if current rumors prove true that the new luxury hotel under construction where the Prado and seawall meet intends to appropriate part of the Malecón for the exclusive use of guests, things could get ugly.

11 *Gardens of the Hotel Nacional de Cuba*

THERE'S OFTEN CONFUSION ABOUT THE hotel scene in Cuba—what's government owned, what's a mixed venture, who runs what, how the profits are split—but about the Hotel Nacional, nothing is fuzzy: this is 100 percent Cuban-owned and operated and is a potent symbol of national sovereignty and pride. Designed by the New York firm of McKim, Meade and White (they of New York's Penn Station and Columbia University), the Nacional opened in 1930 on a rocky outcrop overlooking the Malecón, and was long the preferred place to stay of the rich, famous and powerful. Winston Churchill, Frank Sinatra, and Jean-Paul Sartre all strode the marble and mahogany lobby here, making their way through the heavy doors to the tropical gardens, catching the sea breeze, a stiff rum cocktail at hand. Who didn't stay here was Josephine Baker: the inimitable chanteuse was turned away for being black, whereupon she spun on her heels and checked into the Sevilla-Biltmore, holding a press conference in the spectacular lobby of that hotel, denouncing the Nacional's racist policies. Other stars of sport, stage and screen turned away based on race include Jackie Robinson, Nat King Cole, and Joe Louis.

*

An all-time classic read, out of print but still
available used, is *Sartre on Cuba*.

*

32

Luckily, those days are long behind us. The history of the Nacional runs so deep, the bar tucked away behind the lobby is called Salón de la Fama (Hall of Fame) and is packed with photos of famous guests (Steven Spielberg, Rita Hayworth, Errol Flynn, and Marlon Brando), and vitrines filled with ephemera from golden times gone by. Part of the reason the Nacional is so symbolic and Cubans take such pride in now having full ownership stems from its links to the USA and other developed nations to the north. Designed by a US firm, and a favorite of the global glitterati, the Nacional was also the setting for the climactic scene of Graham Greene's *Our Man in Havana*. But perhaps what sticks most in the Cuban craw are the Nacional's pre-revolutionary mafia ties: notorious mob boss Lucky Luciano convened his cronies here to divvy up the city and its casino, prostitution and other nefarious money-making niches. A handful of years later, Meyer Lansky took over operations at the Parisien, the Nacional's casino and cabaret; today, the Parisien makes a good alternative to the world-famous Tropicana for a hip-shaking, butt-quaking extravaganza.

You need not book a room at the Nacional to experience its seduction—though if it's within your budget, the setting, location, views, and amenities (two pools, an executive floor with added services like a private restaurant, and one of the city's top cabarets) make it worth a night or two. Get a coveted room during the Festival Internacional de Nuevo Cine Latinoamericano (AKA The Havana Film Festival), headquartered here each December and you'll be a fly on the wall for all kinds of star sightings and gossip. Pop in during the festivities and you can get a taste without paying the price. The lobby, with its combination of Moorish, modernist, and eclectic styles is laced with ribbons of cigar smoke, punctuated by the sound of ice shaking in highballs and a polyglot of excitable voices bouncing off the walls. It encapsulates Havana's wicked torpor and promise; no wonder it sets the tropical tone for Pico Iyer's novel *Cuba and the Night*.

Through the double doors lie the hotel's elegant gardens, with wide-angle views of the sea, stately palm trees, and comfortable wicker couches for taking it all in. A cocktail and snack will set you back at least $10CUC—a small price for gaining access to such hallowed ground. The central fountain and grassy expanses leading to the Malecón beyond are popular spots for Cuban *quinceñeras* (girls turning 15, this is a coming-out of sorts, where the 15-year-olds dress like child brides or harlots and videotape the entire affair) to pose and mince; a more kitsch rite of passage doesn't exist—have your camera at the ready. Speaking of kitsch, there's one Havana spectacle that doesn't seem to die, though most of its performers already have: an incarnation of the Buena Vista Social Club plays here three times a week and the music, while not played by original members, is superlative—but then again, if you're listening to bad live music in Cuba, you're doing something woefully wrong. For those looking for history below the neatly clipped gardens of the Hotel Nacional, daily tours of the underground tunnels and bunkers are a unique way to learn about Cuban defensive mechanisms and get beneath the surface of the hotel—literally.

12 *Plaza de la Revolución*

I LIVED IN HAVANA FOR years under the mistaken impression that the giant parade ground that hosts hundreds of thousands every International Workers Day and the occasional pope, high-profile funeral procession (both Hugo Chávez and Fidel Castro were mourned here) and military displays, was constructed by the revolution. But like many buildings, plazas, hotels, and monuments, the Plaza de la Revolución was built by previous administrations, in this case by the infamous Fulgencio Batista. Back in those days, when it was known as the Plaza Cívica, no one imagined eight-hour speeches by Fidel Castro attended by a million admirers or Pope Francisco taking several turns around the plaza, without bulletproof glass or added protection in the Pope mobile, like happened in 2015. The giant sculpture of José Martí looming over the Plaza is one of the few full-body depictions of the "Apostle" in Havana. In 2018, an exact replica of the José Martí statue at the entrance to New York's Central Park, a collaboration between the Bronx Museum and Cuba, was unveiled on Havana's Prado; another one is Marti holding a baby and pointing (accusingly, say folks who like to read into these things) toward the US embassy. Both the Plaza de la Revolución and the "Protestódromo"—the open parade ground along the Malecón directly in front of the embassy—were once the preferred sites for railing against "*yanqui*" policies, but since the ascension of Raúl Castro to the presidency (and by the time you read this, there will no longer be a Castro as President), the rhetoric has been tempered mightily. No one says *yanqui* anymore, for instance; the preferred term for foreigners is Yuma and you'll hear it wherever you go. There are still giant demonstrations held here, however, and if you can catch one, don't miss it for the insight into how Cubans rally en masse.

*

Theories abound as to the origins of the slang term Yuma; most agree it comes from the Hollywood western *3:10 to Yuma*, based on the story of the same name by Elmore Leonard.

*

It always makes me cringe to see folks visiting this monumental space under a blazing Havana sun. Don't make this mistake:

the emblematic Plaza de la Revolución is a wide open concrete parade ground (imagine a football stadium parking lot) completely devoid of shade, your photos will be totally burned out, and the risk of sun stroke is high. Besides, it's one of the stops on the ubiquitous convertible car tours so some randoms from Kansas or Moscow are likely to make their way into your trip photos. At night, on the other hand, the bronze sculptures of revolutionary heroes Che Guevara and Camilo Cienfuegos

are attractively backlit, the Memorial José Martí is illuminated
from below and it will be deserted.

Time a visit on a Saturday night and you can catch the city's
best drag queen extravaganza, Divino, in the Cafe Cantante,
below the Teatro Nacional. Early morning is another good time
to head to the Plaza, when throngs of Cubans in olive green
are arriving at their Ministry of the Interior posts (where the
Che sculpture hangs), and workers are making their way to surrounding buildings, including the Ministry of Communications
(where Havana's main post office is housed) and the National
Library. The one bonus to visiting during the day is you can
access the Memorial José Marti—the giant phallus fronting the
plaza. There's an art gallery on the ground floor and an elevator that takes you to the top of the monument, delivering 360°
bird's eye views of Havana (or more precisely: buzzard's eye
views—the scavengers are constantly circling the monument,
eliciting all manner of morbid commentary). Walk around the
back of the memorial and there are some cafe tables and chairs
and a full on view of the Comité Central, the seat of Cuban
government.

13 Necrópolis Cristobal Colón

I'M NOT A BIG FAN of churches and cemeteries (nor slums or battle sites) as tourist attractions, but there are always exceptions. In Havana, that exception is the Colón Cemetery, a city unto itself, established in 1868 and interring corpses daily since. Like in most high-demand cities, overcrowding is a serious problem—almost every Habanero wishes to be buried in Colón (formally the Necrópolis Cristobal Colón, but unceremoniously clipped to just Colón; Cubans, a profligate bunch in general, are surprisingly parsimonious when it comes to syllables and words). Alas, people keep dying while the cemetery's acreage remains the same, forcing loved ones to disinter their dearly departed after two years and move them to mausoleums. It's not a pretty sight on the day they're digging up remains, the named and numbered streets littered with scraps of clothing, splintered plywood, and dead flowers. You have to be an unlucky soul to witness this sadness—like I did when we buried my friend Odalys a few years ago. On all other days, the cemetery is a quiet oasis in the heart of chaotic Vedado jam-packed with spectacular sculptures and elaborate aboveground tombs. The chapel anchoring the main boulevard, blazing yellow in the midday sun with its terra cotta cupola, calls all photographers; inside is less impressive, unless the resident priest is blessing soon-to-be entombed remains when the apse is charged with a melancholy energy.

Many of the angelic and profane sculptures date back a hundred years or more and the quirky Cuban character is evident even here, in death. There's the "Domino Tomb," the final resting place of Juana Martín de Martín, a fanatic of the game whose tombstone is a three-by-three domino tile; her last game is chiseled into the side of the crypt. Despite being vilified post-revolution and embroiled in a decades-long lawsuit with the Cuban state over the copyright to Havana Club, the Bacardí family pantheon stands tall here, contained inside a wrought iron fence lined with black bats. One of my favorites is the "Faithfulness Grave" of Jeanette Ryder whose devoted dog Rinti padded to her tomb every day following her death, refusing to eat until one day he died right there, beside his beloved owner. Ryder's friends were so moved by the dog's devotion, they raised money to commission a tombstone sculpture with Rinti sleeping contentedly at her feet.

One of the most-often visited graves in the entire cemetery, piled high with flowers, stuffed animals, baby shoes, and written supplications for infant health, is that of Amelia Goyri, familiarly known as "La Milagrosa" (The Miracle). Amelia died eight months pregnant; the baby she carried died with her. They were buried together, the unnamed baby placed at her feet. When she was exhumed some years later, the baby wasn't at her feet, but in her arms. In 1909, a life-size sculpture of the would-be mother with babe in arms was placed at her tomb; today it is festooned with all manner of offerings from parents petitioning miracles for their offspring. Not long ago a friend asked me to do a favor for his neighbor, an elderly *compañera* charged with administering all the offerings: would I be willing to carry the nickels, dimes, and quarters deposited by suplicants in the box at La Milagrosa's tomb to New York in my luggage and change them for bills? (Cuban banks don't change US coins.) The little old lady offered me half for my troubles—around $75. I told my friend I would heft the nearly ten pounds of coins stateside, but I wasn't risking the health of someone's baby purchasing my morning coffee with money offered to La Milagrosa. Another cemetery highlight is the Androgynous Angel statue (who knew?!). You can hire a guide to tour the cemetery, wander independently, or buy the detailed map and booklet *Guía Turística Necrópolis Colón* at the entrance.

14 Jardín Japonés

DON'T BOTHER ASKING YOUR TAXI driver or waiter how to get to the Jardín Japonés (also known as the Isla Japonésa); this is one of Havana's best kept secrets, unknown even to many lifetime locals. Tucked behind the imposing 19th-century mansion housing the unremarkable Restaurante 1830, this little seaside hideaway is perfect for when you need some peace and tranquility mixed in with your hectic Havana days and nights. Constructed entirely of coral, rocks, and seashells, the turrets, bridges, benches, and diminutive caves here are marvelous for beholding a sunset while a trumpeter or two practice their chops in the Moorish cupola overlooking where the Almendares River empties into the sea. I was literally brought to tears the first time I explored this site—granted I was wracked with grief at the time and a friend suggested I head here for some solace. This artificial island officially named Koisima Isla Japonesa (love island) emits a rejuvenating energy that is hard to put into words. Indeed, after I swiped the tears away and headed back home, I discovered I'd lost my keys somewhere amongst the shells and coral and caves, but didn't even care.

No cost was spared in constructing this idyllic isle: the tiles for the mini-mosque were imported from La Cartuja in Seville, Spain and the cupola crown was brought piece by piece from India. Local lore holds that the Jardín Japonés was contracted by the mansion's owner, Carlos Miguel de Céspedes, to keep tabs on his lover who lived across the way, in the mansion known as the Casa Verde, distinguished by its green gabled roof. Perhaps apocryphal, the towers here do provide a direct view of the Casa Verde, a short rowboat ride away, adding weight to the story. Carlos Miguel (who is no relation to the father of Cuban independence, Carlos Manuel de Céspedes) was Secretary of Public Works under President Gerardo Machado, a dictatorial figure who spilled blood indiscriminately. Céspedes oversaw the construction of major projects including the Capitolio, the Carretera Central, the Prado, the Hotel Nacional, and this mansion. Thursday and Saturdays, the patio of Restaurante 1830 facing the Jardín Japonés hosts live salsa bands with raucous dancing and plenty of willing partners. The Torreón de la Chorrera (the stone tower just east of "1830" as it's known here) is a popular seaside spot for beers packed with Cubans at all hours and hosts occasional electronica raves as well.

15 Top Spots for a Havana Sunset

THERE'S SOMETHING MAGICAL ABOUT HAVANA. It's in the sea salt spray caressing the Malecón, the smell of night-time gardenia under a full moon, children laughing in the neighborhood park, and the smile of a grandma as she passes you on the sidewalk. Music pours from Miramar mansions, while a trumpeter improvises jazz under the crown of an old-growth ceiba. It's this magic, I believe, which partly explains the levity Cubans carry when faced with frustrating bureaucracy and interminable lines. It's also why visitors tend to fall fast and hard for Havana, not knowing precisely why. This indescribable energy enriches life here, makes sex better, and soothes grief. It can't be bottled, this unique flavor and swing for which Havana is justly famous, but I hope we can retain, sustain, and grow it moving forward—otherwise, I might have to look for another place to live!

❋

Poet Langston Hughes felt this magic, translating it into prose in his essay "Havana Nights," collected in the thought-provoking collection *Cuba in Mind*.

❋

One way to experience this magic for yourself is to set aside a dusk or two with a good friend or lover, or if you're like me and enjoy your own company, alone, to fully appreciate a Havana sunset. A classic spot is at the bar atop the city's tallest building, the Focsa, on Calles M and 17. Exiting the elevator at the top, site of La Torre restaurant (expensive and luxurious), you'll see the entire western stretch of Vedado spread out below the wall of windows. Settle in with a beer or mojito and you'll have a panoramic vista as the sun goes down in golden, pink, and purple hues. They make decent vittles at the bar, for a fraction of the price of the restaurant. Another iconic building, right on the Malecón, the Riviera Hotel and its iconic lobby bar oozes 1950s mobster ambiance—logical, since this was the pet property of Mafioso Meyer Lansky before he joined the wave of Batista cronies escaping ahead of the winds of political change sweeping the country. Have a cocktail here and gaze through the floor-to-ceiling windows with nothing but glass between you and the Malecón. Speaking of Havana's seawall (nicknamed "the city's sofa" because it serves as an extension of everyone's living room), this is as perfect a place as any to watch the sun go down with a bottle of rum and a quality cigar, if you're so inclined. A hugely popular spot for *habaneros* to swim, neck, and enjoy the sunset is Playa 16 in Miramar. Despite the name, it's not a beach but rather a block-long stretch of coast covered with *diente de perro* (dog's tooth) rock with steps descending into the sea. Carry some flip flops or swim shoes as the shallows are littered with sea urchins. The best access is at Calle 14 and 1ra, where there's a simple cafeteria serving burgers and such, as well as 7 Días, a proper restaurant right on the shore which is hit or miss but occupies a prime sunset location. Two other favorites are La Chorrera, at the western end of the Malecón where the beer bongs are tall and cold and just beyond that the Jardín Japonés (see Chapter 14); both are seaside.

16 Parque Almendares

SOMETIMES HAVANA GETS TOO overwhelming—like today, when my building has no running water and neighbors are knocking down walls accompanied by really bad music. That's when I know it's time for an excursion to Parque Almendares. Languishing on a riverside bench, strolling beneath trees so grand they feel like rain forest, or pumping hard on a playground swing is panacea—for the banal, tiresome, and just plain annoying. I imagine it was precisely this tranquility and escape of which urban planner and landscape architect Jean-Claude Nicolas Forestier dreamt when he laid pencil to draft paper. The legendary French designer responsible for elegant gardens and parks throughout Europe (Champs-de-Mars in Paris; Parc de la Ciutadella in Barcelona) brought his talent to bear on the Gran Parque Metropolitano, to which the Parque Almendares pertains, during the city's halcyon years in the mid-1920s when poets and painters, flappers and dandies fueled by reefer and rum jammed sidewalk cafés and bars to wax eloquent. If you think Havana is wild circa 2018....

Ultimately, Forestier's vision of a corridor of connected parks and green spaces from sea to Boyeros and beyond didn't come to fruition, but a renewed commitment to re-imagining Havana as a sustainable city is now underway and the park is both cleaner and safer thanks to a revitalization project episodically pursued. New riverside landscaping and lighting, fresh coats of paint, and more modern playground equipment have the park feeling downright spiffy these days; if a couple of serviceable public bathrooms were installed and a decent café, this would fast become one of the city's top recreation destinations.

Parque Metropolitano covers 1,700 acres and is known as the lungs of Havana for its expansive tree cover and green space; the heart of these lungs is Parque Almendares, accessed by crossing the eponymous bridge at Vedado's western extent. Immediately upon descending the stairs leading to the park you'll start to see (and smell) part of what makes this park so enigmatic for *habaneros*: the forest running down to river's edge here is an ideal setting for Santería rites and sacrifices and rotting sacrificial flora and fauna dot the cityscape here. Renting a rowboat at the pier (35 cents/hour) and heading down-river delivers an unparalleled excursion through the park's heart and a glimpse of El Fanguito, one of the city's most vulnerable neighborhoods.

The Bosque de la Habana—that of the jungle-like canopy—makes for a cool, pleasant stroll and is a hot spot for Santería rites; should you happen upon one, respect the privacy of the adherents and definitely refrain from taking photos. In 2017, the amphitheater here was re-opened (this lovely, several hundred seat venue saw its last concert in the early 2000s when a Cuban rock guitarist now residing in Spain got too political at the microphone), and there are regular Saturday evening concerts here in the summer. Acerbically droll Cuban folksinger Frank Delgado holds forth here most Saturdays, putting together an entertaining mashup of word and song with invited musicians, poets, and playwrights. The music gets going around 7 p.m. when the sun dips soft and luscious below the horizon—a good option for a cheap, low-key music outing with the kids. Occasionally there are raucous, outdoor music festivals hosted in the parking lots and playgrounds of the park, including the Festival de Salsa each February and Festival Havana World Music in March. Dancing under the stars with hundreds of happy Cubans? Unforgettable.

17 *Parque Lenin*

HILARITY (OR FRUSTRATION, DEPENDING ON my mood) ensues whenever I mention to Cuban friends Parque Lenin and my desire to go to the rodeo. "What rodeo in Vedado?!" they ask me, in a loud voice, gesticulating with their hands like Cubans are wont to do. "There's no rodeo in Vedado. Have you gone mad?" I am then forced to clarify, sounding out slowly, like a

child: "Not Parque Lennon, Parque Lenin: L-E-N-I-N. As in Vladimir Ilyich." Such are the trials of a native English speaker in a Beatles-crazed, USSR-influenced, Spanish-speaking land. Similarly sounding, these two parks couldn't be more different in concept, layout, and purpose. While Lennon Park is easily accessed from any point in the central part of the city, the 1,655-acre park named after the Soviet ideologue is way out on the suburban outskirts, more of a draw for local families and school trips than the stuff of tourist itineraries. Nevertheless, the vast green expanses, varied activities and sites, and chance to mix and mingle with

Cubans of all stripes and types make a good side trip—especially if you're traveling with the little ones.

You'll recognize the entrance to the park when you start seeing grazing horses and a larger-than-life-size statue of revolutionary hero Celia Sánchez Manduley, rifle swung smartly over her shoulder. This multi-purpose park was one of her bright ideas, designed to encourage Cubans to get out and enjoy nature, art, sports, and other healthy pursuits; it's one of the major public projects of the revolution and though a bit rough around the edges in spots—for instance, you're better off bringing a picnic or buying some barbecue from the cluster of cafeterias than visiting one of the depressing restaurants on the grounds—a recent influx of Chinese investment is having an impact. Attending an event here provides some of the most raucous, authentic experiences around and will place your finger firmly on the pulse of Cuban culture. The twice annual rodeo is a hoot, attracting real cowboys (and girls) from the surrounding countryside to compete in heavily contested calf roping events and the like, and the national dog breed show, while not Westminister, is a very serious affair, with well-heeled Cubans parading their pedigreed pooches, including the Cuban-bred Havanese, (called a *bichón habanero* by locals)—a white puff of a lap dog heavily sought after. If you happen upon a pigeon race, held occasionally here, do not hesitate to hang around to see tough looking characters taking bets, adding soiled *pesos cubanos* to growing wads as big as a bagel, while others coo at their birds and brandish heritage papers before potential buyers. When the competitors fly in to view, their owners whoop and holler, running flat out as they coax their birds to the finish line. The last one I went to was a Matanzas-Havana race—these birds flew over 70 miles without breaking a sweat!

*

Internationally sanctioned dog shows happen
in Havana each April and November.

*

There's a small amusement park, a lake for row boating and horseback riding as well here; for something more adrenaline-pumping, you can zoom around the palm-shaded meadows on an all-terrain motorcycle. Directly south of the park is the Jardín Botánico Nacional, with an astounding collection of palms from around the world and the oasis known as the Jardín Japonés, replete with a giant koi pond and the requisite pagoda. If you're out this way, detour to the Parque Zoólogico Nacional, the highlight of which is an African safari bus jaunt with hippos, elephants, lions, tigers, and other exotic animals. Many of these beasts were imported in 2013 thanks to a bilateral agreement between Cuba and Namibia, which donated the animals; their travels and successful insertion into the zoo was splashed all over the news and papers for weeks.

18 *Regla*

RECIPE FOR A PERFECT DAY in Havana: shake off your mojito hangover with a double espresso accompanied by unparalleled views of the Capitolio on the roof of the Hotel Saratoga (preferred hotel of Jimmy Page, Beyoncé, Madonna, and Justin Bieber—who didn't want to vacate the Presidential Suite for Pope Francisco's visit), before heading next door to the Asociación Yoruba de Cuba for a crash course in Afro-Cuban religions—Santería, Abakuá, and Palo Monte. The first is the most popular, practiced widely, while Abakuá is a secret society (membership open only to men) flirting with black magic and ghoulish interventions. In Abakuá, the biblical precept of "an eye for an eye" is taken seriously: violence, sometimes fatal, is rained upon those crossing an adherent. Palo Monte falls somewhere in between, with herbal concoctions and communing with the dead employed to harness supernatural powers. If you've ever wondered why so many people are wearing white, from their head wraps to their umbrellas, this is the place to find out (they're being initiated into Santería—the island's most popular faith by far). Weave your way through Habana Vieja's choked, cobblestoned streets to the new ferry terminal near the Plaza de Armas and hop on the ferry with gaggles of locals to Regla, across the bay.

Known as "Sierra Chiquita" for its revolutionary fervor, Regla transcends time and space when you step from the still-rocking boat. Suddenly, you're in a small Cuban town in the countryside where pedestrians outnumber cars and many homes are listing wooden structures with signs reading *"esta es tu casa, Fidel,"* hanging askew on the front door. Regla is also known as a Santería hotspot. As soon as you disembark, you'll see the spire of the Iglesia de Nuestra Señora de Regla, housing the black Madonna (La Santísima Virgen de Regla). She's a powerful deity, representing Yemayá, *orisha* of the sea and heartily worshipped, particularly on her saint day, September 8, when thousands come to this church to pay their respects and the Virgin is carried through the town's narrow streets. On any given day, you can have your future read via shells by devotees outside the church. Leave some time to wander the narrow streets, where you can drink *pru*, a spicy concoction with a secret formula famous in Cuba's eastern provinces. Folks from Regla are extraordinarily friendly—grab a bench in the town's central park for a little mingling.

II
Music, Arts, & Letters

19 *Taller Experimental de Gráfica*

FOR ART LOVERS, COLLECTORS, AND CURATORS, Cuba is Paradise. There are museums, galleries, private studios, public art, installations, and performances all across the country, enriched by international events including the Bienal de la Habana (see Chapter 85), Holguín's Romerías de Mayo, and workshops at the Instituto Superior de Arte (ISA, see Chapter 25). The last, Cuba's equivalent to New York's Julliard (and free for aspiring Cuban artists), is largely responsible for training and educating generations of the island's top talent.

✳ www.romeriasdemayo.cult.cu

In fact, there's a saying here that if you turn over a rock, half a dozen talented artists will run out—and this isn't simply Cuban hyperbole. While artists can be found in every village, town, and mountain hamlet, certain cities are known for their concentration of fabulous art and artists, such as Santiago de Cuba, Cienfuegos, and of course, Havana. In the Cuban capital, the top places to see art under one roof are the Cuban collection at the Museo de Bellas Artes (see Chapter 21) and the Fábrica de Arte Cubano (see Chapter 30); the best location to buy art for its wide selection from exquisite to kitsch, is the Almacén de San José, a repurposed warehouse with hundreds of different artists and types of art; and the most accessible place to see art being created (and where you can buy what strikes your fancy), is the Taller Experimental de Gráfica.

Founded in 1962, this working lithographic studio in the heart of Habana Vieja is a fun place to visit even if you're not in the market for original Cuban art. Tucked away at the end of a small, cobblestone alley (shared with Doña Eutimia, voted by *Newsweek* as one of the world's top 100 restaurants) in the Plaza de la Catedral, Cuban printmakers create marvels under the languid spin of ceiling fans here every day. The air is thick with the stink of ink and paint, laced with the piquant aroma of uncut Cuban cigarettes, but it's tolerable thanks to the large open space, high ceilings, and positive energy the workshop radiates. The artists here—some self-taught novices, others formally trained and established—are usually happy to chat about their process and craft and will show you around. There's a small gallery upstairs and most of the limited-series prints are for sale. Visitors in town for a month or more should inquire about the printmaking workshops here. Offered regularly, they're affordable and make a great excuse to play with ink and prints while scratching below the surface of Havana and experiencing Cuba more profoundly than most. Participants will take away memories of a lifetime and a dozen prints of their own creation.

20 *Casa de las Américas*

WOMEN HAVE PLAYED A PIVOTAL role in the Cuban Revolution from before the final victory in 1959 until right now, as I type this. There's Vilma Espín, who marshalled resources and organized personnel for the guerrilla war and founded the Cuban Women's Federation (FMC); Espín's daughter Mariela Castro, who directs the National Center for Sex Education (CENESEX) and leads the fight against homo- and transphobia; the tens of thousands of women and girls who taught the country to read and write during the Literacy Campaign; and the genius scientists of the country's biotechnology sector, who developed unique vaccines and therapies unavailable anywhere else in the world. And then there's Haydeé Santamaría. Her life story is heroic, tragic, epic—and eternal, thanks to her bravery and intellectual acumen.

The Cuban Revolution officially got underway during the 1953 attack on the Moncada Barracks in Santiago de Cuba, launched from the Granjita Siboney (see Chapter 68). Two women took up arms in that seminal event: Melba Hernández and Haydeé Santamaría. One of the masterminds of the attack was Haydeé's brother, Abel Santamaría, who was captured, tortured (they cut out his eyes), and killed by thugs in the employ of dictator Fulgencio Batista. Meanwhile, Haydeé and other survivors went to prison on the Isle of Pines (now the Isla de la Juventud; a visit to the Presidio Modelo where they were jailed

makes for a spooky, solitary experience—see Chapter 100). In another turn of luck for the nascent movement, the prisoners were granted amnesty and released, prompting Fidel Castro to deliver his monumental History Will Absolve Me speech; Melba and Haydeé edited, printed and distributed the tract clandestinely. After their release, the motley crew regrouped, went to Mexico, and formalized the Movimiento 26 de Julio (M-26-7), the revolutionary body responsible for all that ensued following the Moncada attack (you'll see black and red M-26-7 flags flying on historical dates). Haydeé followed the directorate to Mexico where plans were laid to topple Batista and fought in the Sierra Maestra alongside Fidel, Raúl, Che, and their crew.

✳

History Will Absolve Me, the speech
that launched a revolution, is widely
available in reprint.

✳

Not long after revolutionary troops entered Havana, hailing triumph, Haydeé established the Casa de las Américas to disseminate and promote Latin American and Caribbean art and literature. One of the hemisphere's most respected cultural centers, the Casa de las Américas is housed in a beautiful art deco building on Calle G near the Malecón. "Casa," as its fondly called, hosts free concerts, book launches, and poetry readings, publishes books and magazines, has an art gallery and library, and each year bestows the coveted Casa de las Américas prize for literature. Haydeé headed the Casa de las Américas for two decades during a time when the intellectual and artistic environment in Cuba was turbulent, reactionary, and random. In the early years, censors worked overtime, prohibiting films, closing magazines, and firing intellectuals. The proverbial shit hit the fan when Cuban poet Heberto Padilla won the Casa prize for a collection of poems in 1968; though the book was published in Cuba by the state-run press, not long thereafter, Fidel Castro pronounced *"dentro de la Revolución, todo; contra la Revolución, nada"* (inside the Revolution, everything; outside the Revolution, nothing) in a meeting with artists and intellectuals. Padilla's poems were subsequently deemed "outside the Revolution." This signaled the death knell for his career and he was sent to jail, released only after issuing a humiliating public apology.

A dark chapter in the history of the Cuban revolution, the "Padilla affair" kicked off what is known as the *"quinquenio gris"*— the five-year "gray period" when writers and artists were shackled by rules regulating content. Many left Cuba and today folks still reference the *quinquenio gris*, sometimes opining that it lasted more like ten years. This episode overlapped with the creation of the infamous UMAPs (Unidades Militares de Apoyo a la Producción), hard labor camps where anyone coloring outside the lines—homosexuals, pastors, musicians, hippies—was sent to instill revolutionary values. It was a short-lived, disastrous initiative for which Fidel Castro apologized publicly in 2010, stating "if someone is responsible it's me." Haydeé didn't witness the evolution of the revolution: she committed suicide in 1980.

*

Pablo Milanés (2016) by Cuban filmmaker Juan
Pin Vilar, won Best Documentary at the 2017
Festival Internacional de Cine Pobre in Gibara
and explores the famous musician's views on
his experience in UMAP.

*

21 *Museo de Bellas Artes*

IT'S NO SECRET THAT CUBA has a surfeit of artistic talent and a long history of creative minds working ahead of the curve—in each of the seven classic genres. Collecting the best, most famous, and commercially viable paintings, sculptures, and drawings by Cuban artists under one roof is what makes the Bellas Artes' Cuban collection the one museum not to miss in Havana. The building itself, with an open patio on the ground floor filled with contemporary sculptures and installations (pieces here by Roberto Fabelo encapsulate Cuban moxie and wit) is well-conceived and executed. The rest of the collection is impressive, as much for its depth as its breadth, which covers the history of Cuban art. Said collection was reduced in recent years when valuable paintings of national patrimony were discovered in private homes in Florida, exposing an art smuggling ring, with Cubans on both sides of the straits implicated in the theft.

Like with many standout museums around the world, you'll need more than an afternoon to see the 1,200 works spread over several floors and 20 galleries here. Fortunately, the collection is organized chronologically, so you can dash straight to the era of most interest (I tend to pass over the grand colonial landscapes and portraits of bourgeoisie *muchachas* in heavy frames, preferring the contemporary and colorful works from the 1950s on). Wilfredo Lam, a surrealist who spent much time cavorting with Pablo Picasso and is Cuba's most celebrated artist (his canvas *The Jungle* hangs in New York's Museum of Modern Art, while another, *Zambezia, Zambezia* is at the Guggenheim), is a good place to start. The Cuban modernist Marcelo Pogolotti, yet one more of the nation's great painters, is exhibited here and his works are worth seeking out. Two other accomplished Cuban artists to keep in mind while visiting are Mariano Rodríguez and Rita Longa.

Pop art relying heavily on primary colors and pro-revolutionary symbolism dominates much of the art spanning the 60s; the canvasses of Raúl Martinez are iconic examples of the Warhol-esque style that defined this period. Successive waves of creative talent emerged once the Instituto Superior de Arte was up and running (see Chapter 25), and the floors of contemporary art are not only fascinating, but a quick and satisfying overview of the development of modern art on the island (you can also hire a guide at the museum, who should speak passable English, at least). The giant canvasses—and penises—of Servando Cabrera Moreno, one of Cuba's most celebrated (and censored, back in his day) artists, are a must-see; the cross between patriotism, eroticism, and fetishism were not kindly looked upon in the early days of the revolution.

A new tendency in Cuban art—hyperrealism—was epitomized by Flavio Garciandía and his painting *"Todo lo que usted necesita es amor"* (All You Need is Love; 1975) of fellow artist (and queen of the contemporary art scene) Zaída del Río, also represented here. Incidentally, both del Río and Garciandía are products of ISA; the latter founded the Bienal de la Habana in 1984 (see Chapter 85). Personally, I can't get enough of the hyperrealist yet psychedelic landscapes of Tomás Sánchez. Jumping forward a generation, other names to look for include Mabel Poblet (from

Cienfuegos), whose star is rising fast, Kcho of course, who hails from the Isla de la Juventud and was Fidel Castro's preferred artist, Ernesto Rancaño, one of my all-time favorites, and Abel Barroso, who constructs wooden machines and objects containing poignant commentary on current affairs.

✳

See a selection of Mabel Poblet's thought-provoking work at www.mabelpobletstudio.com.

✳

Art appreciation, curation, and hobnobbing is best accomplished during the Bienal, when the entire city, including this museum, is transformed into an open studio and street gallery; the next one is scheduled for 2019—that the city's biennial is held every three years tells you everything you need to know about "Cuban time." There's a cute cafe here, a museum shop with unexpectedly interesting items for sale (after you've seen what's typically for sale in Old Havana, I think you'll agree) and a 200-seat theater that is one of the top concert halls in Havana.

22 Casa de Dulce María Loynaz

NO MATTER THE COUNTRY OR context, there's a certain type of neurosis which seems to afflict the extraordinarily cultured and very well-to-do, where they shut themselves away in crumbling mansions, writing, making music, dancing, and creating a universe of their own making and imagination. Maybe you've seen the documentary *Grey Gardens* about the elderly aunt and aging cousin of Jackie Kennedy-Onassis (née De Bouvier) who lived in one room on their Long Island estate eating from tin cans surrounded by packs of cats. It's fascinating in that rubbernecking, train wreck kind of way—a combination of creepy, tragic, and compelling. Cuba has a similar family, educated abroad, well-traveled and better read, full of writers and intellectuals who created their own world in the heart of Vedado, Havana's leafy, bourgeoisie neighborhood, leaving their enclave only sporadically—to enact elaborate dinners in surrealistic settings or to travel overseas. Something in the formula worked to create greatness: daughter Dulce María Loynaz, poetess, travel writer, and novelist, is one of only three Cubans (and the only woman; the other two are Alejo Carpentier and Guillermo Cabrera-Infante) to win the Cervantes Prize, the Spanish literature equivalent to the Nobel Prize.

✳

Get a taste of Carpentier's craft in the novel
Explosion in a Cathedral; Cabrera-Infante is a
clever, talented wordsmith. Check out his
"masterpiece" *Three Trapped Tigers*.

✳

Though she won the prize for her volumes of lyrical poetry
and the novel *Jardín*, inspired by the lush garden of the Loynaz
childhood home, in her estimation, her best work was *Un Verano
en Tenerife* (A Summer in Tenerife), published in 1958 and an
early example of literary travel writing. The family Loynaz was
among the pioneers of international travel, amassing passport
stamps from the USA, Turkey, Syria, Libya, Palestine, Mexico,
various South American countries, and almost all of Europe.
This was between the 1920s and 1950s when international travel
was a long, drawn-out, often laborious endeavor. In 1929, Dulce
María traveled to Egypt and was part of the first delegation to
enter the Tomb of Tutankhamun. This was a privileged *muchacha*
and certainly all that travel informed her craft; it didn't hurt
that literary giants including Federico García Lorca, Gabriela
Mistral, and Carpentier used to hang out at her house, holding
literary salons. Says Loynaz: "We were raised in an environment
of tremendous solitude...we weren't allowed to socialize with
friends or schoolmates, we had exotic plants and animals. We
didn't really need to ever leave the house and so people from the
outside world came to us."

Not everyone was granted passage into the sanctuary, however,
and it seems some visitors harbored rancor. Carpentier calls
the Loynaz women, *"locas,"* prancing around in dresses from

the 1860s, surrounded by unopened crates packed with treasures brought home from exotic locales. Eusebio Leal, Havana's revered city historian, makes a kinder assessment: "They weren't crazy but anachronistic, with their ball gowns and solitude. They knew what they were doing and the world they were creating."

*

The 12-minute short, Últimos Días de una
Casa, explores the world and home of the
Loynaz family.

*

You can get a taste of that world by visiting the family homestead, on Calle 19 and E, now the Centro Cultural Dulce María Loynaz, fully restored in 2005 and looking as it might have nearly a century ago. In a word: fabulous. Several of the rooms, including the private chapel and parlor, are preserved as they were, Persian carpets, Louis XV furniture, piano, and all, and are open to the public; don't miss the grand hand fan collection, the rocking chair where the authoress habitually sat (her shawl and cane at hand, as if awaiting her return) and the marble sculpture *The Headless Woman*. This work of art was stolen from the family home and when it was returned, Dulce María chopped off the head to ensure it was never stolen again.

There are conferences and book launches here, poetry readings and other intellectual events befitting the history of the house. But to get the real flavor of how this award-winning writer lived out her later years, head to Línea and Calle 14—there in the middle of the block, you'll find a grand wooden house, listing in a frightful, tumble-down way, the lattice busted and rotting and a handful of chickens pecking at the dirt. It's now occupied by multiple families crowded into illegally partitioned apartments, a seamstress or two, cobblers, various domestic and farm animals, and termites to the gills. It makes for a stark and chilling contrast. Welcome to *Grey Gardens*, Cuban-style.

For a more in-depth look into the Loynaz family, check out the Centro de Promoción y Desarrollo de la Literatura Hermanos Loynaz, in Pinar del Río where the collected works, unpublished manuscripts, letters and other literary ephemera from the Loynaz children (María Dulce's brother was an even better writer by some accounts) are collected.

23 *Papa Hemingway's Havana*

IT'S ARGUABLE WHETHER ONE OF literature's greatest misogynists, philanderers, and machos deserves a place in a book celebrating travel for women, but Hemingway is a major figure in Cuba and you can love the writing, if not the writer, as I've learned (the hard way). Ernest Hemingway spent two decades in Havana, which is not surprising considering the city's prevailing creative environment and permissible, debauched culture during his tenure here from 1939 to 1960. This was the heyday of Batista—who Hemingway called a son of a bitch—when casinos and brothels, bars and corruption attracted American hordes; Hemingway was in his element, writing, fishing, and drinking like a fish in bars that today attract American hordes, notably El Floridita and the Bodeguita del Medio.

*

Meticulously researched and chock full of delicious Papa gossip (and his favorite cocktail recipes), *To Have and Have Another* by Philip Green is a treasure trove of Hemingway lore.

*

Hemingway was prolific during his residence in Room #511 at the Hotel Ambos Mundos (where a chunk of *For Whom the Bell Tolls* was written) and even more so once he bought his home, Finca Vigía in San Francisco de Paula, a far-flung suburb of Havana. In this modest farmhouse, restored by Wife #3 Martha Gellhorn (an accomplished writer and reporter in her own right, known for her coverage from World War II to the Vietnam War), Hemingway wrote *Islands in the Stream*, containing descriptions of Cuba's richest fishing grounds and *A Moveable Feast*. It was also here among the mango and ceiba trees that he wrote his master-piece exploring the limits of human strength—mental, physical, spiritual—*The Old Man and the Sea*. In 2014, a unique collabora-tion between US and Cuban Hemingway curators resulted in the digitization of 2,500 mouldering documents that had been discovered in the basement of Finca Vigía, including an unpub-lished epilogue to *Islands in the Stream* and perhaps more revealing: bar bills, recipes, and hurricane logs.

*

Fun fact: the first royalty check from *For Whom
the Bell Tolls* went to buy Finca Vigía.

*

Today you can visit the writer's home, now a museum replete with a gift shop stocking all manner of Cuban kitsch, none of it Hemingway-related, curiously, and picnic on the grounds prowled by six-toed felines known as Hemingway cats. Be sure to board *Pilar*, his fishing boat, built in Brooklyn, captained to Havana, and in dry dock at Finca Vigía for decades.

Once upon a time, Hemingway moored *Pilar* in Cojímar, the quaint seaside village just east of Havana, where a world-record-making 21-foot-long great white shark was caught in 1945. Cojímar, a laidback, quirky kind of place, is where Hemingway took to the sea to fish with First Mate Gregorio Fuentes, the Old Man immortalized in his book—or some say. Fiction is a tricky mistress and most characters are an amalgam of different people, a device used to protect the innocent and guilty alike (writer included); Hemingway professed that the Old Man was not based on any one person, but Fuentes embraced the fame and benefits provided by the friendship until his death at age 104. By all accounts, Hemingway and Fuentes were as tight as brothers and after a day hooking dorado and marlin, they'd set up at the long, hardwood bar at Las Terrazas to throw back a few. Fast forward to 2018 and every day, tour buses rumble past the bronze bust of Hemingway along Cojímar's seaside drive and idle at the curb long enough for tourists to jump out and down a mojito at that same bar, which is thriving thanks to its literary notoriety.

When I first visited Havana in the early '90s, you could still pop by Gregorio Fuentes's home to chat about his relationship and adventures with Papa Hemingway. His heirs keep up the family tradition/business, the living room peppered with ephemera, but it has lost its luster since Fuentes died in 2002. Still, if you want to experience a bit of Hemingway nostalgia, Havana hosts the Hemingway International Billfishing Tournament in May. The contest, held every year since 1950, attracts tag and release sport fishing enthusiasts who compete to catch the biggest tuna, marlin, and wahoo. In 2017, more than 50 boats from 13 countries participated, including the US, which usually fields a boat or three. Awards go to those catching the most and biggest fish, as well as best female and youngest anglers. Real Hemingway diehards might want to snap a few selfies alongside life-like creations of the author: there's a bust on the shore in Cojímar (forged from brass boat hardware donated by the town's fisherman upon learning of the writer's death) and a life-sized replica of him sidled up to the bar at the Floridita in Habana Vieja.

❋

A good book to carry while exploring
Cuba is the *Complete Short Stories of Ernest
Hemingway, The Finca Vigia Edition*

❋

24 *Alma Mater*

SITTING AT THE CREST OF a majestic hill above the decidedly pro-
saic crossroads of Calle L and San Lázaro, where Vedado meets
Centro Habana, the University of Havana is, was, and always
shall be Cuba's lodestar of bright ideas. Standing guard over this
intellectual incubator is, not surprisingly, a woman: Alma

Mater, the symbol of wisdom.
Curiously, the sculptor, Mario
Korbel, was Czech and the base, also
festooned with female forms, was
imported from New York—a similar
statue sits at the entrance to Columbia
University. Although the University
of Havana (known as UH) was founded
in 1728, it didn't move to this location until 1902. Even back then,
some 15 percent of the student body
was women; today, more than 60 percent of all Cuban university graduates
are women. The University of Havana enjoys exchange programs
with dozens of US universities, so don't be surprised if you hear
a smattering of English here and there. The *escalinata*—grand
staircase—leading to the main campus is one of Havana's stunning outdoor concert settings; consider yourself lucky if you're

in town when X Alfonso, Buena Fe, or Descemer Bueno are holding forth here (free!).

UH has always been a hotbed of student politics and protests (nowadays Young Communists promote, rather than question, the dominant paradigm) and just downhill from Alma Mater sits a monument to the university rebel of legend, Julio Antonio Mella. Not only was he courageous, charismatic, and pre-curve—organizing demonstrations against corrupt university administrators in the 1920s and co-founding the Federación Estudiantil Universitaria, still active today—he was also one sexy revolutionary. A definite RILF in my book. Needless to say, the monument doesn't do his good looks justice.

Another revolutionary hottie is Camilo Cienfuegos, who my friend Mabel calls The Man. I know this sounds incredibly vapid, so I just paged through a reference book to deepen my under-standing of these men and learned that Camilo Cienfuegos was born to Spanish parents. And Julio Antonio Mella's mother was Irish, his father Dominican. What a surprise, to learn that two of the super revolutionaries were yuma! When I shared this revela-tion with Cuban friends, they were stunned; they had no idea these major figures they'd been learning about their entire lives were not Cuban by birth.

Foreigners fighting for Cuban causes are an odd and recur-ring theme in the island's trajectory, often overlooked. But Camilo Cienfuegos and Julio Antonio Mella were in good com-pany. Other foreigners who made their mark on Cuban history include: Máximo Gómez (Dominican) and Henry Reeve (New Yorker) fighting valiantly in the First War of Independence; the ever-popular Ernesto "Che" Guevara (Argentine), an integral figure in the Revolution who still resonates today (and whose visage is emblazoned on t-shirts from Habana del Este to East

Timor); and in the world of letters, Ernest Hemingway, to mention just a few. It's more than a bit ironic that so many foreigners have left an indelible imprint on the culture and history here, but today are largely reduced to "ATMs with legs" (a common moniker for visitors) or a visa out of the country. You've been warned!

25

ISA

THE FOUNDING OF CUBA'S FLAGSHIP ART UNIVERSITY, the Instituto Superior de Arte (ISA), is one of those wild, stranger-than-fiction tales written only in countries led by dreamers; if John Lennon reigned somewhere, he might have created a free university for students to explore and develop their artistic talent. But the revolutionary government took their idealist, anti-imperialist, anti-capitalist outlook to another level when construction began on the ISA in the early 1960s. First, was the site chosen for the school. Perhaps you've seen the photo of the world's most famous bearded guerrillas Fidel Castro and Che Guevara hitting the links (if not, you can buy black and white postcards of the one-off historic moment all over the island). This shot was snapped at the Havana Country Club, where the elite used to meet before they all fled to Florida or were kicked out.

Seeing those immense stretches of green ringed by coconut palms and framboyan trees gave birth to a crazy idea to convert the golf course into an art school. Then there were the architects contracted to design the buildings—destined to house schools of modern dance, music, theater, ballet, and visual arts—these were vanguard, almost avant-garde, visionaries. This is evident as soon as you step on campus where the glass-paned domes, soaring Catalan vaults, red brick colonnades and courtyards, and sexy, sinuous lines of the classrooms and performance spaces evoke Dr. Seuss and Stanley Kubrick. ISA, now short-listed for UNESCO World Heritage Site status, sprang from the imaginations of Cuban architect Ricardo Porro (a disciple of Corbusier and Gaudí) and Italians Vittorio Garatti and Roberto Gottardi. Porro's contribution—the schools for modern dance and visual arts—were completed and the music and ballet schools designed by Garatti were almost finished. Gottardi's school of theater, however, never saw its curtain go up, construction abandoned when money and patience ran out in 1965.

Historically, ISA has been plagued by dogma and political entrenchment. With construction well under way, it was determined that the designs were too outré, not "communist" enough (there was a time when Cuba wanted more Soviet, less Seuss), and the project was halted mid-stream. Not surprisingly, this embittered the architects; Porro left for Paris and Garatti, who was accused of spying, returned to his native Milan. Gottardi, meanwhile, stayed in Cuba, dying in August 2017 at his home in Havana. Of the drama surrounding the school's origins and construction, he said his design and ideas "were never censored. I could do what I want and spend what I needed. Perhaps it was too much liberty, too Utopian, all of it."

✳

Unfinished Spaces, the most in-depth
documentary made to date about ISA,
reveals the fascinating creativity and contro-
versy surrounding the flagship school.
www.unfinishedspaces.com

✳

Despite the school's aborted construction, it opened (but not until 1976, giving you an inkling of resistance to the project) and began training future generations of Cuba's extraordinary artists—and continues today. But the cultural clash wasn't over yet. The mosaic fountain installed in the center of the school for visual arts was deemed pornographic and its removal demanded by a band of Cuban matrons. Apparently they found the giant vagina, with water spouting from the tiled clitoris and running over the oversized labia, offensive. But art—good, bad, mediocre—tends to incite emotions of all hues. One of the remarkable sights at ISA is precisely the half-built buildings and practice rooms that have been colonized by invasive plants, stray cats, and the shattered illusions of Garatti, Gottardi, and Porro. Walking around here while the throaty tones of a saxophone expertly played drift over the glass domes, and theater majors strut their funky style while leaping over art installations, is a Havana experience altogether different. Called "the world's most beautiful school," the campus exudes a palpable peace and electric energy unique in this chaotic city. And I'm happy to report that the vagina is back in place and the fountain functioning, except when it's used for performance pieces—and sometimes even then.

26 Ballet Nacional de Cuba

CUBA HAS PRODUCED SOME POWERFUL women. Vilma Espín, veteran of the guerrilla war, wife of Raúl Castro, and founder of the Federation of Cuban Women, was entirely pre-curve in her fight for gender parity and sexual diversity. Another veteran of the war in the Sierra Maestra mountains, Celía Sánchez, was a master strategist who served as Fidel Castro's confidant, secretary, and right-hand woman; she's upheld as the archetypal revolutionary to this day. And then there's Prima Ballerina Assoluta Alicia Alonso, along with her (former) husband Fernando and his brother Alberto, who founded the Ballet Nacional de Cuba (BNC) in 1948. Although almost entirely blind and on the far side of 90, she remains the director of the famous company which she rules with an iron fist (with the help of fully sighted underlings who interpret dancers' performances and stage presence). The BNC performs regularly in Havana at the fabulous Gran Teatro, recently restored and renamed the Gran Teatro de la Habana Alicia Alonso. For less than you'd pay for a couple of cocktails in San Francisco, you can see extraordinary works like *Giselle, Swan Lake, Don Quijote,* or *Corsair.* Each December, the BNC offers several performances of *The Nutcracker.* Updating the repertoire beyond the classics has become a priority recently; one of the stand-out offerings is the beautiful, but creepy, *Dracula.*

The National School of Ballet, the company's feeder school, identifies talented children at the age of six, whereupon the best of them begin a grueling twelve-year training program. Future dancers are hand-picked from all over the country and are enrolled in the rigorous program; the most gifted go on to the prestigious BNC, known for its technically brilliant dancers, with opportunities to travel and perform (and sometimes join companies) all over the world. Veterans of the Cuban program include Lorna Feijóo, who made her mark with the Boston Ballet, and Carlos Acosta, once of London's Royal Ballet, which hosted a ground-breaking performance in Havana in 2009. Trailblazer Acosta established Havana's premier independent contemporary dance company and school in 2016; top dancers clamor for a spot on his roster and performances by this electric, talented company sell out fast. José Manuel Carreno, another of Cuba's ballet stars, was a principal at the Royal Ballet and American Ballet Theatre and is the only Cuban (other than Alicia Alonso) to win *Dance Magazine's* annual award recognizing individual contributions to ballet. All these stars are a product of the BNC.

❊ www.acostadanza.com

In addition to catching a performance, there are other ways to experience the impact of the BNC while in Cuba. The Museo Nacional de la Danza (Línea and G Street, Vedado) is dedicated to documenting the life of Alicia Alonso and the trajectory of the Ballet Nacional de Cuba. Professional and aspiring dancers showing aptitude can take master classes and work-shops—practical and theoretical—as part of the BNC's annual International Dance Program. In April 2017, the Ministry of Communications issued a limited series of six stamps celebrating the founding of the BNC and the premiere of their work *Antes de Alba*. Stamp fans can pick up these and other funky stamps at the philatelic window at Havana's main post office just off the Plaza de la Revolución.

27

Ediciones Vigía

MOST PEOPLE KNOW THAT CUBA is a cultural powerhouse. But what can be a total surprise is how the island's talent manifests—in genres so diverse and random, it makes you wonder what's in the water (bacteria and amoebae aplenty, that's for sure). There are puppet theaters, regular performances of *Cats* (in Spanish), opera, fierce jewelry making and fashion design, even tobacco art and artisanal garden gnomes. In the sleepy, Swiss-clean town of Matanzas, just over 62 miles to the east of Havana, is a workshop of unparalleled creativity and talent. Ediciones Vigía is a bookmaking studio where every limited edition book is a work of art, hand-crafted and of museum quality. Indeed, a selection of the art books created here are in New York's Museum of Modern Art and the Library of Congress. Founded in 1985 by Cuban designer Rolando Estévez Jordán and poet Alfredo Zaldívar, Ediciones Vigía is an independent venture that's part studio, bookstore, workshop, publishing house, and gallery— and is worth a special stop. Given that all travelers headed to Varadero from Havana must pass through Matanzas, planning to visit Ediciones Vigía and have lunch in this lovely city is an added-value travel experience. A super savvy local recommends El Bacán for food—"best service in Cuba and the portions are Midwestern-style" (i.e. huge). Matanzas also makes a good destination for a day trip from Havana; the stalwart may consider riding the Hershey Electric Railway, Cuba's only electric train, which leaves from Casablanca and terminates in Matanzas, passing through stereotypical tiny towns and picturesque landscapes along the way.

✳ vigia.missouri.edu

Now for the books. They're extravagant and intricate. Elegant and original. A book from Ediciones Vigía will not only be the coolest souvenir from your Cuba travels, it will become a family keepsake—these are real collector's items. Each edition is limited to 200 copies and is handmade by local craftspeople who work in the multi-purpose space, giving visitors a glimpse of magic in the making. Here you can find titles by Cuban authors, of course, but also classics by Emily Dickinson, Ernest Hemingway, and other writers of similar caliber. Authors with a special connection to Cuba also have titles here among the hundreds available, including poet and scribe Margaret Randall, who lived in Havana for nearly two decades and raised her children here before moving back to the United States. All the books here are hand-bound and created from handmade paper and natural objects—flowers, sticks, bark, seeds, and leaves. They're textured and layered and may incorporate buttons, coins, or sections of string, zippers, and lace. The texts are handwritten or painted and the covers are marvels of paper engineering with tricky folds and secret windows, using a fair amount of trompe l'oeil. These books are as much a pleasure to behold as to read.

✳

To Change the World: My Years in Cuba is Randall's
memoir of her life on the island.

✳

28 *Los Beatles*

ONCE UPON A TIME, FOR A VERY LONG TIME, the music of The Beatles was verboten in Cuba. Not that it was an actual law or anything, but everyone knew: play the mop tops and risk the snitching and cold shoulders of your neighbors (many no-nos are like this in Cuba to this very day—unwritten but understood). It's hard to fathom this kind of ban now, with kids blasting Beyoncé and Coldplay and since the Rolling Stones gifted a phenomenal free mega-concert to Havana in March 2016.

✳

Havana Moon is a rockumentary of the
Stones' historic Havana concert.

✳

But back in the thick of the anti-communist, anti-hippy era, when Cuba was still finding its revolutionary feet, the four boys from Liverpool were considered a bad influence, subversive even. For those who remember the early days of rock 'n' roll, the vibe wasn't dissimilar from what parents told their children as they snapped off the Ed Sullivan show at the first gyration of Elvis Presley's hips; paternalism knows no nation, it seems. It was a minor coup, therefore, when a concert dedicated to The Beatles was held, with local musicians doing their best (some terrible) renditions of classics like *All the Lonely People* and *Why Don't We Do It On* [sic] *The Road?*

I'm sure it was a surreal, exultant moment for those who attended the 1990 concert to see those hippy hordes singing and dancing to an all-live Lennon/McCartney soundtrack in the middle of Havana.

*

Renowned Cuban filmmaker Robert Chile cobbled together footage from the historic 1990 concert; his documentary, *Lennon en la Habana*, is available on YouTube.

*

But what really sealed the deal was when Fidel Castro unveiled the uncannily life-like statue of John Lennon in the park at the corners of Calles 17 and 6 in Vedado in 2000. Lennon (as well as Lenin) is esteemed here and the preferred Beatle of Cubans for his humanism and poeticism, his politics, intelligence and talent. Today, Cubans and tourists (some not even deigning to alight from their candy-colored, chauffeured convertible) flock to his park to pay homage and take pictures sitting beside the Beatle who has his own security guard—the emblematic wire-rimmed glasses fashioned by the artist have been stolen and roughed up repeatedly; the security guard keeps them in his pocket and will gladly fit them onto John's face if you ask.

A handful of years later, The Yellow Submarine was inaugurated. A live rock 'n' roll club just a few steps from Parque John Lennon, the entire décor, from the bright yellow doors with portholes to the Blue Meanies and Fab Four in full Technicolor regalia, oozes Beatlemania. On any night of the week, it's one of the city's most swinging hotspots, with good music, cheap beer, and Cubans from 18 to 60 getting their groove on. On the club's opening night, when the bands were required to play from The Beatles songbook, Minister of Culture Abel Prieto (a long-haired poet and writer) wryly observed: "The Beatles used to be banned; now they're obligatory." The resounding success of The Yellow Submarine format led the Cuban government to open Beatles-themed clubs, all with live music, across the country. Known as "Los Beatles" (pronounced Beet-el-ehs), these venues attract locals and foreign fans looking for a good time in Bayamo, Holguín, Trinidad, and Varadero—check out the statues of John, Paul, George, and Ringo at the entrance to the last. Qué horror! Obviously, the sculptor of Havana's Lennon had nothing to do with this work, which looks nothing like any of them. Rumor has it that there are plans to put one of these clubs in every major Cuban city. And for anyone appalled by the fact that The Beatles were ostensibly banned here, it's worth remembering that they were also boycotted in the USA and declared anti-American, once upon a time.

29 The Female Music Mystique

BEFORE THE BUENA VISTA SOCIAL CLUB, before the *nueva trova* movement, before Desi Arnaz, even before the pulsating rhythms of mambo, rumba, and chachachá reached foreign shores, Cuba was a musical heavyweight. Composer and violinist Amadeo Roldán (1900-1939) spearheaded the Afrocubanism movement, incorporating Afro-Cuban elements into classical music, crackerjack pianist and composer Ernesto Lecuona (1895-1963) penned over 600 compositions and went on to worldwide fame, and blind *tres* player Arsenio Rodríguez (1911-1970) was a giant of traditional *son montuno* to which he added robust horn sections, laying the groundwork for what we know as salsa. Cuba's musical heritage goes way back, its influences imprinted on international genres from baroque to rap, jazz to pop. In some cases, modifications by Cuban musicians to standard styles created new genres altogether, including Afro-Cuban jazz and salsa. Before the revolution, female musicians were mostly singers, chanteuses like Rita Montaner (Cuba's transvestites dig deep into her repertoire), the inimitable Elena Burke (still covered by Cuban crooners), Celia Cruz AKA the Queen of Salsa who left Cuba after the revolution never to set foot on the island again, and Omara Portuondo, who got her start with super group Anacoana, an all-female orchestra, and re-gained superstar status with the Buena Vista Social Club. The advent of free, universal education, including in the arts, where the most talented Cubans from across the country were invited to study at Havana's flagship art university, the Instituto Superior de Arte (ISA, see Chapter 25), changed all that. Tapping into national talent the breadth of the island unleashed a wave of creativity that resonates and stimulated a boom in phenomenal female drummers, bassists, pianists, and singers.

＊

Cuba and Its Music: From the First Drums to the Mambo by Ned Sublette is considered the definitive reference on the evolution of Cuban sounds and their global influence.

＊

While some more (literally and virtually) connected musicians can be found on iTunes and YouTube, many of Cuba's notable music makers are just beginning to surface on the global radar. But here on the island, we're enjoying the sultry sounds of all sorts of talented women and you can too—if you know for whom to keep eyes and ears peeled.

Omara Portuondo (known affec-
tionately as Omara here) is still going
strong at 87 years of age, thanks
mainly to her exceptional, carefully
tended voice and re-found fame with
the Buena Vista Social Club. Her concerts are always packed with talented
musicians of all ages and often spark
collective singing and dancing from
the audience.

The tradition of powerhouse female singers continues to thrive among the younger generation; currently bearing the torch is the raven-haired knockout Luna Manzanares, who Cubans adore across the board, and rap-turned-pop star Diana Fuentes, who, while not as universally popular, has a distinctive voice suited to her street roots. Telmary, who staked her claim on the Havana music scene with Interactivo a decade or so ago and has since gone solo, is a spunky, fun artist who raps and sings audiences into the zone.

Many Cuban singers belt out tunes in English—badly. What a relief, then, to discover young blues-rock singer Zule Guerra, who sets the bar so high for singing in English, she will not be surpassed any time soon (though the lead singer for the rock band Sweet Lizzy Project has got a set of pipes on her to rival anyone). For the beauty of their harmonies and arrangements, not to mention their stage presence, Sexto Sentido is a quartet of young Cuban women worth catching.

I've saved my absolute favorites for last: Yissy and Yusa (Cubans have an obsession for names beginning with Y; a friend has amassed a list that now surpasses 1,000 Cuban names that start with Y). Both women of color subverting the dominant paradigm, they each have their own bands and play instruments traditionally the purview of men. Yusa, who you'll be lucky to catch since she's often touring in Europe, Japan, or Argentina, was formally trained on the *tres* before she picked up an electric bass. She composes, writes lyrics, sings, and holds everything together with her funky, fun bass playing, though she also wails on the guitar and *cajón,* a traditional percussion instrument that is essentially a box with a sound hole. Yissy is a ferocious drummer, who together with an all-star group of musicians known as

Bandancha (keyboards, bass, guitar, and DJ with some congas thrown in for shits and giggles), rip the roof off whatever room they're playing. The synergy and energy generated by these musicians is more palpable than most—there's no ego or posing with Yissy and Bandancha, just extraordinarily talented musicians who love what they do and want to share that joy with their audience.

❋ www.yissygarcia.com/en

30 La Fábrica de Arte Cubano (F.A.C.)

OPENED WITH LITTLE FANFARE IN 2014, the F.A.C. started as a multi-genre art space with several bars, a cafe, two musical venues, and a lot of corners and crannies for kanoodling and chilling. Set in an old cooking oil factory (hence the Fábrica moniker), most of the cobbled together spaces are constructed from re-purposed shipping containers, the furniture is made of pallets like they use in Home Depot to shuttle around merchandise, and there are collapsible wooden stools scattered around so groups of friends can grab several to create their own hangout area. Permanent installations also dot the multi-tiered space; don't be surprised if you stumble upon a giant fiberglass tongue or towering sculpture representing the Republic as you explore the different galleries and patios while sipping your mojito smoothie. On any given night here you can see photo exhibits, dance performances, live music, with the occasional fashion show, hairstyling competition, or documentary film sprinkled among the regular programming. Top DJs from Cuba and around the world are often invited to spin their best sets here and the live music on offer is always A-list. This makes sense since the "Fábrica," as Cubans call it, was founded by X Alfonso, part of the Alfonso musical dynasty headed by his parents and leaders of the decades-old group Síntesis. X was born, raised, and grew up listening to and making music, and that life-long education is reflected in the quality of the acts gracing the F.A.C. stages.

Community-building and outreach is also part of the Fábrica mystique: there's a free concert for neighborhood children the first Sunday of every month, and every summer, there are free workshops for kids and teens, who can sign up to learn anything from photography to belly-dancing, graphic design to video production. There is simply no other venue in Cuba—though others have tried to replicate it in one form or another—like the Fábrica.

And therein lies the problem: after receiving an avalanche of foreign tourists, press, and investment, the Fábrica has become unsustainably popular. Since opening, the space has expanded exponentially, with new galleries, a fine dining restaurant, and a VIP section added to the original structure. Unfortunately, the narrow hallways have nowhere to grow, the bathrooms often become overwhelmed with use, and the mobs of drunken European and American youths attract a certain type of Cuban not interested in art or music. And this is a huge turn-off for Cubans just looking for a fun night out with friends.

The hustle hits you hard at the Fábrica, and signs advise patrons to hold on tight to their entrance card. No money changes hands inside the venue; you pay the $2CUC cover and are given a cardboard card; all your purchases made within the space and among the different bars are noted on the card; and you pay the total when you leave. A common scam is to steal someone else's card, drink to the hilt on the heisted card, and then hand over an empty one upon leaving. The line to get in can be two hours (or longer), depending on who's playing, but is usually more tolerable Thursdays and Sundays—many Cubans I know will go only on these days, when crowds (and the hustlers they attract) are more manageable. Since the space only opens at 8 p.m. Thursdays to Sundays, one strategy to beat the tiresome line is to eat at Tierra, the gourmet restaurant inside; another is to pay off the bouncer, but this is a sure way to piss off every Cuban who bears witness.

*

The best online resource for cultural happenings in Havana is What's On: www.lahabana.com.

*

Note that the F.A.C is closed January, May, and September. Regardless of whether you love or hate the Fábrica, it reflects Havana's new economy, culture, and vibe—for better or worse. Word on the street is that another one is going to be opening soon, not far from the original. Stay tuned.

III

Popular in the Provinces

31 *Cienfuegos*

FROM HAVANA TO MATANZAS, GUANTÁNAMO to Nipe, one of the reasons early explorers (and exploiters) were so enamored of Cuba was the presence of deep, navigable bays allowing for easy off-loading of slaves and packing of ships with the sugar they were forced to cut and process. Cienfuegos, known as "the Pearl of the South" has one of the country's deepest bays and while once a bustle of agriculture and industry (including a nearly finished nuclear power plant financed by the USSR, which has been left to the elements for decades, making for a fascinating photo shoot), today, it's lifeblood is art and tourism. And the deep, navigable bay is proving a cash cow now as in colonial times: cruise ships dock regularly in Cienfuegos and live aboard sailboats with everything included set out from the modern marina here—circumnavigating the island with an all-Cuban crew must make for one of the Caribbean's all-time greatest family vacations. The eponymous capital city meanwhile, can be desultory, but is peppered with artist studios and galleries, while top-flight dance and music performances are hosted at the Teatro Tomás Terry, a marvel of late 1800s architecture anchoring the tranquil Parque José Martí in the heart of the city.

Strolling Cienfuegos's spiffy, bustling streets or taking sunset cocktails from a wooden porch along Punta Gorda reveals the sensual enchantment of this small, archetypal Cuban city. Along the main drag, there's a Coppelia outpost for an ice cream fix, a life-like statue of musical icon Benny Moré (known as "the barbarian of rhythm," he hails from the country town of Santa Isabel de la Lajas in Cienfuegos province), and along the water, a mini-Malecón where local youth neck and gossip as night falls. As you might expect from a town so closely linked to all activities maritime, Cienfuegos has a modern marina where fully crewed live-aboard sailboats can be contracted and where foreign sailors dock for some R&R.

*

You can hear the sublime tones of
Benny Moré singing Santa Isabel de la
Lajas Querida on YouTube.

*

An old saying in Cuba, "plant a broomstick and it will grow," is an axiom brought to life at the sprawling Jardín Botánico Soledad, home to over 2000 plant species and an oasis of green wedged between an abandoned sugar mill and active cement factory 11 miles from the city center. Originally founded to study different species of sugar cane, Cuba's largest botanical garden was in the care of Harvard University researchers in the early 20th century and now is a center for studying and cultivating endemic and imported flora. The boom-bust sugar cycle, US interests profiting off island resources, and Cuban researchers stepping into the void serve as metaphor for the island's contemporary history. Using Cienfuegos as a base—to dive on the southern coast, for hiking to El Nicho (see Chapter 57) and other waterfalls in Topes de Collantes (see Chapter 54), to contract a live-aboard for seafaring adventures—is a practical, rarely implemented travel strategy.

32 Trinidad

ONE OF CUBA'S NINE UNESCO World Heritage Sites, Trinidad and the Valle de los Ingenios nearby encapsulate Cuba's history of slavery, sugar, and colonial imperialism wrapped in a jaw-dropping landscape. In fact, Trinidad's history reads like a CliffsNotes version of the history of Latin America. The town was founded in 1514 by none other than Diego Velázquez, the explorer who followed Columbus's caravan and founded Cuba's first settlements: Baracoa, Bayamo and then Trinidad. This was the boonies back then, completely isolated and prime territory for buccaneers, bandits, and swashbucklers. Despite its remote location, legend holds that the first mass Fray Bartolomé de las Casas ever delivered was in Trinidad. He would go on to travel throughout the region delivering impassioned sermons; his appeal to the King of Spain for more humane treatment of indigenous populations in the Americas earned him the appellation the "Protector of the Indians."

✳

Witnessing the execution of Cuban indigenous
leader Hatuey and similar barbarities
led Bartolomé de las Casas to pen *A Brief
Account of the Destruction of the Indies*.

✳

Time passed and Trinidad's aggressive, active slave trade assured the necessary labor to produce the sugar cane for which the area is famous (at its height, there were 75 sugar mills here), making the plantation owners extraordinarily rich in the bargain—hence the palatial homes lining the city's colonial center. Many of these landowners were of Basque descent (like Iznaga, of the famed Iznaga Plantation in the Valle de los Ingenios), who were followed by French colonists fleeing the slave revolt that led to Haitian independence. It's estimated that 25,000 French people and their descendants sought refuge in Cuba when all hell broke loose in Haiti; you'll see traces of this European heritage in museum collections, furniture in finer homes, and in the blond hair and light eyes of the original settlers' descendants. Anyone interested in the sugar boom that converted Cuba from an island backwater and pirate stopover to a colonial powerhouse should check out Trinidad.

Some towns absorb tourists well, their foreign tongues carried away on the tropical breeze, the bus tour hordes blending seamlessly into side streets, galleries, and plazas. Trinidad isn't one of them. Since the tourist explosion detonated over the island (a record-breaking 4 million foreigners visited Cuba in 2017) Trinidad likewise has exploded—some would say imploded. It makes sense that so many people want to visit Trinidad since it's one of Cuba's only cities with a unique mix of architecture, history, verdant landscapes, and white sand beach all within close proximity to the *casco histórico* (historical core). Along with Cienfuegos (see Chapter 31), Trinidad also has a vibrant art scene, with studios lining the cobblestone streets and artists-in-residence welcoming the public with coffee or a shot of rum. This is the type of town where you can ride a bicycle to the beach one day, horseback ride the next, visit half a dozen museums in an afternoon, eat sumptuously at night, and dance until daybreak.

The Tourist Train, running on the old tracks which once carried loads of cane, makes a four-hour loop through town and valley with a couple of stops at sites of historic interest; the scenery is dynamite. Day trips to dazzling spots in the Escambray (see Chapter 54) can also be arranged from Trinidad. One of the most common 10-day itineraries starts in Havana and loops through Cienfuegos (see Chapter 31) and Trinidad ending in the capital. If this appeals, a couple of words to the wise: bus tickets sell out days before, travel times are longer than they appear on the map, and lodging in Trinidad is booked solid months in advance.

33 *Santa Clara*

WELCOME TO THE CITY OF Che, the City Gay: the bulk of visitors making their way to Santa Clara, two and a half hours from Havana, are queer folk or communists

(or both, though one orientation usually remains on the down low since it's the rare Cuban who can bridge both worlds easily). Sympathizers with the cause and history buffs include Santa Clara on their itineraries, a dull, charmless city truth be told, because of Ernesto "Che" Guevara. One of the brave—some might say crazy—82 souls who set out from Mexico in the *Granma*, a dubiously seaworthy boat not unlike *The Minnow* of Gilligan fame, he helped launch a revolution that resonated around the world.

On paper, the adventure was doomed from the start, damned by bad weather, a man overboard (recovered after six hours), and a less than auspicious landing in a mangrove-choked swamp. Upon attaining terra firma, the ravaged fighters were met by well-equipped and -trained Batista troops. Only 11 survived the ensuing battle, including Juan Almeida, a beloved revolutionary whose words during the fight, "*¡Aquí no se rinde nadie!*" ("Here, nobody surrenders!") are still invoked. Another *"barbudo,"* as the bearded revolutionaries were known, who escaped into the Sierra Maestra was the one, the only, Che Guevara. In addition to acting as doctor and dentist (he was an MD, after all) for the revolutionary troops bivouacked in the mountains and the surrounding population (an experience that led to the creation of Cuba's universal health system), he and his column took the city of Santa Clara in December 1958. This marked the beginning of the end for Batista; the final blow was struck when Che and company commandeered the "Tren Blindado," a train filled to the hilt with armed government forces. It took the 18 *barbudos* less than 10 minutes to overtake the 400 troops huddled inside.

Today the train is a museum, but Santa Clara's five-star attraction is the Monumento Ernesto Che Guevara, a giant sculpture of the revered guerrilla in a blazing hot plaza on the outskirts of the city. The mausoleum in the base of the museum complex is one of the most peaceful, moving spots in all of Cuba. Dimly lit, with a fresh flower in front of each of the 38 niches housing remains of those slain in the failed guerrilla uprising led by Che in Bolivia, it exudes an undeniable energy, regardless of your political proclivities.

But Santa Clara is famous for another spot. Just as revolutionary as the sites where Che and troops made history is El Mejunje. An indigenous word meaning pastiche or potpourri, this was the first club in the country to openly declare itself a space celebrating sexual diversity. It quickly gained notoriety for its drag shows (the first one was held in 1992 during a homage to Freddy Mercury) and LGBT programming, including the annual Miss Travesti pageant (March). Opening El Mejunje in 1984 was a gutsy move by founder Ramón Silverio—back then, homo- and transphobia were par for the course in macho Cuba,

and this cultural center provided both succor and refuge for any
and all who identified as different.

*

For the straight dope on gay life in Cuba,
the blog www.paquitoeldecuba.com
is the go to source.

*

Just as you need not be a revolutionary to appreciate the
accomplishments of Che, you need not be gay, bi, or anywhere
else outside the heteronormative paradigm to have a great night
out at Mejunje. Housed in the ruins of an old mansion, with a
shabby-chic patio shaded by giant jacarandas where you can sip
mojitos under the stars, its part gay dance club, part community
center, part bohemian bar. In short, El Mejunje feels like San
Francisco and Berlin got together and had a Cuban lovechild.
Here, you're just as likely to happen upon live *trova* or salsa, as
a *quinceñera* or drag show. Luckily, we've come a long way from
when Allen Ginsberg was asked to leave the country for cruising
Che Guevara.

34 Remedios

WHEN THE FIRST EXPLORERS STUMBLED on Cuba, they hit the jack-pot: first they founded Baracoa (1511), one of Cuba's most majestic towns, followed by Bayamo (1513; see Chapter 64), a vibrant city recently renovated and the envy of the country, and then Trinidad (1514; see Chapter 32), the epitome of a colonial gem, pristinely preserved. And Remedios, founded in 1524 a stone's throw from the Villa Clara coast, is a contender for the loveliest of all. The 16th-century architecture, the narrow streets where elder gentleman walk hand-in-hand with their granddaughters, and the slow pace, plus the easy access to Cayo Santa María, distinguish Remedios from other colonial towns. What really puts Remedios over the top, however is the annual festival known as Las Parrandas, held every December 24th usu-ally lasting several days. The festivities kick off just before mid-night when the two opposing neighborhoods, San Salvador and El Carmen, debut their pyrotechnic, multi-tiered floats topped with gyrating dancing girls, spinning wheels, and telescopic, mechanized geegaws. The display is accompanied by non-stop fireworks until dawn, filling the town's main plaza with smoke and accompanying piquant sulfur smell, while littering the ground, bushes, and benches with multi-colored confetti. It is one of Cuba's best parties, for which Remedios prepares all year, tapping friends and family abroad for materials and money to put their neighborhood's best foot forward in the competition for top float. In 2016, the Parrandas were cancelled to observe the nine days of mourning following Fidel Castro's death and in 2017, a fireworks malfunction sent over 30 onlookers to the hospital. It is very difficult to get reservations at this time of year and sleeping (or rather, losing consciousness) in the main park is not unheard of; if you can't make it to Remedios for Las Parrandas, the Charangas de Bejucal, a small city 25 miles southeast of Havana, are held every December 17th.

There's not much to do in Remedios but wander around, get to know the neighbors, and admire the architecture. Therein lies its charm (if nightlife and street scenes float your boat, Trinidad is a better option). Literary travelers should consider grabbing a quick drink at El Louvre, where poet Federico García Lorca used to tie one on. After a couple of cold ones, the place to start sightseeing is Parque Martí, the heart and soul of Remedios. Not one, but two gorgeous churches flank the park. The more spectacular of the two is San Juan Bautista de Remedios. Originally built in 1545 at another site, the church standing here today was constructed in the 1700s, with the bell tower added a century later; the interior was restored in 1946 and warrants a look for its gilded altar and pregnant Virgin Mary. Hmmmm. That's not how the story goes, is it?! If you can't make it for the grand fiesta on December 24th, pop into the Museo de las Parrandas Remedianas to ogle winning floats of years past and learn about the history of this cultural tradition.

35 Camagüey

CAUGHT BETWEEN THE CENTRAL PROVINCES and those in the Oriente, Camagüey is Cuba's third-largest city and suffers from something similar to "middle child syndrome." It's not the biggest (like Havana) or the second-biggest and birthplace of the revolution (like Santiago de Cuba). Despite being a UNSECO World Heritage Site, it's underestimated by travelers who treat it more as a convenient stopover, breaking cross-country trips here, than a destination in itself. Meanwhile, Cubans I know from Camagüey have called it everything from "Cuba's most racist city" to "full of *gusanos*"—literally meaning worms, this was a term used at the height of the Cold War to describe anti-government factions and now largely out of fashion (except when it comes to Camagüey apparently). Sounds bad, right? It certainly doesn't sound like one of the 100 places in Cuba women should go. But it is, because Camagüey is a unique city, riddled with hidden, unnamed streets and colonial plazas popping up around blind corners. The architecture is neck-ache stunning and the pace friendlier and mellower than its big city counterparts to the east and west.

Train buffs will have a field day at the old train yards and the adjacent train museum currently under construction. And if the Ballet of Camagüey is performing at the dazzling Teatro Principal, jump on the opportunity to see this, Cuba's foremost company after the Ballet Nacional de Cuba. In Camagüey, the charm lies in slowing down, getting lost, exploring, and diving into local life at art galleries and cinemas.

*

The history of railway development in Cuba and its intersection with US interests on the island is explained (and meticulously documented) in Louis A Perez's *On Becoming Cuban*.

*

Founded in 1514, Camagüey was designed to hoodwink and trap rapacious pirates who continually laid siege to this strategic

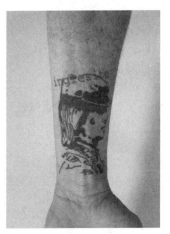

city—one of the original seven established by Diego Velázquez. Narrow, cobblestone streets dead end (there's an actual street in the colonial core named "No Exit"), while wider streets double back on themselves. Still others bend around corners to continue anew farther up the way creating a labyrinthine city center as confusing to modern-day visitors as they were to the likes of Henry Morgan and company back when pirates of the Caribbean were a real threat. In addition to baroque churches and columned mansions with cool interior patios, Camagüey is strewn with *tinajones*, giant clay pots laid on their side that were used to collect scarce, coveted rainwater in colonial times; today they're used to adorn gardens and porticoes, but the pressure is on to restore their functionality as Cuba faces periodic drought and the effects of global warming.

One characteristic that jumps out immediately upon entering Camagüey is the number of streets, buildings, and sites named after Ignacio Agramonte. In the roster of war heroes, Agramonte ranks high, for his bravery and leadership skills during the First War of Independence. This first, failed attempt at liberation from Spain was fought with machetes and grit, clever tactics, and bold maneuvering. Agramonte led by example, one taken to heart by Henry Reeve, his most valued column leader who charged into battle valiantly, gaining ground and motivating his cavalry to soldier on. Wounded six times in one fight, he faked his own death until the enemy retreated, strapped his legs to his horse and kept fighting.

The curious history of Cuba is studded with foreign war heroes who are not Cuban but sympathize with the cause— Máximo Gómez, who distinguished himself in both the First and Second Wars of Independence hailed from the Dominican Republic, and then there's Che Guevara, of course. And so it is with Henry Reeve, a young man from New York who made his way to Cuba in the 1800s to fight for the cause of liberation. He fast became a household name in these parts and the Cubans dubbed him "El Inglesito" (the little Englishman; Cubans were a bit geographically challenged back then). Outside of central Cuba, this New Yorker and freedom fighter was largely forgotten to history until 2005, when his name was immortalized by Cuba's newly formed Henry Reeve Disaster and Epidemics Brigade, a rapid response, post-disaster medical team which has saved lives from Pakistan to Haiti, Guatemala to Sierra Leone. In 2017, the World Health Organization granted this team its Public Health Award for its cumulative work, most notably fighting Ebola in West Africa.

Since the city celebrated its quincentennial, the government has pumped serious money into local infrastructure to upgrade Camagüey's technological and cultural offerings. Today there's a "Cinema Street" with art galleries, movie theaters, new media centers, and headquarters of the annual Festival Internacional de Video de Camagüey. The Paseo Tecnológico, meanwhile, is nerd central, with Wi-Fi access, high tech video games, IT stores and the like, which the government spent $50,000CUC to create in 2017.

"Demand has surpassed all expectations," the national press reported that summer, as the Bosque Tecnológico proved on a recent visit, the shady benches under the crowns of grand trees crowded with local youths on their portable devices. Ironically, the "Technology Forest" is one of Camagüey's greenest spaces— the dearth of shade and foliage here is something of which urban planners are keenly aware, creating massive ex-urban parks to compensate. The city center does boast one grand dame of a tree however: in Parque Ignacio Agramonte grows a 115-year-old ceiba, protected by wrap-around iron railings and an inscription reading, "This ceiba was planted on May 20, 1902 to represent the genuine fighting tradition and aspirations of all Cubans." Though Camagüey suffers from a lack of trees, it is known all around the country as producing the island's best cheese; take advantage of men emerging from the bush along the highway selling blocks of semi-hard, white, salty cheese for $1CUC a pound.

36 *Holguín*

LET ME ADMIT RIGHT OFF that I'm biased about Holguín—both the province and the capital city. This soft spot is due to the many close friends I have from here, people who are part of my "central" (a central is a sugar mill and since these form—or rather, formed—the backbone of the culture and economy for so many centuries, Cubans say: "Those who have friends have a central," meaning they get by with a little help from their friends). Technically, according to cartographers and meteorologists, the eastern part of Cuba known as the Oriente starts in somnolent Las Tunas. In reality, Las Tunas is just building momentum for Holguín, where the Oriente, with its trademark hospitality, down home cooking, and party atmosphere, actually gains purchase. Hitting this vibrant city after the long, hot, boring road through Las Tunas is like a shot of good, strong coffee followed by a whiskey chaser. Known as "the city of parks" for the four major plazas delineating the city center, Holguín has fewer than 300,000 inhabitants, who spend their spare time strolling between plazas, popping into galleries and artisan bazaars, and embroiling themselves in heated games of dominoes, moving the tables under streetlamps at night. At the same time, this is a working city of industry and agriculture with a palpable hustle and flow that views tourism as an afterthought. This is what also attracts about Holguín: despite its proximity to tantalizing

Gibara and the mega-resorts in and around Guardalavaca, it's not all tarted up for tourism and is surprisingly hustler-free.

May and August are the best times to drop into town. The one-week, blowout cultural event known as the Romerías de Mayo transforms Holguín into an art party every May, with quality improv theater, art openings, concerts, and dance performances that bring people flooding in from around the country and the world. Ostensibly founded as a religious festival with a dedicated Mass and pilgrimages to the Loma de la Cruz overlooking town, the ecclesiastical roots and purpose have been eclipsed by the cultural programming now distinguishing the Romerías. The third week in August (considerately scheduled so as not to conflict with the August 13th birthday of El Comandante Fidel Castro), Holguín goes completely bonkers with its annual blowout Carnaval festivities. Rides, floats, live music, and dancing are accompanied by an endless flow of rum and locally produced Mayabe beer, which at 75 cents a can is Cuba's best cheap brew. For dining, it's roast pork, followed by more roast pork and when hunger pangs hit, even more roast pork. It's a bit disconcerting to be in Holguín around Carnaval, when the death squeals of pigs being slaughtered are heard into the pre-dawn hours, but boy are they mighty tasty once they're slipped off the spit; my apologies to my vegetarian readers, but Cuba is, after all, a decidedly carnivorous place. This is something you'll have to plan for and get used to if you're a vegetarian—or even more challenging, a vegan—traveling to the island.

No matter when you find yourself in Holguín, a trip to the top of the Loma de la Cruz is compulsory. Ascending the 902 feet via 495 steps is a searing hot slog, but the views over town are worth it. You can drive up here, but that's kind of cheating, considering the cross was erected here to draw pilgrims seeking relief from drought. As the saying goes, "Be careful what you wish for"—in September 2017, Category 5 Hurricane Irma hammered Cuba, affecting 15 of the country's 16 provinces; it wrought millions of dollars in damages, but returned Cuba's reservoirs to robust levels, providing respite from a 70-year-long drought.

37 *Gibara*

THIS ENCLAVE A QUICK HOP from Holguín is marked with a purple asterisk on the most recent edition of International Travel Maps' Cuba, indicating it's a Point of Interest. The description says: "Friendly harbor town." This is like saying "Donald Trump's presidency is a wee problematic"—in short, a huge understatement. Fifteen years ago, Gibara was a fairy tale princess gone to seed, a forgotten crumbling town on the northern coast where old men sold shots of oysters for 15 cents from rickety carts and even the horses lacked the giddy-up to swat flies. Back then, only a couple of houses rented rooms and the one mouldering hotel in town was boarded up, laced with cobwebs. Then, miraculously, Gibara transformed. The "friendly harbor town" rose from the ashes to become Cuba's Sleeping Beauty, the new place to go and be seen—for those in the know, it was cooler than Habana Vieja, more sophisticated than Trinidad (see Chapter 32).

This rebirth is a result of the Festival Internacional de Cine Pobre (International Budget Film Festival), established by Cuban director Humberto Solás, who discovered the town in the late 1960s and like a catchy pop song, couldn't get it out of his head. The global attention this premier festival has garnered over the years motivated local and regional authorities to invest in Gibara, fixing up plazas, restoring the old hotel and constructing new ones, and improving infrastructure. As one local told me: "Thank god for Humberto Solás," without him and the money and interest the festival garners, she implied, Gibara would have continued its downward slide.

*

In 1968, Humberto Solás filmed his master-
piece, *Lucia*, in Gibara. The splendor of the town
stuck with him and is now HQ of the annual
International Low-Budget Film Festival.
www.cinepobre.com

*

This is particularly true since Hurricane Ike ripped through the town in 2008, projecting roofs and trees and front doors clear across town and battering Gibara's mini-malecón. Says Rafaelita, a life-long resident: "It was the most terrifying night of my life. Nine of us spent eight hours huddled in the bath-room until the wind stopped roaring. When we came out, we couldn't see the street the debris was piled so deep. The entire town was without electricity for 15 days."

Head up to the lookout point above Gibara and you can still see gaping holes in roofs and lots where entire houses were swept away. I wouldn't be surprised if residents toward the upper reaches of town took refuge in the Cueva de Panaderos—a mas-sive, 19-gallery cavern system with rock climbing possibilities in the entry galleries and a pool for swimming farther in.

Today, you slide through verdant hills on what feels like a backcountry road to the seaside town and are greeted by brightly colored skiffs floating in the bay, the distant mountains rippling toward the horizon providing a cinematic backdrop. Colonial houses oozing quaint, centuries-old charm beckon with their room for rent signs and fanning out from the main streets are unpaved lanes making their way to the upper reaches of town where panoramic vistas unfold. Even in August, Gibara remains cool, caressed by sea breezes for which it has gained famed; hence, the windmill farms down the coast.

I should stop here and say point blank that foreigners without permanent residency are prohibited from buying property in Cuba. I'm sorry to have to interrupt the narrative, but Gibara is the kind of place that engenders love at first sight and dreams of relocation (think Merida or San Miguel de Allende in Mexico)—a tranquil seaside town with gorgeous colonial architecture, a warm and open populace, nice beaches just up the road, and a burgeoning foodie scene. What's more, Gibara is located just 30 minutes from a major city and international airport. And every April, everybody who is anybody in Cuban cinema, plus film folk from Hollywood, New York, Buenos Aires, Tehran, and beyond, descend upon Gibara to inject it with high-quality movies in a hotly contested competition.

It reminds me a bit of San Sebastián in Spain, minus the killer pinxos (though with the abundance of seafood here and restaurants that are lauded as far away as Havana, they'll probably soon be on the menu). Still, there are some fabulous places to eat in Gibara and while I'm loath to devote word count to restaurant recommendations, a couple of local secrets are worth mentioning: Vista Azul (locals call it "Paladar Pelly"—the restaurant sign has a picture of a Pelly, the Cuban Cheez Doodle) at the top of the hill overlooking town, quite near the picturesque arches of an abandoned Spanish fort, provides 270° views while you dine. Cueva Taína, on the outskirts toward Playa Caletones, is tucked back on a dirt lane and is a national treasure (peruse the wall of photos featuring famous Cuban diners as you sip a beer). They have their own organic garden, startlingly intricate and educational sculptures depicting the history of Gibara and its indigenous (Taíno) roots, a re-creation of a traditional *bohio*, where kids can pretend they're living in the campo, donning a hat and making pretend coffee in the *tetera*, and exuberant plants all around. At either of these places a complete meal with your choice of shrimp, crab, lobster, fish, or octopus, freshly caught of course, will cost a mere $5CUC.

Coastal life is alive and well around Gibara; Playa Caletones, a darling beach 11 miles up a dirt road west of town, is exploding since it got electricity in 2016. Every August, there's a three-day rave held here that brings DJs from as far as Havana.

38 _Baracoa_

AH, BARACOA. THIS REMOTE SEASIDE town on Cuba's eastern tip is so enchanting a local saying holds that "Anyone who swims in the Río Miel, will forever stay in Baracoa." You may be tempted once you've awoken to a Baracoa sunrise, the nearby mountains peeking through the lifting mist—iconic El Yunque chief among them—wondering whether to romp in rivers or hit the beaches, hike into the woods or go for a scenic drive, stopping to dine on unique regional dishes along the way. With so many things to do and see in the area, this town of 40,000 people punches well above its weight; were this book limited to the top five places to go in Cuba, Baracoa would be among them. Pulsing with myths, legends, and history hewn by a tough, resilient populace where traces of indigenous roots can still be seen in the face and countenance of some, Baracoa is the loam from which travel adventures root and flourish.

Part of Baracoa's seductive mystery lies in the fact that the town was completely cut off from the rest of the island until 1965, when the Farola (touted as one of Cuba's Seven Engineering Wonders) was completed. Before this road connected Baracoa to towns on the southern coast of Guantánamo province, there was more contact with other Caribbean islands and points north than with Cuba. Says native Baracuense Ana María Navarro: "When I was a young girl growing up in Baracoa, boats plied the waters every day between here and Florida, Jamaica, and Haiti. Our perspective fanned outward, to other countries; it didn't feel isolated to us."

Yet, Baracoa's isolation is real—making it charming, but also vulnerable, as witnessed by the events of October 4, 2016 when Hurricane Matthew battered this and nearby towns with winds of 137 miles per hour, accompanied by heavy rains and flooding when the ocean breached Baracoa's seawall. As the Category 4 cyclone ripped across this knob of Guantánamo, trees snapped like matchsticks, land and rocks and flora tumbled from the mountains, making roads impassable, and bridges washed out, cutting Baracoa off, once again, from the rest of the country. Disaster response was organized and rapid, but the region's geography, combined with massive damage to buildings and infrastructure, means there are still homes without roofs, people without homes, and sacks of cement, bricks, and other building materials stacked three feet high in Baracoa, more than a year later. Reminders of the destruction are everywhere: entire swaths of mountains stripped of trees, coconut palms missing their crowns, and caved in houses where people live under ceilings propped up with salvaged wood. National environmental authorities estimate that 75 percent of old-growth forest was downed in the storm, while almost the entire coconut and cacao harvests—two mainstays of Baracoa's economy—were lost. Baracoa is tinged with an 'edgy, survivalist hue it didn't use to have as a result and the trauma is still fresh in people's minds. "Donations took too long to get to us. All the rivers were choked with leaves and debris, contaminating the water, but purification tablets like these weren't distributed until eight months later," Miguel Suárez tells me, holding up a box of pills. Spanish-speaking visitors will share many hurricane-related conversations and exchanges like this one while traveling in and around Baracoa.

Restoring tourism infrastructure was a priority in Hurricane Mathew's aftermath and Baracoa is very much open for business: there are lovely sea- and bayside rooms with a view for rent, restaurants and tours are up and running, and the perennially popular Casa de la Trova on the town's pedestrian boulevard still holds raucous live music and dance parties almost every night. Hiking—through Parque Natural Majayara, to the top of El Yunque or along trails in the Parque Nacional Alejandro de Humboldt (see Chapter 63)—is still a major draw, despite the damage to local flora and fauna. The coastline was altered significantly by the storm, but the beaches at Playa Duaba and Playa Maguana are two beauties within striking distance from town drawing locals and visitors alike. Farther afield, numerous beaches out toward Boca de Yumurí (see Chapter 62) along a winding country road dot the coastline; even in August, when Cubans flock to any water source to beat the heat, you might find you're the only soul strolling their dark sands.

One of the allures of Baracoa is that it's one of the few places in Cuba with a definitive regional cuisine—sweet relief after so much pork, rice, and beans. There's a Cuban saying that "When you get tired of rice and beans, switch to beans and rice," and after just a few days on the island, you'll be slavering for Baracoa's fish in coconut milk, almond toffee, 50-cent bars of pure chocolate, and spicy mounds of teeny tiny *tetí*, a fish found only in the rivers of the area. Served up whole, some hundreds of these fish the size of a fingernail clipping make a meal—look closely and you can see their pinpoint black eyes among the onion and peppers. You can still get Baracoa's signature "*cucurucho de coco*" (sweet, flaked coconut wrapped in husk cones), but they're less densely packed and more expensive since the hurricane took out 90 percent of the area's coconut palms. They cost 25 cents apiece if you're coming via Moa (AKA Cuba's most depressing town), $1CUC if you drive the fabulously picturesque La Farola (see Chapter 91). Though Hurricane Irma, a Category 5 monster that struck Cuba in September 2017, didn't hit Baracoa directly, heavy rains lashed the seaside town and the ocean breached the seawall anew, further complicating Matthew reconstruction efforts.

39 Chivirico

THIS IS WHAT I CALL a "told-you-so town." Perfectly situated on Santiago de Cuba's southern coast, where the foothills of the island's highest mountain range drop down to the sea and the surf roils up on crescent after crescent of clean, black sand beaches, this could easily be backcountry Hawai'i rather than remote Cuba. And you should go there now, before it gets discovered by hustlers, drifters, and beach bums—before anyone can say "It was better back when..." Relatedly, plan to spend at least double (or triple!) the time you originally thought you might like in this neck of the woods, otherwise you'll leave wanting more; then I'll be perfectly justified in saying "I told you so."

Guidebooks miss the point of little Chivirico, population 6000, calling it "a small dusty fishing village" (Moon) with "little to offer" (Lonely Planet). On the contrary, Chivirico has plenty to offer, something cyclists and a handful of adventurous surfers have known for years and who are going to lambast me for sharing.

After dipping down to the coast from hectic, fume-choked Santiago de Cuba, the road ribbons between mountain and sea, dotted with caramel-colored beaches, white-sand beaches, and beaches entirely lined with smooth, multicolored rocks. As you weave between billy goats and cows debating at which beach to stop for a swim, barefoot kids riding bareback gallop by, waving from the shoulder; offshore islands floating in the sea distract from the gorgeous mountains inland; and farm bounty mounded at roadside stands—mangoes, bananas, and soursop—gets mouths watering. And then you enter a tidy town, heralded by a giant conch shell sculpture, strung along a trio of dark sand beaches, each prettier than the next.

Welcome to Chivirico, where the public park boasts (fast) Wi-Fi, the few rooms for rent are clean and well-equipped, and there's never a line at the local Coppelia. The sounds of Chivirico are as remarkable as the vistas: this was the first time in weeks of traveling we heard no reggaetón, instead falling asleep to the crashing of waves and the clip-clop of horses' hooves, the preferred mode of travel down this way.

Chivirico is a great combination of gateway and home base. From here you can hit local breaks, explore the Cuevas de Murciélagos (Bat Caves, populated with thousands of the flying mammals—don't worry, they won't hit or hurt you), and explore farther down the coast, what is commonly known as "Cuba's Most Beautiful Road" (see Chapter 99). There are so many pocket beaches in this area, they don't even bother to name them. Head out of Chivirico on the roller coaster of a road for three miles and just before Río Grande (which locals know but which appears on no map that I've found) is a grassy plateau plunging down to a deserted beach that nearly disappears at high tide. "It has no name," young Wilfredo told us sitting atop his mule. "No one goes down there. Not even the fishermen." We eyed the tree on the cliff and the precipitous slope leading to the inviting scoop of sand. Did we have enough rope? We did. Would the tree hold our weight as we hand-over-hand made our way down? It would. But the light was fading, the sky streaking summer sherbet colors behind the closest mountain and the next curve in the road. It was one of those sane, but difficult travel decisions to not descend to what we dubbed "Playa Toby"; instead, we hopped on the Harley and headed back to Chivirico, facing another difficult decision: fresh crab, octopus, fish, or conch for dinner?

IV

Travel With Niños & Niñas— of All Ages

40 *Coppelia*

KNOWN AS HAVANA'S ICE CREAM CATHEDRAL, Coppelia is a Havana institution—people may not be able to tell you where the Museo de la Revolución is located or how to get to the Víazul bus station, but everyone knows Coppelia sits on the corner of Calles 23 and L. A visit here makes for a down and dirty education in Cuban culture—from the hour-long (or longer) line to the psychological hunger evidenced by your tablemates inhaling 20 scoops of ice cream in mere minutes. A brisk black market exists for Coppelia ice cream ($10CUC a tub), and if you keep your eyes peeled—especially in the downstairs counter section—you'll see Cubans spiriting the 5-liter containers out the door. It's common for a couple of family members to hoof it to Coppelia to enjoy an ice cream "salad" (five scoops of whatever flavors are on offer for under 50 cents) while directing the waiter to fill whatever makeshift container they've brought with as many scoops as will fit for enjoying at home. There are several entrances offering at most three different flavors; choose the shortest line or the one with the flavors you favor. There's also a section with no lines, proffering more variety for four times the price, but there will be no Cubans there, making it four times less fun and educational.

Strategies for beating Coppelia's crowds include: lining up right when they open at 10 a.m.; heading there during dinner

hour or when it's raining; timing your visit for when the night-
time soap opera is heating up; or hitting Coppelia whenever a
"cold" front rolls in (anything below 24°C/75°F is considered
cold by Cuban standards).

Any Cuban city of respectable size has a Coppelia outpost, so
if you're not up for the wait and hassle at its Havana headquarters, try the one in Nueva Gerona on the Isla de la Juventud (see
Chapter 100), which is a marvel in itself with its enthusiastic use
of locally quarried marble—everything from the floors to coun-
ters and tables are made of black-ribboned marble. Here, service comes with a genuine smile. The Coppelias in Santiago de
Cuba and Santa Clara (see Chapter 33) are large, breezy buildings and extraordinarily popular with locals as you might expect,
but the lines aren't nearly as onerous (and the staff not nearly
as ornery) as in Havana. Cienfuegos (see Chapter 31) also has a
Coppelia, on Calle 37—what locals universally call "the Prado"—
the main avenue leading into the city and to the bay, but it's
lackluster somehow, more an obligatory nod to the national ice
cream mania than a protagonist in the city's narrative. Pinar del
Río has its Coppelia as well, but folks from that part of the island
say the Coppelia in Palacios, 40 miles to the east, is much better.
One of my favorite Coppelia parlors is in the tiny seaside town
of Chivirico (see Chapter 39) on the southern coast of Santiago
de Cuba, where they open early, the ice cream never runs out,
and you never have to wait in line.

41 El Palenque

INSPIRED BY HAITI'S SLAVE REVOLT, which led to the founding of the first independent black republic in the hemisphere in 1804, Cuban escaped slaves, known as *cimarrones*, took to the mountains and carved out communities known as *palenques*. Today, the term has been co-opted for tourist attractions, bars and restaurants and El Palenque, in Havana's upper crust neighborhood of Siboney (another historic term denoting Cuba's pre-Columbian population), is where Cuban families of all classes and colors escape the kitchen to eat well and cheap. Here, there's something for every palate, from charcoal roasted pork by the pound and garlic shrimp to pizza and chicken fingers. There are coin-operated rides and games to keep kids giggling while waiting for their vittles and lots of cute dogs snaking between tables (*es Cuba* as we say here). For the quality and variety, the ice cream parlor here is one of the city's best. At $1CUC a scoop, it's expensive by local standards, but even Cubans swoon over the dark chocolate truffle, pistachio, hazelnut, wild berry, and other exotic flavors.

Pabexpo, the convention center adjacent to El Palenque, hosts annual events providing another good reason to head out this way. During the first two weeks of May, for example, the showrooms here swarm with Cuban shoppers looking for something for Mother's Day during La Feria de Mamá. This is a great opportunity to snag an original, handmade souvenir of better quality and creativity than anything sold in tourist markets. Almost all the wares here are made by Cuban artisans with a couple of stands selling bohemian togs from India or Ecuador; these get swarmed by locals looking for cool, comfortable clothing. The Feria de Mamá also makes for an excellent (and cheap) education in the newest trends in Cuban handmade shoes, furniture design, and accessories; I've received compliments from archetypally aloof socialites walking along New York's Fifth Avenue in my mega platform shoes made in Cuba and purchased for $25 at the Feria. In December, a similar fair, FIART, is hosted here and is a great destination for holiday shopping. A visit to El Palenque and Pabexpo can be easily combined with Fusterlandía (see Chapter 44).

42 Playgrounds

HAVANA IS A PHENOMENAL DESTINATION for traveling with children—Cubans adore kids and the super social context means your little ones will make instant friends and playmates. Nevertheless, the emphasis on colonial architecture, art, and history means kids can get bored; mixing up activities and sites with some strategically timed naps to keep children engaged and entertained makes a good approach. Kids of all ages adore tours in classic convertible cars, and if you've got a bag of preferred snacks on hand, you're golden; lack of kid-friendly food is a major, common complaint. Havana is peppered with playgrounds that provide a great break from boring adult stuff as well. They also allow kids to let off steam and make new Cuban  *amiguitos* in a fun, natural way. Now for the caveat emptor: some Havana playgrounds are so dilapidated they are more dangerous than enjoyable and none have the safety features you're used to (you won't find any wood chips or padded mats under Cuban jungle gyms, for instance). Still, decent swings and seesaws, slides and climbing towers are dotted around town.

Parque Almendares is a solid choice, with plenty of room to run around and some decent equipment. One of the best, most modern playgrounds in Havana is in the heart of Vedado, at Calle 5ta and F. For pure whimsy, the hairstyling-themed playground Barbe Parque (scissor seesaws, slides shaped like straight razors and the like), designed and built by master stylist and community activist Papito, creator of many neighborhood projects including a salon school and this playground, is a good bet in Habana Vieja (across the street from the Museo de la Revolución). Look for the red, white, and blue barber poles.

Head toward the Malecón in this part of town to Parque La Maestranza, right on the seafront, where kids can enjoy pony rides, bounce houses, jungle gyms, and a carrousel. Lines can be long at this, one of Havana's most popular kid spaces, but the sea breeze is refreshing and good people watching helps pass the time. Jalisco Park on the corners of Calles 23 and 18 in Vedado is much more than a compact playground and mini-amusement park: the oldest playground in the capital, for Cubans it represents nostalgia and a carefree childhood. So indelible were lazy afternoons spent by generations at Jalisco Park, it moved Cuba's international rock star Carlos Varela to write a song about it. There's also a new boulevard between Calles 23 and 25 and Calle M in Vedado with inflatable bounce houses, a pool, lots of kid-friendly food and a café for parents who need to re-energize while the little ones run wild.

43 Parque Ecológico Monte Barreto

WHEN DONALD TRUMP SENT DOWN advance troops to scout locations for his Cuban hotel and casino in the mid-2000s, they looked upon this wide-open park in the privileged Miramar neighborhood and started fantasizing about how they would capitalize on one of Havana's most expansive green spaces (a friend was their translator, paling as they described their vision). Dream on Donald: Cuban decision makers are not going to jump in with such strange bedfellows and certainly not to allow casinos for cavorting Americans (casinos were outlawed with the Revolution, though gambling—on everything from car and pigeon racing to dog and cock fights—continues with fervor).

Of all my favorite spots in the city, Monte Barreto tops the list; it's the perfect antidote to loud, gritty, and hustler-ridden Centro Habana and Habana Vieja. And herein lies the rub: this park's setting, size, Miramar location just blocks from the sea, and low noise pollution/litter factor creates a peaceful psychic space, which is a high commodity in frenetic Havana. At Monte Barreto, you can kick off your shoes and bury your toes in clean, springy grass without crunching upon a cigarette butt. There are regular pickup games of basketball here, and the adjacent handball court is popular, too. There's a small botanical garden on the park's western extent, which also provides a full frontal shot of the first post-revolution hotel run by a US firm—Sheraton's Starwood property overlooks the park.

Sundays are family days at Monte Barreto, and a visit on the weekend means pony rides, picnics, and mingling with Cuban families of all shades and ages. Recent additions to recreational offerings here include inflatable ball houses, four-wheeled motorcycles, and other modern fun stuff that will make kids scream with delight and their parents blanch in terror. This is also a popular destination for kiddie birthday parties, so don't be surprised if there are balloon sculptors, clowns, and packs of Cuban kids hopped up on cheap sugar running around. Monte Barreto is a great destination for a bike ride—take shady 7ma Avenida (carpeted with multi-colored blossoms in spring) until you hit the park where you can flop on the grass with a cold beer and fried chicken for $3. Alternatively, La Corte del Príncipe restaurant on the southern border of the park is popular with diplomatic wives and other foreigners for their variety of hand-made pasta and mix and match sauce options (pesto anyone?!).

44 *Fusterlandia*

KNOWN AS CUBA'S "GAUDÍ" (with a little of that other zany Spaniard Salvador Dalí thrown in for good measure), artist and gadfly José Fuster began transforming his home and studio a couple of decades ago by constructing wild, gravity-defying sculptures and covering them with multi-colored mosaic tiles. If you've seen the Sagrada Familia or Casa Batlló, you'll likely find the Gaudí comparison overblown, but there are certain similarities—and you don't have to pay an arm and a leg like you do in Barcelona. In fact, you don't have to pay anything to ogle the giant palm trees, arches, and domes covered with celestial bodies, and children at play—including a larger-than-life Elian González who stands guard over the pool at the artist's home. What started as a pet project at Fuster's home has launched a neighborhood phenomenon.

Today, it seems everything in this neck of the woods is canvas for Fuster and his crazy mosaics: the family doctor's office, nearly every home on adjacent blocks, the local park, street markers. In fact, you can tell the holdouts and NIMBYers by the glaring absence of tiles on their houses. Wandering the streets here is an excursion into Surreal Havana. There are giant mosaic chess sets if you're up for a match, love seats replete with big hearts and messages of *amor*, a nautical theme on retaining walls featuring massive crabs and fish (wholly at home in seaside Jaimanitas), and terrestrial animals of all sorts.

Visitors are welcome at Fuster's studio (though he's rarely in residence these days; his son and colleagues hold down the fort) where his latest work is on display and you're given access to where the tiles are created and fired. Take a good look at the floor of the aforementioned pool: it, too, is decorated with mosaic art that serves both form and function. As Fuster explained to me, he put in this pool years ago when you needed special permission to do so, which he didn't have. When inspectors showed up he told them: "That's not a pool. See the tile image on the floor? It's art." Cue the pool parties! This has become a major tourist attraction and during high season the tour buses run five deep on the narrow streets—an early morning or late afternoon visit is best at these times.

45 Take Thee Out to the Ballgame

Mojitos. Salsa. Cigars. Indomitable resilience and moribund humor. Intractable politics. Cuba is famous for many things. Once upon a time, baseball was among them. Jackie Robinson played here, with black and white colleagues in 1947, before donning his Brooklyn Dodgers' jersey to break the color barrier in the United States. When baseball was still an Olympic sport, Cubans took gold—repeatedly—and never failed to medal. Everywhere you went, there were pickup games and little leagues, improvised diamonds and boys playing catch with dad (again, gender roles are so ingrained here, in 16 years, I've never seen a girl playing ball with dad and forget about mom). But Cuban baseball has been on a rapid and steady decline in recent years. The reasons are sundry for the plummeting enthusiasm for the national sport, but the primary culprit is the meteoric ascension of soccer (known as football everywhere outside the USA). Passions run extra hot for certain teams and when Barça and Real Madrid face off, streets are deserted and you can hear a pin drop. Then someone scores a goal and a roar erupts from Cubans huddled around TVs following every move with baited breath.

Emigration of baseball talent has gutted rosters, it's true, but damage has been wrought as well by a change in how Cuban teams are composed. For decades, players were limited to playing in the provinces in which they were born. Fans knew the entire lineup by heart, their stats, even where they lived—they would run into each other buying chicken or coffee. It engendered a familiarity and loyalty to team and players that became diluted when trading began. As happens in the major leagues, the best-equipped and esteemed teams contracted the top players from around the country, completely altering a team's makeup. When your favorite player gets traded, for instance, do you follow him or the team you've been rooting for your entire life? What if he's traded to your traditional rival? As with everything in Cuba, it gets complicated. But wait, there's more. Due to economic straits, night games—which require lights—are largely a thing of the past, and so are prime time broadcasts of games, meaning a much reduced viewing audience. According to my baseball buddy Alfredo, the financial resources needed to get together a baseball team, which needs gloves, bats, balls, and a slew of umpires is prohibitive, whereas with football/soccer, set up a few sticks for goals, grab a ball, and you're good to go.

But for the visitor, little of this internal strife matters: a baseball game is a wonderful way to mix with Cubans and measure the pulse of the game for yourself. It's a wholly different experience from baseball in other climes; traditionalists sometimes refer to the Cuban sport as "pure baseball," since there is no advertising, zero corporate sponsorship at ballparks, no Jumbotrons, no merchandise for sale, and the stands are cement benches (people spend a lot of time on their feet at Cuban baseball games). Food sold in the ballpark is limited to sandwiches with ham product (if you're lucky), popcorn, and hard candies. Beer may or may not be available; most Cubans come with their own snacks and a Tetra-Pak of rotgut rum. Entertainment is provided by the fans who bring congas, *claves*, trumpets, and other instruments to the ballpark to create as much music and noise as they can throughout the nine innings.

✳

Check out Havana Curveball, a documentary about
13-year-old Mica Jarmel-Schneider and
his quest to bring US baseballs to Cuba.
www.havanacurveball.info

✳

In Cuba, baseball is also truly for the masses, as there is no financial barrier to catching your favorite team: the local price for a ticket is 2 *pesos cubanos* (about six cents); for tourists it's less than $1CUC. Each province has a team, so no matter where you are, you'll be able to catch a game—except in the off-season. Recent adjustments were made to the schedule, which incenses some Cubans as well. The first part of the season starts in late August where all 16 teams face off for 45 games. After a hiatus of indeterminate time, the top eight teams from the first part of the season play another 45 games (and those eight get to choose three players from those teams that didn't qualify for the second half of the season). This is followed by the playoffs. Although Havana's team—the Industriales, also known as the Lions—is the most famous, and has the biggest stadium, it has suffered especially from players emigrating to the United States; the team has failed to make the playoffs several years running as a result.

*

Full schedule available at:
www.beisbolencuba.com

*

The teams to watch these days are the Crocodiles (Matanzas), the Orangemen (Villa Clara), the Tobacco Farmers (Pinar del Río), the Stallions (Granma, 2016 and 2017 champions), and the Tigers (Ciego de Ávila). Even if you're here in the off-season, the *esquina caliente* (hot corner) is a fascinating forum of loud, passionate debate about anything and everything baseball-related. Havana's hot corner takes place in Parque Central; in Santiago de Cuba, you can catch it in Plaza de Marte.

46 *Parque Escaleras de Jaruco*

WITH SO LITTLE TOURISM FOR SO long and a chronic domestic transportation problem, Cuba is riddled with wonderful off-the-beaten-path attractions that many Cubans don't even know about. These are waiting to be discovered (and developed) and provide prime opportunities for one-of-a-kind travel experiences. Many of these hidden spots are within easy reach of Havana—if you have private transport, whether it's car, moped, or bike (or in my case, an antique Harley-Davidson). This park, a mere 40 miles or so from Havana and less than 20 miles from the beach town of Guanabo (see Chapter 73), is a perfect example and makes a fine getaway for a day, especially if you're traveling with the kids. There are a couple of restaurants here, including one in a quirky Moorish palace at the park's highest point, but the picnic possibilities are varied and rich. Many roads lead to the Parque Escaleras de Jaruco; no matter which you choose, there will be green pastures with grazing horses, thick stands of trees and country homes dotting the landscape. Design a loop route and it makes a perfect languid drive. Head here mid-week and you'll likely have the place to yourself.

You'll notice things move slower in Cuba (this damned heat!) and it took me 15 years to finally make the trip into this hinterland. After leaving the picturesque road behind and entering the park proper, the road begins to climb, rambling through gardens and recreational areas including Cuba's most whimsical playground with all kinds of oversized, brightly colored animals and insects to climb on and around. Keep following the road around and up until it terminates at a spectacular scenic overlook taking in a fecund valley dotted with palms and farms. One of the highlights here is the extensive cave system in which you can lose yourself for a day—literally: I have Cuban friends who have become lost here in the miles of caves surrounded by dense forest. Adventurers should be particularly careful if the weather turns threatening, when it's all too easy to become disoriented. When the local cowboys are feeling up to it and arrive to work, you can rent a mount and horseback around the park. Disregarding the faux indigenous theme here, ask yourself once again: Why are these beautiful natural landscapes so woefully underused in Cuba when they are so perfect for genuine ecotourism (Jardines de Hershey nearby is another example)?

V

Natural Splendor

47 *Valle de Yumurí*

MOST PEOPLE ONLY BEHOLD THIS palm-studded valley from the lookout point of the Puente de Bacunayagua, sipping overpriced piña coladas on their way to Varadero. If that's all your itinerary has got to give, take it, but this little-explored, quintessentially Cuban valley makes a picturesque detour where you can meet down-to-earth locals with time to sit down for coffee and a chat. This valley straddling Mayabeque and Matanzas provinces is a tropical pastiche of emerald, chartreuse, and palm-frond green as beautiful as the shimmering blue sea beyond. It is so dazzling, German explorer, ecologist and geographer Alexander von Humboldt, dubbed it "the loveliest valley in the world" when he set eyes upon it at the turn of the 19th century. Fifty years later, poet William Bryant Cullen said, "The sight of [this valley] is worth a voyage to the island." And what's so wonderful about the Valle de Yumurí: it looks much the same today as it did back then—worth the trip.

Legend holds that the word Yumurí is rooted in the language spoken by the indigenous Taíno that once inhabited the valley; it was the word they yelled before leaping to their deaths, preferring suicide to succumbing to Spanish domination. True or not, it makes for good lore and the soaring cliffs on either side are indeed perfect for a death leap. The five-mile-wide Valle de Yumurí retains a secret, timeless feeling, worthy of jealous protection and guardianship, a spot to explore but not share. Until recently, the valley saw few visitors save for intrepid cyclists and nature-starved university students escaping from pollution-choked Havana for a weekend. Evidently designers of Cuba's tourism strategy fail to see the potential in developing naturally stunning places like this for genuine eco-tourism—or maybe they're just asleep at the wheel. I predict that the Valle de Yumurí, so close to Havana, halfway between the capital and Varadero, won't hover below travelers' radar much longer.

One of the reasons the Valle de Yumurí is so off-the-beaten-track is limited accessibility since you can only get there by train or your own wheels—whether they're on a bicycle, motorcycle, or car. What's more, the valley doesn't appear on any hardcopy map that I've found and guidebooks give it short shrift, if they mention it at all. Sure, so-called "jeep safaris" are offered by all-inclusive resorts in Varadero to give guests a couple of hours in one of Cuba's most beautiful landscapes spread thick with endemic plants and the iconic royal palm, the country's national tree. But nothing gives you a better sense of place than slowing down, taking a hike, and spending a night or two immersed in that landscape—it's the difference between looking at it and living it, the difference between observational and experiential travel.

Having your own wheels is the best strategy for maximizing adventure here, but the Hershey Electric Railway departing from Casablanca across the bay from Havana is an entertaining and educational way to get to the Valle de Yumurí. It's also a test in patience: the train makes more than 35 stops on the 75-mile route between Casablanca and its terminus in Matanzas, which is slow-going but provides a good, close look at all the tiny towns along the way. Alighting at Mena puts you as near to the valley as you can get riding the rails; you'll have to walk about a mile from the station to begin accessing parts that make this spot so special. Horseback riding is a possibility here and the Río Yumurí and Río Bacunayagua beckon swimmers on a hot day. Rugged types like to make the half-day hike from the valley to the sea; hikers can pick up the Abra Trail near the Hotel Casa del Valle for the easy hike along the Río Bacunayagua.

48 *Parque la Güira*

THERE'S A MOMENT IN THE Cuban evening when the streets are deserted, calm descends on every city, and the only detectable sound is the hum of innumerable televisions tuned to the same channel. This is *telenovela* time, when everyone is planted in front of their set watching the night-time soap opera. This is Cuban church, the altar at which the nation worships and the melodrama typical to all soaps seems to run in Cuban blood. The back story of Parque La Güira is a case in point: this marvelous park was built by multi-millionaire lawyer José Manuel Cortina in 1920 to provide a cloister and home for his mistress whose name is lost to history. Touring the extensive, luxurious grounds, with its plantation house, Zen garden, mini-Versailles, re-creations of Greek statues, and lake, bridges, and meandering paths, you have to wonder what charms and spells this woman worked on her lover. He literally built her a castle, with a grand stone entrance replete with turrets, massive wooden doors, and a sweeping driveway—the only thing missing is a moat. The spread gets grander the more you explore.

Parque La Güira makes for a wonderful family outing and Cuban families flock here on weekends to enjoy the pool, eat well for dirt cheap, and pose for photographs in front of Chinese pagodas, the pet monkey, and peacocks, and to play billiards on the regulation-size pool table. But this is just a small slice of this 54,000-acre protected area leading into the Sierra de los Órganos mountain range; pick a rarely traveled road or path in these parts and you'll have the place to yourself. There are hiking opportunities (without a guide!) within the park proper for those craving nature including an easy-to-moderate three-mile loop hike featuring wild mango trees and fragrant stands of pine, *guayabita*, a small fruit from which a local liquor is made, and views of the surrounding *mogotes* (limestone hills).

With your own transport, you can explore even farther up in the hills, where ruins and caves lie hidden among the jungle-like growth. For a truly unique experience, try the back road between here and Viñales (see Chapter 49) via La Palma—you likely won't see another soul and the only noise will be birdsong and mangoes plopping to the ground. This road calls to cyclists who have the stamina for the rise and fall of the deserted macadam. A southern branch of this road goes from La Palma to La Cueva de los Portales, a national monument and extensive cave system where Che Guevara set up headquarters during what Cubans call the October Crisis; the rest of the world knows this debacle of brinksmanship as the Cuban Missile Crisis. There are simple cabins for rent in La Güira and a *campismo* at the caves should you want a more immersive experience. A young Cuban who hails from these parts says you haven't visited San Diego de los Baños (see Chapter 88) if you haven't been to Parque La Güira.

49 *Viñales*

AY, VIÑALES. A VALLEY OF singular beauty and geologic splendor, where tobacco grows as tall and strong as the farmers working the fields, Viñales is becoming a victim of its own majesty. Over the past several years, this valley dotted with unique pin cushion hills just a stone's throw from Pinar del Río and 110 miles from Havana, has become (there's no delicate way to put this) overrun with tourists. According to provincial authorities, 80 percent of the local population works with tourists—either in the food and lodging establishments that host them, or as guides, drivers, or fixers. And herein lies the problem. The foreign influx, say experts, is affecting local crafts, the economy, and food supply. They offer various examples as evidence. There's the perception that foreigners prefer a more modern "look," driving a trend toward abandoning traditional furnishings made from locally-sourced wood and cowhide in favor of generic furniture from Ikea; prices have spiked for transport and staples (when you can find them; tourists and the businesses receiving them strip stores bare of necessities like toilet paper, beer, and coffee); and private restaurants and homes renting rooms to foreigners buy most of the fresh fruits and vegetables available, often at elevated prices, obligating locals to travel many miles to access produce.

Nevertheless, the popularity of Viñales has injected sorely-needed funds into the town and led to improvements in infrastructure, housing stock, and environmental protection. Finding the balance between protection and preservation of culture and environment, while attracting sorely needed tourist dollars, is a difficult equation and it's not only Cuba struggling to figure it out: a recent article in the *Wall Street Journal* entitled "Tourism Boom Bogs down Iceland" sums it up, saying "the tourism explosion has caught the government unprepared, leaving infrastructure strained and Icelanders complaining about scarce housing, rising rental prices and roadside litter." Sounds familiar.

But when you have a place of unequaled beauty, everyone wants a piece of it; for outdoor and nature enthusiasts, Viñales is a must. Here you can hike, horseback ride, swim in wild rivers, and rock climb. The last is particularly popular, with DIY Cubans opening routes along the vertical rock faces of the *mogotes* (the bulbous hills for which Viñales is famous) and nurturing a nascent climbing community *poco a poco* (little by little). The problem is rock climbing can be dangerous and there have  been accidents; way out here, a fairly serious fall requiring an ambulance ride to the nearest hospital—in Pinar del Río—taps scarce resources destined for the country's universal health system. This is the official reason authorities aren't too keen on this adventure sport, but I suspect there are others, like how to monetize this fiercely independent sport. Anyone interested in scaling some rock while here should bring their own gear and consult with locals about current conditions—and regulations.

*

The guidebook *Cuba Climbing* orients
climbers for island adventure on the rocks.
Get it and connect with local climbers at
www.cubaclimbing.com.

*

Visits to tobacco farms, replete with weathered campesinos
hand-rolling cigars, are also possible here. Two "attractions"
definitely worth a miss are the Mural Prehistórico—a 400-
foot rock face painted with dinosaurs, giant sea monsters,
and humans, which the artist determined would be as "high as
the tallest building in Havana"—and the Cueva del Indio, an
over-exploited cave run through with a river where tourists are
shuttled along on a motorboat. If you're into caves, though,
Viñales is a good base to explore Gran Caverna de Santa Tomás,
Cuba's largest mapped cave system with more than 40 galleries
spread across eight levels. Not all are accessible to visitors, but
the handful of miles open to non-specialists traverses several
different levels and are full of mind-blowing formations, giant
stalactites in pristine condition, multi-colored pools made psychedelic by eons of mineral filtration, and a lot of tight spaces.

50 *Soroa*

THE AIR STARTS TO CLEAR and the perfume of cedar and pine laces the breeze winding through the foothills of the Sierra del Rosario Reserva de la Biosfera as you approach Soroa, 52 miles west of Havana. This mountain range was Cuba's first natural area to receive UNESCO Biosphere Reserve status, in 1984, and is kept pristine by strict conservation policies. Settlements here date back to colonial times, with a few historical sites including old coffee farms and processing mills, but the area wasn't aggressively developed for visitors until the mid-1940s. The backdrop of verdant peaks—the highest reaches a mere 1640 feet but is no less picturesque for its modest altitude—combines with nearby rivers and waterfalls to create a natural tableau unrivaled in this part of the country. Covering more than 61,000 acres thick with mahogany, pine, teak, cedar, and coffee, a lot of it leggy and growing wild, the reserve is seriously underutilized. This could be prime eco-tourism territory if authorities were keen to stoke responsible nature travel, backpacking, and camping; after extensive research into the issue, including talking to various tourism authorities, it appears golf resorts and cruise arrivals take priority, unfortunately.

While backcountry hiking and wilderness camping are seriously discouraged—two types of travel that are arguably more sustainable and attract an ecology-minded crowd intrinsically motivated to protect the environment—there are opportunities for getting into the woods here. For those craving nature, hikes from simple, quick loop trails to a 10-mile trek to the mountain village of La Rosita can be arranged from the only hotel in town, Villas Soroa. Officially, all hikes must be guided. The 72-foot-tall Salto del Arco Iris waterfall is a bracing destination for a quick hike, accessible from the road beside the hotel. It will be gushing or dribbling depending on the time of year and global warming; your best bet for catching a voluminous cascade is the May-October rainy season.

One of Soroa's major attractions is the Orquidiario de Soroa, the country's flagship orchid garden with nearly 500 species, more than a third of which are endemic. According to Dr. Brian M. Boom, who heads up the Caribbean Biodiversity Program at the New York Botanical Garden which enjoys ongoing scientific exchanges and collaboration with the Soroa Orchidarium, "at least 32 species of Cuban orchids are threatened due to various factors such as habitat modification and climate change." Botanists here are working hard to protect the island's orchids and if you venture out this way in Cuban "winter" (that global warming thing again), from November to February, the volume and variety of blooms will blow your mind. For other hiking possibilities, see Las Terrazas, also within the Sierra del Rosario Biosphere Reserve.

✳

Cuba's National Orchid Show is
held each year in March.

✳

51 Las Terrazas

UNIQUE IN ALL OF CUBA, this experimental eco-community nestled in the Sierra del Rosario Reserva del Biosfera (designated a UNESCO Biosphere Reserve in 1984) was the forward-thinking pet project of Osmany Cienfuegos—brother of national hero Camilo Cienfuegos, a member of the *Granma* expedition which launched the revolution and an integral part of the brain trust until his plane disappeared under mysterious circumstances in 1959. Las Terrazas's original master plan, initiated in 1971, included artist studios, nature hikes, and architectural design melding seamlessly into the surrounding landscape, accompanied by economic opportunities for residents (in tourism, as docents and guides, and community farming).

Today, Las Terrazas boasts a zipline that rockets you over palm trees and lakes, darling houses for rent, and a vegetarian restaurant more like something you'd find in Berkeley or Brooklyn than the Cuban countryside. There's also a burgeoning art scene here, with artists creating in studios open to the public—Lester Campa is a favorite and Ariel Gato Miranda teaches local kids to handcraft paper with natural materials, selling them in his studio. Browsing the studios is a great way to meet the community and bring home a one-of-a-kind souvenir. Add to this nearby Soroa (Cuba's orchid capital) and you have an ideal day trip from Havana, a short 52 miles away. For my money, a night at La Moka, Las Terrazas's only hotel—with a giant mango tree growing through the lobby and the island's most blissful bathrooms—is salve for body and mind. If there's no space at the inn, ask about rooms for rent in town, where accommodation takes full advantage of the locale's natural beauty.

After too many boring miles of fields and fallow land, the Sierra del Rosario mountain range appears in the distance, its 61,775 acres of woodlands, coffee, waterfalls, and hiking trails beckoning. That's the good news. The bad news is that all hikes must be taken with a guide—while in theory an enviable approach (for protecting the environment and informing hikers about local flora and fauna), in practice it can be a crap shoot depending on the quality and training of your guide (to say nothing of foreign language skills). This can be frustrating for travelers with extensive hiking experience, but the guide policy is strictly enforced and there are no markers or signage for the rogue Swiss and Aussie folks taking to the trails unaccompanied.

The longest official hike covers 13 miles, ending at the bracing pools of the 66-foot-tall San Claudio waterfall; other shorter, tamer hikes are also possible, including the 5-mile El Contento loop passing a few abandoned coffee mills, and a 2-mile stroll to the San Juan River, with mini-waterfalls and pools for cooling off. This place gets mobbed with Cubans June–August; you've been forewarned! There are simple cabins on stilts with shared bathrooms if you wish to spend the night, but book early, especially in the summer—reservations can be made at La Moka.

52 *Playa Larga*

NEW YORK, CALIFORNIA, SPAIN, MAURITIUS: no matter the city, country or context, it seems most coastal locales have a "long beach." In Cuba's case, Playa Larga is something of a misnomer since the beach is small and the mud-colored sand rather a disappointment if you've been to any of the powdery white beauties typical of the north coast. On the upside, at least there *is* sand; much of Cuba's southern coast is lined with an ankle-twisting, biting kind of rock known as *diente de perro* (dog's tooth) more hospitable to hermit crabs than humans; the exception is Playa Ancón, very close to Trinidad (see Chapter 32), which boasts soft, white sand complemented by a verdant mountain backdrop. While not the most attractive beach destination in the classic sense, Playa Larga offers terrific scuba diving and birding, with some of Cuba's best fly-fishing grounds in nearby Ciénaga de Zapata (see Chapter 53). Playa Larga also holds an important place in Cuban, nay the hemisphere's history, since it's perched on the northern bend of the infamous Bahía de Cochinos.

*

In late 2016, the CIA was forced to release
Volume V of its official version of the Bay of
Pigs invasion; the agency kept it secret for years
stating "it would confuse the public."

*

English-speakers with historical memory know this as the Bay
of Pigs, the site of the first military defeat of the United States
in the Americas—something proclaimed on billboards dotting
the area. Say Bahía de Cochinos to a Cuban, however, and you'll
receive a blank stare or quick correction to Playa Girón, as it's
universally known here. In fact, nearly 1,500 US-trained and
CIA-backed Cuban émigrés invaded at both Playa Larga and
Playa Girón in April, 1961; the latter, on the eastern side of the
Bahía de Cochinos, has a museum detailing everything from the
plan of attack to the shoes worn by the town's victims.

Animal lovers visiting down this way between April and July
will have a bitter pill to swallow since this is the annual
great crab migration, when the road becomes
an undulating sea of red, the crunch and
pop of lives snuffed out audible, accompanied by a putrid stench wafting from
the hot macadam. It's impossible to avoid
the tsunami of crabs—they're even scrab-
bling up the sides of buildings. Some 3.5
million crabs die during this four-month
period, trying to make their way to the sea to
lay their eggs. The road constructed between Playa Larga and
Playa Girón had such negative effects on this migration that
Cuba's environmental protection agency teamed up with international organizations to bore a couple of tunnels in an effort to
encourage the crabs to go under, rather than over, the road and
hopefully save some lives. File this under Epic Fail—the crabs are
still dying in droves, proving once again that when you fuss with
natural habitat, the flora and fauna suffer. This isn't the only
place in Cuba where disruption of the ecology for human ends
has had negative effects: the causeway built to Cayo Sabinal (and

other cays off the northern coast) have wrecked marine habitats and the animals calling them home.

Luckily, the marine life is rich and varied around the Bay of Pigs and scuba diving is a major highlight. There are several well-equipped outfits in and around Playa Larga offering shore dives where angelfish, parrot fish, barracuda, grouper, Technicolor sponges, and coral clinging to drop-offs and swim-throughs abound. Since most of the action is located a quick 10- or 15-minute swim from shore and at depths between 20 and 100 feet, this area is also a good destination for snorkelers. More advanced divers can contract a guide to take them into the dark and spooky El Brinco cave, a flooded, inland cave known as a cenote. This is a tricky, deep dive between 100 and 125 feet which only highly experienced divers should attempt; head in around high noon and you'll be rewarded with a shaft of bright, white sunlight piercing the cave roof; this is when visibility is best. Another cenote, Cueva de los Peces (literally Fish Cave), is, as you might imagine, packed with spectacular fish and feels like swimming in a tropical aquarium. Located halfway between Playas Larga and Girón, this is a prime snorkeling spot.

The southern coast is calmer year-round (especially from October-May), making it a better bet for good conditions than northern diving spots. If the sea isn't cooperating or you're more into birds than fish, Las Salinas Wildlife Refuge is a major fly-through for migratory birds from August to April, with sightings peaking in October. Birders will definitely get an eye- and earful at nearby Ciénaga de Zapata, where more than 200 species have been reported and 83 percent of Cuba's endemic species call home.

53 *Ciénaga de Zapata*

I REMEMBER GLEEFULLY RIPPING PAGES from my guidebook to get a campfire started the first time I backpacked through Latin America, watching the flames lick the paper: "Now I definitely won't have to read you drone on about birds and their rich habitat anymore!" That was decades ago and while I still carry on similar conversations with myself on the road (long-term solo travel tends to do that), I've come to appreciate those charmed moments when I spot a rare bird in the wild and have even dedicated precious pack space to a small pair of binoculars just in case. I have to admit, putting those field glasses to my eye and snapping a hawk or woodpecker into focus is pretty exhilarating, but it's more of a serendipitous event, right place at the right time, that kind of thing—I still struggle to understand the passion for sitting under a tree or beside a river for hours waiting for something winged to show up in order to check a box on a "birds bagged" list. Nor do I understand the attraction of spending hour after hour knee-deep in a river or marshes casting a line over and over and over again to try and get something on the hook. Friends have tried to explain their passion for fly-fishing, but its allure continues to escape me. Don't get me wrong: I'm all for a day on the water fishing with friends, a cooler of icy potables and toothsome picnic on hand to break up the monotony, but I wouldn't take an entire fishing vacation like some people I know. But if birds or fishing float your boat, Cuba's Ciénaga de Zapata, both a UNESCO Biosphere Reserve and Ramsar Convention site, has you covered.

This gigantic *ciénaga* (literally: swamp) is one of the richest and most diverse breeding and migratory habitats for fish and birds in the entire country. Measuring over 1.5 million acres, this wetland veldt is also the largest of its kind in the Caribbean; a boat tour through the mangroves here inserts visitors into one of Cuba's most remote natural settings and gives an idea of the sheer massiveness of this swamp wilderness. The pristine condition of the Ciénaga, combined with the favorable climate and tasty flora/fauna, makes this a veritable all-inclusive for fish and birds of all types. The biodiversity here is remarkable: there are over 900 species of plants, more than 100 of them endemic and nearly 200 bird species calling the swamp home, along with a dozen types of mammals (rare in an island ecology like Cuba). Plus there are some 30 species of reptiles, none of them venomous.

The variety of birds here is boosted during the August to November southern bird migration, when thousands of birds including several types of heron, ibis, pink flamingoes, cranes and other waterfowl stop to refuel here.

✳

Birders visiting Cuba will be well served with
Aves de Cuba by Orlando H. Garrido and
Arturo Kirkconnell, the definitive reference,
complete with color illustrations.

✳

Visitors can also glimpse manatees, Cuban crocodiles—subject of intense study by biologists at the nearby research center—turtles, iguanas, and *manjuarí* (a prehistoric fish called an alligator gar, it has an alligator's head and a fish's body, like something you'd see out of Jurassic Park). If you're quiet and lucky, the dwarf *jutia*, a pygmy tree rodent that is threatened with extinction might trundle into view. This is indisputably the best place for wildlife watching in the country, particularly since few visitors even know it exists; no chattering suburban housewife or drunken frat boy is going to startle away that endemic *gallinuela de Santo Tomás* or bee hummingbird as you slide out your camera. The fly-fishing here is world-class and so underexploited, you'll feel like a true pioneer angling in the shallow, clear-as-glass waters of the Río Hatiguanico and the Laguna de las Salinas. Tarpon and other species like snook ply the waters here, but the real prize is bone-fish, a wily, faster-than-a-*cubana* fish that can run out hundreds of yards of line in seconds. Experts consider this area some of the best bonefishing grounds in the world and cite it is as one of the prime spots for snagging the coveted grand slam. Fanatic fly-fisherman Tom Stienstra explains that this is when "a bonefish, the fastest of all fish in the world, the tarpon, the most acrobatic, and the permit, the most elusive," are caught in single day. All fishing here is catch and release.

*

For more on bonefishing, riding the rails, and other true tales from the island, *Cuba: True Stories* edited by veteran traveler Tom Miller, makes a great on-the-road read.

*

Two annoyances not to take lightly when you visit this area are the dogged mosquitoes (it is a swamp, after all) and the toxic *guao* tree. Cubans will share hilarious stories about *compañeros* being stung silly by this innocuous looking tree, but it's no laughing matter. Speaking from experience, the tears shed after tangling with a *guao* (pronounced "wow") won't be from joy. If you start to itch like mad and break out in welts that won't go away, ask locals to find you a *contra guao*, the antidote to the dastardly *guao*.

54

Sierra del Escambray
& Topes de Collantes

SINCE THE REVOLUTION TRIUMPHED IN 1959, Cuba has been a bone stuck firmly in the craw of US policy makers, Cuban émigrés, and counterrevolutionaries on the island who weren't down with the new program. Beginning in 1960, the CIA funded and armed bands of locals to fight in this mountain range squeezed between the southern coast and Villa Clara, Sancti Spíritus and Cienfuegos provinces. Their goal? "A guerrilla war to beat Castro at his own game," according to the scrupulously researched *Cuba: A New History* by Richard Gott. At the height of fighting there were 800 farmers and country folk armed with rifles and delusions of toppling the nascent revolution, with supplies air-dropped by the CIA. What US strategists didn't account for was the tenacity of pro-revolution Cubans—the same approach, sending in Cuban exiles trained and armed in the USA to establish a beachhead, with air support provided by the CIA, backfired miserably at the Bay of Pigs. It was a tense, violent moment in the early history of the Cuban revolution and anyone over 60 in this part of the country participated in the fight against the "bandits"; it was also a proud rout and you will be regaled with first-hand stories of bravery and derring-do if you show interest. One of Trinidad's (see Chapter 32) most iconic and photographed buildings—that of the colorful bell tower—houses the Museo Nacional de la

Lucha Contra los Bandidos, dedicated to this bellicose episode in contemporary Cuban history.

On the perkier side of things, the Escambray, with its cool(er) mountain climate, abundant shade and fertile soil, is one of Cuba's major coffee growing regions. Even the one peso shots sold in the smallest towns are robust, smoky and brewed from freshly roasted beans that come down from the slopes of this mountain range. On short and long treks or slow drives, the glossy green leaves and bright red coffee cherry are visible to the naked eye and fairly mouth-watering. Coffee is a commodity crop in Cuba, with all stages of production in the hands of state enterprises and farming cooperatives, meaning there are no little roadside stands selling beans in nifty little bags, nor quaint cafés featuring locally grown coffee like in Guatemala or Hawai'i. Here the coffee experience is more direct, with locals spread across the slopes harvesting the ripe cherry in the chilly months toward years' end and the coveted beans laid out to dry on large cement patios in front of wooden houses. Stop for a salutation and a chat and you'll likely be invited in for a cup of the sweet, strong, dark brew typical to Cuba (made the old-fashioned way, in a *tetera*, a burlap cone set in a wooden stand, filled with grounds over which hot water is poured).

The Casa Museo del Café in Topes de Collantes is a bare bones café where you can learn about the area's coffee culture; there's a garden nearby with more than two dozen coffee plant varieties. The mountains here are also home to the Teatro Escambray, an avant-garde theater group founded shortly after the revolution to bring theater to rural populations; it thrives to this day, with a countryside theater and school nestled between Hanabanilla and Cumanayagua.

For hikers and nature enthusiasts, the Escambray, the country's second-highest mountain range after the Sierra Maestra, and specifically Topes de Collantes nature reserve, make a great home base for a trekking adventure. There are well-kept, easy to moderate trails fanning out from the monstrous Kurhotel, including the phenomenally popular 3.75-mile roundtrip hike to the Salto del Caburní, 203 feet of crystal clear waterfall pouring into a series of bathing pools. This trail is clearly the beaten path, but if you've got some goat in you, scramble up toward the top of the falls for some peace and tranquility away from the maddening crowds. Another hiking highlight here passes through the best scenery available in Topes (as locals call the reserve), including full frontal views of Pico San Juan, via a network of trails in Parque Guanayara. The trails begin 9 miles north of the Kurhotel—hoof it for some pretty vistas or hitch a ride. If you do only one hike in these parts, head to the Salto de Rocío, a wide set of several falls with individual pools at the bottom. This is a great area for intrepid campers.

55 *Embalse Hanabanilla*

THIS MASSIVE RESERVOIR TUCKED INTO a valley in the Escambray mountains is a marvel of modern engineering and one of Cuba's best spots for solo hiking (i.e., without compulsory guide), boat trips and appreciating the pace and flavor of country life. The 22-square-mile reservoir was created in the 1950s by an American firm that flooded the valleys and towns in the triangle range of mountains between Cienfuegos, Trinidad, and Santa Clara to create a hydroelectric project. The populations of these remote villages were relocated and the remains of their dear, departed loved ones in the cemetery removed and re-interred elsewhere; the cemetery itself is now under water. When the revolution triumphed and the US and Cuba broke off relations, the project was only 70 percent done, whereupon the Cubans saw it through to completion, with the aid of Czechoslovakian specialists. Today, the hydroelectric plant here is connected to the national electric grid and generates between 40,000 and 60,000 watts annually. The drought—the island's worst in decades—was ameliorated by 2017's Hurricane Irma, but the reservoir is still far from capacity, as evidenced by the exposed bright blue water markers climbing up the reservoir's steep slope. An elder who has lived her entire life here told me: "The lake is very low, it's so sad." But in typical Cuban fashion, she followed this with enviable optimism: "But it has been lower than this before. It will come back."

There are many ways to enjoy the charms of this reservoir—Fidel Castro knew this well: he had a country home on floating  pontoons he used as a refuge for unwinding from the stress of leading. There are various hikes, none too strenuous, including a stroll around the shoreline with its golden sands and bountiful butter-flies and a five-mile roundtrip trek to a lookout point pro-viding views of the entire basin and to the Río Negro beyond. The trail to the overlook, called El Reto a Loma Atahalaya, starts to the right of the Hotel Hanabanilla. In late spring, the path is littered with mangoes and mamey, a hiker's delight; in the fall, the wild coffee plants will be budding with cherry. White, bright quartz winks up from the path and once in a while a feral cow will crash through the brush. It's a criminal offense to kill cows in Cuba—not for religious or animal protection reasons, but because cattle stock are strictly controlled by the state to guaran-tee milk rations for every Cuban under seven years old and those with certain chronic diseases on a doctor-prescribed diet. Slaying a cow carries a minimum four-year sentence, which is why you rarely see beef in markets or on menus. Nevertheless, stories are rife in this part of the country (and other similar grazing grounds across the island) about cows escaping or meeting "accidental" ends. In this way, legal ramifications are avoided and there's enough beef suddenly available to feed a village.

Serious hikers should consider the 9-mile trail crossing the mountains to El Nicho and surrounding waterfalls. In countryside vernacular, mountains are known as *las lomas,* a handy tip when getting directions. If physical activity and exertion are far from your idea of a good time, consider a boat trip—a low-impact alternative for getting a taste of the natural beauty around Hanabanilla. My preferred captain leaves from the pier below Paladar de Ever, where you can take a lake tour to waterfalls and caves or make a beeline directly to El Nicho (see Chapter 57). Bring an appetite: Ever and crew serve up Cuba's best pork chunks and chicharrones, cooked over a wood fire, complemented by rice and beans, salad and chips for $2CUC.

56

Presa Jibacoa

I'M ONE OF THOSE PEOPLE who keeps on going when the road ends. Sometimes it means I end up tangled and bloody in a nasty bramble or bushwhacking my way back to civilization, with no grand view attained, no new path forded. But once in a while, pushing beyond where most turn back, I've discovered secret caves and deserted beaches, little hidden hamlets and the perfect clandestine camping spot. Regardless of the outcome of such ventures, it always feels like I'm embracing the journey, rather than just focussing on the destination. But I won't lie: discovering that abandoned cave or tucked away cascade brings a jolt of joy and achievement all travelers must feel when they break through the forest cover to behold a spectacular view or river valley, a cluster of thatch-roofed houses or golden scoop of sand.

This is precisely what happened when we gunned the 1946 Harley-Davidson past the last cluster of homes and up the steep, rocky slope delineating the southeastern extent of the Embalse Hanabanilla. My fear that we would pop a tire on the sharp stones or skid backwards on the precipitous grade melted away when we came to a level clearing and gazed upon the sparkling waters of the Presa Jibacoa. A pair of row boats bobbed in the shallows, verdant hills ringed the shoreline, and a level grassy meadow anchored it all; shoreline camping below the towering peaks of the Sierra Escambray was now firmly on the travel itinerary.

Similar to the Embalse Hanabanilla, this reservoir has been at dangerously low levels in the past, regaining some capacity when tropical storms and hurricanes pass through this area (which are not as typically hard hit as coastal areas). You can tell how healthy the water levels are by the markers driven into the rocky slope stepping down to the water's edge. And despite a faded warning sign painted by the Ministry of Public Health urging people not to swim here, two local lovers showed up at sunset to doff their clothes and take a cool dip while we explored. Otherwise, we had this beautifully pristine place to ourselves, sitting on the boulders between forest and shore skipping stones, watching the sun dip and slide between hills, and cooing over the earth-toned striped shells that litter the ground. So captivated were we by the surrounding landscape, we didn't have enough sunlight to find the Cueva de Guanajo (Wild Turkey Cave) that locals told us was just beyond the house at the top of the stairs.

Jibacoa is a remote mountain town where the well-to-do get around on horseback and the rest go around barefoot—any kind of packaged or processed food (pasta, soda, crackers, cookies) are treasured here for providing novel variety and offers to share will be reciprocated, no matter if you're enjoying an afternoon with the horseback or barefoot set. This is coffee territory, and you'll see cement drying platforms by the side of the road; here, the aroma of roasting beans mixes with the perfume of pines and is a prime opportunity to procure some quality Cuban coffee straight from the source. You'll definitely need private transport in these parts (surprisingly, there's a gas station along the burg's one road), but the reward of beating your own path will be worth it.

57 *El Nicho*

THE BEAUTY AND NATURAL SPLENDOR of this waterfall and the individual bathing pools linked by a succession of cascades are known far and wide around Cuba. From Havana to Pinar del Río, Holguín to Baracoa, Cubans grow dewy-eyed at the mention of El Nicho. Nevertheless, even folks from nearby Santa Clara or Cienfuegos may never have actually played in the falls' cool spray or smelled the perfume of the mountain pines. This so-near-yet-so-far status of one of Cuba's most glorious natural settings is thanks to its difficult access along a precipitous mountain road that leaves even modern cars smoking on the narrow shoulder. In fact, on a recent adventure into the Escambray, local cowboys were jibing the taxi driver who had to ask four tourists to walk up the steepest grades while his late-model Chinese import cooled off, the engine ticking and knocking with the effort. But folks from these parts brag proudly about how the road to El Nicho— especially the 7 miles dotted with dramatic skidding car signs and bright yellow markers with black exclamation points!—has been completely repaved. It was in good shape as of this writing, but best to have your travel buddy with the most mountain (or San Francisco) driving experience piloting your vehicle. And take great care in any kind of foul weather; even a slight mist can cause a dangerous skid-out or backslide.

El Nicho is a gorgeous double cascade linked to the Río Hanabanilla—the river feeding the Embalse Hanabanilla. The area officially open to visitors (wink, wink) includes the "Lover's Pool," an oasis of turquoise blue surrounded by verdant forest and giant boulders, over which hangs a rustic wooden bridge. Rivaling this romantic tableau is El Nicho itself, a series of waterfalls draped with curtains of glistening green ferns moistened by the powerful cold spray caroming off the rocks. The volume of the falls depends largely on annual rainfall (and hurricane action), but are still beautiful and a panacea for the heat—even during drought. The trail skirting El Nicho leads straight up to another, smaller set of falls with a big swimming hole and ends at a lookout over the valley to the Embalse Hanabanilla beyond. If you pass through the rustic gate to the left of the trail where a team of Red Cross lifeguards hangs out, ready to run to anyone requiring aid at the falls below, you enter *tocororo* (Cuban trogon) territory. With a distinctive song and emblematic red, white and blue plumage, it's a real treat to see Cuba's national bird in its natural habitat. Cuban blackbirds, and ruby-throated and bee hummingbirds abound, making this a good birding area in general, including for photography. You'll hear them trilling through the forest as you hike and swim.

The trail is fairly short, but with swimming, taking in the views, romping in the falls and snapping selfies, you can easily burn an entire day at El Nicho. There are rudimentary campgrounds here for the truly determined and strong cyclists make this trip on two wheels. Across from the official entrance, there are more cascades and pools where you can get some distance from the maddening crowds; this is a good strategy on summer weekends when Cubans pour into El Nicho with powerful portable speakers and (on the whole) terribly banal music.

58 Guajimico

TOURISM IS CHANGING THE FACE and pace of Cuba. Just a handful of years ago, US travelers to Cuba had to meet very strict requirements for their trip, work with a certified travel provider, file pages and pages of paperwork, have a full, scheduled program of activities directly related to their visit, and fly via a charter flight. The charters were outrageously expensive, with the 45-minute flight between Miami and Havana costing $400 round trip. When President Obama signed an executive order in 2015 allowing for 12 categories of "legal" travel to Cuba for US citizens and residents, visiting became a matter of jumping on the internet, booking a regularly scheduled commercial flight and clicking the appropriate boxes. Suddenly, a round trip from Miami cost half of what it used to and folks were flocking to Cuba for long weekends and records were broken for number of foreign arrivals. Despite many confusing US news stories, these categories of legal travel remain in place, as do the commercial flights (though several routes have been scaled back or cut altogether), assuring the popularity of the loop route from Havana-Cienfuegos-Trinidad. If this quick, common itinerary appeals, don't make the mistake of blowing by the best of what this part of Cuba has to offer—the southern coast between Cienfuegos and Trinidad. This stretch of coastal road is dotted with little pocket beaches fed by freshwater rivers running down from the

Escambray where you can camp, picnic and get to know Cuban families day-tripping to the beach.

The first place you hit once the road out of Cienfuegos dips down to the coast is Guajimico. Cloistered on a series of turquoise inlets, this scuba and snorkel camp with individual rooms in the surrounding forest gets my vote for best kept secret in this part of the island. The accommodation is affordable and serviceable and the reefs healthy. Dives can be organized here or bring your own snorkel gear for an independent adventure. While the food can get repetitive, there's a pool with a view overlooking the ocean, caves worth exploring, and kayaks for rent, making this an attractive option for family travel.

Since few people other than in-the-know Europeans venture out this way, Guajimico is also a good spot for an intimate getaway; I've always found carnal delights mix well with nature appreciation. With a car, picking your way along the coast stopping at whatever beach strikes your fancy is highly recommended. I camped this length of coast more than a decade ago and returned just a few months before the book you hold in your hands was published; the beaches were smaller, narrower, and at least one was no longer visible at high tide. According to local environmental authorities, this section of the Cuban coast is losing almost five feet of ground every year. Though Cuba has national beach recovery, dune-building and native beach planting programs, and is signatory to the Paris Climate Change Accords, saving the nation's beaches from further erosion is a race against time—take your kids here now; some of these beaches might not be here when they're grown.

59 *Cuba's Highest Waterfall*

YOU'VE LIKELY TIRED OF THE refrains already and if not, you surely will once you set down in Cuba: *"de Alto Cedro voy para Macarné, llego a Cueto, voy para Mayarí."* *Chan Chan*, the classic *son* revived from the dusty annals of Cuban song by the global phenomenon that became the Buena Vista Social Club, is performed from New York to Shanghai, Barcelona to Veracruz. It's the one tune recognizable to tourists, though most couldn't find Macarné or Mayarí, let alone Cueto or Alto Cedro, on a map. Guidebooks tout this quartet of backwater towns in central Cuba as the "Chan Chan Route" for which diehard fans and musicologists pay good money to traverse. Little do they know—or even the Cubans taking them there—that tucked among the mountains, high above the pine trees that dominate the forest here, hides one of Cuba's most magnificent natural landscapes. Indeed, criss-crossing the island in conversation with Cubans from all walks of life, no one, aside from a few fellows linked to tourism in Holguín, had ever heard of Salto de Guayabo or Salto de Berraco, the pair of waterfalls secreted among the mountains of the Parque Nacional la Mensura. This is doubly ironic given that none of the dusty, hot towns invoked in what has become Cuba's signature song have anything to recommend them—except perhaps for ice-cold, fresh-pressed sugar cane juice, the one reliable potable in this land where cane is king.

But turn off the main street in Mayarí toward the mountains, steady yourself for a hard drive or pedal (only strong cyclists need try), and start heading up. And up and up and up, along the "Loma de Bandera." The stuff of legend, Flag Hill used to be so narrow a flag was planted at the bottom as a way to manage traffic: if you arrived at the base of the hill and the flag was there, the road was clear and you could proceed—but you had to take the flag with you. Arriving at the top with a sigh of relief, travelers enjoyed panoramic vistas of the Sierra Mensura and the Sierra Cristal beyond, whereupon they replaced the flag for the next driver. If you arrived at the base of Flag Hill or were sitting at the top and there was no flag, you had to wait until the person on the road appeared from above or below and passed it off. The rock-rutted road, now widened, mostly paved and in decent repair, climbs nearly 1,640 feet in only a handful of miles and is slow going still, even for modern vehicles with all- or four-wheel drive. Indeed, I saw tractors and heavy duty trucks specifically designed for the mountain terrain struggling here. Take care, especially if there has been recent rain.

Several miles beyond where the Loma de Bandera tapers off into more manageable inclines is the entrance to the Salto de Guayabo—you'll hear the rush of the parallel falls before ever glimpsing them. The visitors center here is a paradigm of Cuban country hospitality and you'll be offered a frosty beer or fresh brewed cup of coffee upon stepping through the gate; in fact, after traveling over 1,500 miles across Cuba, my travel partner and I agreed: among all the incredibly nice people we met during our adventure, the kindest of all were up here. Gorgeous views of the falls are to be had from two lookout points, providing clear sightlines to Salto de Guayabo (318 feet, and the even more impressive Salto de Berraco, 417 feet). This is eco-travel at its best: the structures here are made from all natural materials, the guides and rangers are true environmental stewards and the only sound you'll hear are the chirping of birds and the gush of the falls. Not a strain of reggaetón for miles!

The trio of trails are perfumed by wild yellow and white ginger lilies (called *mariposas*, the latter is Cuba's national flower)

and even reluctant hikers will want to take the short route to the natural pool fed by a series of cascades; bobbing in the chilly mountain water, while gazing upon the green-fading-to-blue peaks in the distance with the falls as soundtrack, is therapy to

any tormented soul. Another trail leads to the top of Salto de Berraco, touted as the highest waterfall in Cuba, though detractors contend that Salto Fino, in an inaccessible part of Parque Nacional Alejandro de Humboldt, is higher. Keep an eye peeled for the red, white and blue *tocororo* (Cuba's national bird) and the just as colorful Cuban tody as you explore up this way. The third trail dives steeply through dense woods with prehistoric tree ferns, pine trees, and coffee plants as tall as an NBA center, heavy with ruby red cherry (good for a quick energy burst while hiking), to the bottom of the falls. The natural pools here are deep and cool, the color of milk chocolate thanks to the crimson earth typical to this region, with plenty of opportunities for hydro-massages more powerful than anything reproduced in a spa; in my experience, bathing suits are optional!

60 *Jardines de la Reina*

IF YOU'RE A FAN OF *Shark Week*, you already know about the marvels (and dangers) inhabiting the waters surrounding this necklace of coral islets off Cuba's south-central coast. This area is known for its large, brazen shark population, with several species plying the waters around the "Gardens of the Queen," including bull, blacktip, great white, hammerhead, and silky sharks. Giant whale sharks are also seen in this neighborhood, typically between November and December. In short, if sharks are your thing, this is your place. So well-protected is this marine habitat that Anderson Cooper hosted a lengthy *60 Minutes* special here a few years ago. Watch either of these US-produced programs showcasing this rarely visited, but highly esteemed marine wildlife sanctuary, and it will get your travel fantasies rolling.

✳

"Cuba's Gardens of the Queen," the
underwater odyssey filmed for 60 Minutes,
is available on YouTube.

✳

Experienced scuba divers cherish the Jardines de la Reina for swimming with sharks, naturally, but also for the challenging open water dives afforded here, featuring everything from moray eels to eagle rays, giant jewfish to turtles languishing among infinite types of coral, sponges, and gorgonians. The underwater landscape is fascinating in itself with platforms and ledges dropping off into the big blue, plus caves and spookily deep channels for working up a sweat in your wet suit. Conditions are superb here year-round, with terrific visibility and nary a current to kick up the sands or pull you away from whatever Technicolor delights you happen to be enjoying at the time. In addition to diving, anglers can also cast for bonefish—the fastest fish in the world.

The cost and hassle of getting to the Jardines de la Reina, combined with its limited access and accommodation options, ensure casual tourists won't just show up like an unwanted house guest. The protected area here measures an awesome 2,361 miles and is considered one of the healthiest, most intact marine habitats in the world. This is partly by design and partly due to circumstance: geopolitics have kept US-Cuba boat traffic at bay for decades; the prohibitive cost keeps Cubans and other budget travelers from getting out this way; and importantly, aggressive conservation whereby nearly 20 percent of Cuba's coastal environment is officially protected, all play a role in maintaining the health of these waters and surrounding islands. It helps that commercial fishing has long been banned in this national park and that all the cays are uninhabited.

Permits for who can bring visitors to this underwater paradise are severely restricted. Currently only two agencies, Avalon, running live-aboard trips out of the marina at the down-at-the-heels fishing town of Júcaro and Windward Islands Cruising Company, sailing from the surprisingly modern marina in Cienfuegos, are authorized to pursue fishing and diving at Las Jardines de la Reina.

✲ cubanfishingcenters.com

For a long time, the only accommodation and diving was offered aboard the Hotel Flotante Tortuga, a hulk of a two-story houseboat with several cabins, all equipped with air conditioning and private bath. The Tortuga is a serviceable alternative, if a bit long in the tooth, and is the only live-aboard option moored offshore. Avalon has four other yachts of differing sizes and levels of luxury docked at Júcaro; the biggest and best is the eight-cabin *Avalon Fleet One*, with on-board Jacuzzi, if you're looking for modern amenities. Fully crewed, live-aboard sailboat trips are the bread and butter of the Windward Islands Cruising Company—consider one of these for a unique family vacation or (dare I suggest it?!) a company retreat. This is not a trip you can plan on the ground once you're in Cuba so get your ducks in order if Jardines de le Reina is on your radar; I have some very frustrated California friends and scuba pros who can attest.

✳ www.windward-islands.net/en/yacht-charter
  -caribbean/cuba

61 La Gran Piedra/ Parque Baconao

THE CULTURE! THE MUSIC! THE HISTORY! Some people adore Santiago de Cuba. I'm not one of them. I find the narrow, hilly streets (where it's impossible to walk two abreast) a pain, the motorcycle taxis buzzing like swarms of mosquitoes annoying and dangerous, and the aggressive hustlers tedious. When I need a break from Santiago de Cuba's modern headaches, I head into nature and back in time. At 4,048 feet above sea level, La Gran Piedra, (The Big Rock) didn't hold much attraction at first. Sure, it's a very big rock, but not challenging as a summit goal and has few hiking possibilities regardless. It's more a Mount Washington for the lazy scenario: you drive to the top, get out of the car, and snap a few photos before buying the bumper sticker: "This car climbed Mt. Washington." But like with so many travel experiences, the majesty of La Gran Piedra lies in the journey rather than the destination.

As soon as you turn off the access road about a dozen miles from Santiago de Cuba, you enter a delicious microclimate; breathing comes much easier here after the suffocating heat and humidity of the city. Winding ever upward through a densely forested landscape, the sound of tropical fruit splashing to the asphalt mixes with birds singing and leaves whistling in the wind, evoking Hawai'i rather than Cuba. A few miles along, wonderfully odd metal, wood, and brick sculptures begin to materialize by the roadside. Known as "Sculpture Boulevard" (Prado de las Esculturas), they make a perfect justification for a pit stop, especially if the curvaceous road is wreaking havoc with your stomach. Just before arriving at La Gran Piedra for the money shot, the botanical garden featuring regional fauna is worth a pause if plants get your blood flowing. Once you reach the top, you're awarded with panoramic views over the entire valley and coast; for the best look, come in the morning or early afternoon before the clouds roll in.

I'm starting to think that Cubans are obsessed with the pre-historic (this is *not* a commentary on the political system). There's the Prehistoric Mural in Viñales—a great example of how to mar a beautiful natural landscape—re-creations of indigenous villages with young metrosexuals dressed up like pre-Columbian Indians, and the Prehistoric Valley in Parque Baconao, 15 miles from the city of Santiago de Cuba. While I wouldn't spend a minute of precious travel time visiting the first two, the Prehistoric Valley here is a gas and worth a detour.

There are all kinds of sites in sprawling Parque Baconao, declared a UNESCO Biosphere Reserve in 1987, including a car museum, artists' colony, and a desert ecosystem world's away from the cool, mountain climate of La Gran Piedra. But for me, the star of the show is the Valle de Prehistoria—Cuba's quirkiest, queerest attraction. Spread out over a giant 27-acre field are 200 enormous dinosaurs of all types. Made from cement by prisoners from the nearby jail, these beasts include brontosaurus, tyrannosaurus, triceratops, and more, in various attack poses and states of repose. It's the perfect place for a picnic or romantic interlude and kids (of all ages) love running around here and sitting inside the dinosaurs' mouths. An excursion to La Gran Piedra can be combined easily with Parque Baconao. The entire mountainous and coastal area around Santiago de Cuba calls to adventurers and if you're going to hire a driver or rent a car for a spell in Cuba, this is a good place to do it.

62 Boca de Yumurí

RÍO TOA, RÍO MIEL, RÍO DUABA—part of the magic infusing the region around Baracoa is a result of the numerous, voluminous rivers coursing through the land. They're a source of income, respite, recreation, and solace. Riders bathe their horses, bats flit amongst eerie caves and cliffs overhanging the banks, and there's a sweet, but savory feel to the rivers as they meet the ocean. Follow the rivers upstream and you'll discover natural freshwater pools for cooling off. Each river has its charms, and every Baracuense will profess a different favorite, but there's something ethereal and eye-opening about a trip to *my* favorite, the Río Yumurí. Out here, you can lounge on a beach as if it were your own personal domain, nary a hustler or hawker in sight. The insidious, insipid beats of reggaetón may still be making the rounds in your head, but the soundtrack here is strictly birdsong and surf. The scenic road traverses hill and dale, green with coconut palms, before dropping down to the coast lined with black sand beaches, one after the other. Here, locals cook up fresh octopus, crab, fish, and other ocean fare, evoking the South Seas more than one of the world's last socialist states. Out here, the river meets the sea at Boca de Yumurí, one of the most popular day trips out of Baracoa and a point of pride among locals for its singular beauty. The gorgeous setting and easy access (Boca de Yumurí is just 16 miles from Baracoa via a good, paved road) means this spot can get crowded, but stop anywhere before the town and village and you won't be disappointed.

One of the startling sites along the way to Yumurí is the preponderance of sturdy, modern churches (no holes in these roofs!), freshly painted and fenced in, next to sagging wooden houses covered with palm thatch, a skinny mutt lying in the bare earth trying to get cool. Grand Pentecostal churches set among poor villages are a common site in the rest of Latin America, but not so in Cuba, where they're a recent phenomenon of some concern to government authorities, as much for their divisionary doctrine as their deep pockets and socio-economic sway. You'll see well-dressed locals streaming to catch a sermon as you travel this road.

After gliding amongst the wooded hills where 2016 hurricane damage is still evident, the coast comes in to view and then at once, is close enough to touch. The entire coastline here is carved through with dark sand beaches—take your pick where to indulge in a Caribbean fantasy. My two favorites are Playa Guillermo, a secret scoop of paradise accessed via a stairway right after the Paso de Alemanes, a natural, tree bough arch straight out of *The Hobbit*, followed closely by Playa Cascajo, just beyond, with just enough *uva caleta* trees (sea grape) for a shady respite; at low tide you can walk between these two beauties, collecting stones smoothed by the elements along the way.

About a quarter of a mile down the road is the town and riverside site of Boca de Yumurí, where the river rushes forth from a deep canyon to meet the sea. Trips upriver are possible and aggressively promoted by local touts. They'll try to get you to dine, too, but don't miss the chance to shrug into a bright blue Adirondack chair on a private crescent beach on the road back to Baracoa where you can choose from all manner of fresh seafood, cooked while you gaze upon sea, mountains, and sand. If I had to have one last meal, I'd likely dine at La Flaca (The Skinny One), who has the regional delicacy *tetí* (a miniscule river fish available only in this area) on the menu and homemade hot sauce on the checker clothed table set into the sand. Yuneisi (aka La Flaca) tries to entice us to pitch camp and see the sun rise and set from this little beach—one of the few spots in Cuba where this is possible. It's a shame we have to move on: she's about to star in the Cuban episode of the reality motorcycle/chef TV show *One Tank* and it won't be long before you'll have to wait for your place in one of her Adirondack chairs. If you make it out this far, consider traveling just over a dozen miles farther down the road to Punto Maisí, earning you a notch on your traveler's belt since you will have made it to Cuba's most eastern point.

⁂ www.onetankadventure.com

63 Parque Nacional Alejandro de Humboldt

NATIONAL PARKS, WILDERNESS PRESERVES, Ramsar Convention Sites and UNESCO Biosphere Reserves: Cuba has its fair share of protected marine habitats, forests, coastlines, and mountain ranges. But it's safe to say that none rival Alejandro de Humboldt, which is both national park and part of the Cuchillas del Toa UNESCO Biosphere Reserve. The 373 miles of forest and 16.5 miles of mangrove and coast protected within this park located halfway between Moa and Baracoa led UNESCO to categorize the Parque Nacional Alejandro de Humboldt as one of the most biodiverse tropical ecosystems on the planet, with the last stand of virgin rainforest in the Caribbean. Part of the reason for the international accolades and distinction is the park's high density of endemic flora and fauna—905 endemic species dwell here—including the Cuban trogon, Cuban tody and Cuban parrots, the world's smallest frog which would sit comfortably on your pinkie nail, and thousands of native plants, including 75 species of edible plants used in traditional medicine as well as in the kitchen. The 175,037 acres of the park also harbor endangered species like manatees who gently ply the waters of Bahía de Taco and psychedelic polymita snails clinging to trees and plants; these brightly striped mollusks are crafted into jewelry and sold in tourist markets, despite prohibitions against collecting them.

Luckily, hiking and exploring this natural wonderland is now a possibility. When I first visited in 2002, there was no visitor center, no hiking trails open to the public, and we had to beg the apathetic ranger to let us pitch camp along the idyllic shores of Bahía de Taco with the resident cow. Now that the economic potential of eco-tourism is becoming more apparent, there is a proper visitors center with surprisingly informative displays and biologists on-staff, four hikes (all guided), and daily excursions from Baracoa. This is a hard-fought victory: a handful of years ago, a hydroelectric project was slated for the mighty Río Toa. Designed to tap into the country's most voluminous river, the project would provide juice to the national electricity grid—cutting through the heart of this park in the process. Cuban and international environmentalists sounded the alarm, rallied, and successfully persuaded authorities to shelve the idea.

With the hydroelectric project dead in the water so to speak, environmentalists on the island breathed a sigh of relief—until Hurricane Matthew tore through the park in October 2016, dramatically reducing forest cover and downing great swaths of trees. The damage is still visible, with dead trees scattering the hillsides leading to the park entrance. Experts predict that it will take generations for the park to return to its previous glory, but there are still a handful of wonderful hikes available to get a taste of one of Cuba's greatest protected areas. From easy to moderately difficult, these combine treks through Cuban pine and evergreen forests, superb birdwatching opportunities, and exploring and swimming in Cuba's most perfect crescent bay, Bahía de Taco. A colony of West Indian manatees still calls these waters home and rangers are dedicated to protecting them and their environment.

The example of the Parque Nacional Alejandro de Humboldt underscores the problematic state of environmental protection in Cuba, where, like in other developing countries, unrelenting economic crisis often eclipses ecological considerations. While the government has aggressive tree planting programs, for example, reforesting nearly 10 percent of national lands over the past several years, it also recently approved Latin America's biggest golf resort abutting sea turtle nesting site and UNESCO Biosphere Reserve Península de Guanahacabibes. So when you roll up to Parque Nacional Alejandro de Humboldt and are asked to fork over $10CUC for entry and then additional hiking fees, keep this dilemma in mind. If more people hike and fewer people golf—sorry golfers, but your sport, pastime, and hobby wreaks havoc on habitat—maybe we can collectively make a difference.

VI

Republic & Revolution

64 *Bayamo*

SOME YEARS AGO, WORD STARTED making its way around the island that historic Bayamo—the island's second oldest city and birthplace of both Cuban independence hero Carlos Manuel de Céspedes and the Cuban national anthem—was the "it" city to visit. Every Cuban of reading age knows Céspedes, Bayamo's most famous son, who boldly freed his slaves from his Demajagua

sugar plantation on October 10, 1868, sparking the First War of Independence. No matter that the initiative failed: it set events in motion, the impact of which are still felt today—and not just because October 10th is a national holiday, providing yet another good reason to kick back with a Cristal. Céspedes, a lawyer-cum-revolutionary (not unlike that other famous son, Fidel Castro), inspired centuries of Cubans to fight for what's rightfully theirs or die trying.

He rallied his fellow Bayameses to take up arms to liberate his hometown from Spanish overlords, but as soon as the ragged rebel army smelled defeat, they torched Bayamo rather than see it re-occupied. Watching your city burn instead of letting interlopers profit from it gives you an idea how deeply the principle of sovereignty runs here and goes a long way toward explaining Cuba's position vis-à-vis the United States.

The events of October 1868 ignited a flame of self-determination in the hearts of all Cubans, including Bayamese Perucho Figueredo, who penned "La Bayamesa," the country's national anthem, first belted out just ten days after Céspedes freed his slaves. "To arms, quickly, Bayamesans! All Cuba looks to you proudly. Do not fear a glorious death. To die for the homeland is to live," run the anthem's opening lines, sung at the beginning of every school day, at every political rally, during each meeting of neighborhood blocks associations known as Comités de Defensa de la Revolución and played every night when TV channels sign off. In short: Bayamo is invoked every day across the island, in one form or another.

Then suddenly, unexpectedly, Bayamo became the talk of the town—around domino games in Pinar, dinner tables in Havana, and park fountains in Sancti Spíritus. Friends returned from the Oriente (as all lands east of Camagüey are collectively known) lauding the progress of Bayamo, the cleanliness of the streets, the efficiency of government and commerce, and the all-around feel-good vibe. Revitalization of Cuban cities like this one happen when there's a major anniversary or visit, spearheaded by someone with the authority and grit to see it through properly, in this case Lázaro Expósito, the First Secretary of the Cuban Communist Party (i.e.,: the top dog and political bigwig in the area). The mastermind of the city's revamp was Expósito, and the event justifying the project was Fidel Castro's speech here in 2006—his last before falling ill, as it turned out.

For history buffs, Bayamo is a must: there's the Plaza de la Patria with statues of independence heroes Céspedes, Máximo Gómez, and Antonio Maceo; Parque Céspedes, with a bust of anthem author Figueredo, inscribed with the lyrics; and the home where Céspedes first drew breath. This is also one of Cuba's friendliest cities, as a stroll along Paseo Bayamés, a boulevard inlaid with colorful mosaics and lined with public art, will attest. At the southern extent of this pedestrian-only street is the Museo de Cera, a quirky wax museum worth a stop (and not just for the robust air conditioning—this province regularly records Cuba's hottest temperatures). Astoundingly life-like renditions of Cuban greats including musicians Bola de Nieve and Polo Montañez, champion boxer Teófilo Stevenson, and the apostle José Martí pack the two floors here; locals proudly share tales of how this former state laundromat was transformed into a museum of note, each of the sculptures created by a family from nearby Guisa.

"You should have seen when they inaugurated Juan Formell. The entire family came from Havana and his wife was reduced to tears when it was unveiled—he's even wearing the actual watch, rings, and chains he wore in real life," Jorge the cookie seller tells me as I munch on one of his delicious *mantecados*, a traditional butter cookie also known as a *tortica* or *polverón*. From Formell, founder of the legendary salsa band Los Van Van to Che Guevara and Gabriel García Márquez, Bayamo's wax museum is a pantheon to Latin American greatness. "They're going to have to expand soon; I don't even know how they fit Luis Carbonell in there (another Cuban musician of global impact, unveiled in 2017)," Jorge says. Trailing cookie crumbs, I leave Jorge and his neighbor Hugo debating if the museum should build up or acquire the small parcel adjacent as I continue my ramble along the boulevard.

65 *Casa Natal de José Martí*

IF THERE'S ONE NAME EVERYONE should learn before traveling to Cuba, it's José Martí, journalist, poet, publisher, orator, and the father of Cuban independence. You'll see him at every turn: on the one peso coin and bill, in front of every school, on billboards, standing in defiance of the US Embassy, and in institutions dedicated to studying his work and philosophy. There are streets, theaters, and parks named after him. Indeed, you probably alit at Havana's Jose Martí International Airport. He's claimed as ally by revolutionaries and dissidents alike, his writings liberally quoted to validate their respective causes.

Along with being a prolific writer—he began publishing a newspaper at the tender age of 16 and his collected works fill 30 volumes—he was also an ex-convict, having been sent to prison for his pro-independence agitating and organizing. He was deported as a condition of his release, traveling to Europe and Central America before landing in the United States. He set down roots in New York, spending 14 years in the Big Apple marshalling resources to free Cuba from Spain's grip. When all was said and done, Martí, too, was an exile. For all his virtues, Martí was not cut out for the actual fight: he was the first casualty in the Second War of Independence (known as the Spanish American War in the USA), shot from his white stallion on May

19, 1895 at Dos Ríos. Martí: writer, organizer, fighter, exile, and finally, martyr. Cubans on and off the island, regardless of their political bent, revere him above all other historical, political, and cultural icons, living or dead.

✻

Poet Martí penned two classics, *Simple Verses* and
Ismaelillo, while his children's book, *La Edad de Oro*,
is read by every Cuban kid. The *José Martí Reader* is
a collection of essays giving a good overview of his
thoughts on the state of colonial America.

✻

Martí was both a prescient political analyst and keen observer of history. Indeed, just a year before he was born, the United States, France, and England sat down and decided "we are thoroughly convinced that an immediate and earnest effort ought to be made by the government of the United States to purchase Cuba from Spain at any price for which it can be obtained." They tried to do just that, repeatedly and unsuccessfully. After residing in the United States where he raised funds and forces for Cuban independence, Martí underscored the imperialist designs of the United States, writing: "I have lived inside the monster and I know its entrails"—this observation is invoked on the island still. His vision of "Cuba Libre" was realized in 1902 when the island finally gained independence—sort of: Cuba was not present at the treaty signing, and certainly wouldn't have acquiesced to the inclusion of the Platt Amendment, which stated that the US could intervene militarily in Cuba whenever it saw fit. The Platt Amendment also allowed the annexation of a large corner of

Guantánamo province—home for more than a century and still, to the notorious US naval base and detention center.

The interventionist Platt Amendment paved the way for US business interests to carve up the island and amass fortunes from sugar, coffee, and real estate; American economic and political power was consolidated with the help of (and kickbacks to) one puppet president after another installed by Washington. Perhaps it was Martí's experience living in exile in New York that motivated him to write "an economic theory without an ethical base is destined to bring forth monsters"—something current leaders are keeping in mind while ongoing reforms flirt with a mixed socialist-capitalist system. Martí's political philosophy also put a fine point on socio-economic and gender equality, something Cuba has struggled to forge, with mixed results.

Given that Martí is such a larger-than-life figure, it's surprising to see the modest childhood home where he grew up. Located on the margins of Havana's historical (and truth be told, actual) red-light district at Calle Leonor Pérez #314, this yellow and blue house, now fully restored, became the island's first museum when it opened in 1925; in 1949 it was designated a National Monument. Yes, he was as short as his single bed implies and the ephemera, from his preferred pen to the cup in which he drank his morning *café con leche*, provides a fascinating glimpse into "The Apostle's" origins. Many of his hand-written documents are also on display.

His spectacular tomb in the Santa Ifigenia cemetery in Santiago de Cuba, with regular changing of the guards in full regalia, attests to his near-beatification amongst those on the island. One of Martí's most enduring recitations, still quoted liberally, is that every man (and woman, I wonder?) should do three things in life: raise a child; write a book; and plant a tree.

66 Birán—Birthplace of the Castro Clan

As I write this, it's almost 91 years to the day that Lina Ruz gave birth at Finca Manacas to a healthy, hardy boy she named Fidel. Where a legend is born, a museum is sure to follow, and the Finca, located in the boondocks of Holguín in the tiny town of Birán, has been completely restored and serves as pilgrimage site for those wishing to pay homage or get a glimpse of where it all began. Located after miles of interminable sugar cane, far from anywhere of note, you have to make a real effort to visit the Museo Conjunto Histórico de Birán (its formal name), which is why they only receive a handful of visitors on a busy day. But what we learned (and didn't) on the obligatory guided tour by our docent Virgen was enlightening. Castro patriarch Ángel came to Cuba from Galicia, Spain as a poorly paid, over-marched soldier to shore up Spanish colonial holdings on the island. Beholding the fertile lands of central Cuba convinced him wealth was to be sown here and he determined to set down roots along the colonial road linking island commerce from east to west. He acquired parcel after parcel—initially leasing much of it from the omnipotent United Fruit Company, which his rebel son eventually booted from the country—building a sugar and agricultural empire that covered more than 27,000 acres when all was said and done.

Part of the Castro penchant to think big must be genetic: Ángel constructed an entire town to house, entertain, educate, and support his family and workers, while serving merchants traveling along the strategic commercial route. There's the red roofed plantation house and hotel, their lemon yellow clapboard contrasting smartly against the green palms and mountains behind; a bar which served tipples to thirsty travelers, while providing sharks an opportunity to make some quick cash at the billiards table; and the telegraph and post office next door which "could communicate with the entire world," Virgen says, trying to inflect her memorized spiel with reverence. After 20 years giving the same tour, her monotone belies her enthusiasm. There's the company store (Virgen pointedly shares no details of the store's terms for the Haitian workers toiling in Ángel's fields) and the one-room schoolhouse where Fidel learned to read and write at age five. Little brother Raúl was also enrolled here, but declined to attend after a spell, saying it was too close to the watchful eyes of his parents; he opted for military academy instead. The school walls are hung with historic photos—a seven-year old Raúl in his school military uniform, Fidel with his high school volleyball team—providing clues into the Castro brothers' character. Raúl has an easy smile and Fidel, even at a very young age, had a way with the girls.

✳

National Book Award finalist *Telex from Cuba*
by Rachel Kushner, set in this part of the country,
captures the sweet and sour essence of the island's
pre-revolution sugar economy.

✳

Visitors get only a brief look at the main house, which was rebuilt and restored after a careless smoker burned it to the ground several decades ago (Worker? Squatter? Saboteur? Virgen doesn't expound and we don't ask). The bedroom with iron bed and crib where Lina gave birth to seven children, including Fidel, is spine-chilling. Virgen tells us these weren't easy births, with the strong and willful midwife sweating hard through the process as Lina, a diabetic, had babies weighing 10 pounds or more. What becomes evident as the tour progresses is that the real story here is about Castro matriarch Lina. The family maid and cook, she first lived in quarters befitting her station in the plantation house, before properly marrying Ángel and moving to "Fidel's house," built with the intention of housing Fidel and his family once he finished law school. The plan derailed when the young man went rogue revolutionary in the early 1950s; seems once he left for high school in Santiago de Cuba, he never looked back.

The 1918 crank-motor Dodge Lina drove is parked between the stilts holding up the house and pictures of the stalwart campesina—alongside the car, tending goats, on the farm—adorn the walls of the house. As we roam through the gigantic tiled kitchen equipped with a six-burner charcoal stove and state-of-the-art (for the time), kerosene-fueled refrigerator, her presence and the esteem in which she was held breathes life into the quiet home. Ángel and Lina kept separate bedrooms (the latter is the only room where photography is prohibited) and the rifle Fidel used in the Sierra Maestra fighting Batista's troops is encased in a vitrine nearby. Though Fidel never lived here, it's clear mother and son shared mutual admiration: hanging in the closet in the guest bedroom is the Adidas tracksuit he was wearing on the day he died. Cue goosebumps.

I had so many questions for Virgen but it was hot and late, the workers were waiting for us to leave so they could go home for the night, and it occurred to me that what's revealed on a tour of the historic compound is as intriguing as what isn't. Indeed, when I asked a friend who lived at Birán for six months as part of the restoration team for the inside skinny, she told me: "Some stories aren't for sharing in the book, Conner."

67 Historic Beachheads

FIRST CAME NOMADIC INDIGENOUS TRIBES making their way from other tropical climes and islands to Cuban shores—most notably the Siboney, followed by the Taíno.

✳

Indigenous words, names, and even foods are still a daily reality in Cuba: there's Hatuey beer; casabe, a tasteless flatbread made from yucca; and Radio Taíno, ironically the "tourist station" broadcasting in English, French, and Spanish on 93.3 FM.

✳

Then came the explorers: Christopher Columbus, who thought he'd found passage to India, and then colonizer extraordinaire Diego Velázquez, who established Cuba's first original seven cities (in order: Baracoa, Bayamo, Trinidad, Sancti Spíritus, Camagüey, Santiago de Cuba, and finally, Havana). Rich colonists were swiftly followed by pirates, buccaneers, and corsairs of the coarsest sort who laid waste to Spanish galleons loaded with coffee, sugar, and chocolate setting sail for Europe. No matter what dramatic event in Cuban history you choose—slavery, the arrival of la Virgen de la Caridad (see Chapter 97), the explosion of the *Maine*, the Bay of Pigs (see Chapter 70), the

Mariel boatlift, the Elián fiasco, the rafter crisis—it is always intricately linked to the sea. Not surprising, given that Cuba is the Caribbean's largest island and pre-industrial age technology limited invasions and incursions to the water. But what is curious is that the two most definitive moments in the nation's history, what set the stage for everything that followed and which defined the tenor and flavor of events for centuries down the line, took place on south coast beaches, in some of Cuba's most remote reaches.

Cuba's Second War of Independence (called the Spanish American War in most US textbooks, obliterating Cuba's role entirely like a revisionist bitch slap) finally jettisoned the yoke of

Spanish rule over the island. It was a long, hard, expensive struggle led by Cuban Renaissance man, José Martí, who campaigned, wrote tracts, raised money, and rallied troops for the cause. He also was one of the six freedom fighters, including decorated veteran from Cuba's First War of Independence (aka The One That Failed), Máximo Gómez, who rowed to the beachhead at Playita de Cajobabo on April 11, 1895.

Given what this area looks like today, it's hard to fathom how inhospitable it must have felt nearly 125 years ago. Guantánamo is so arid even the cacti and scrub cower, surrendering to their sere-induced fate, the heat clasps a chokehold around your throat, and you might as well stare into a solar eclipse without protection—your retinas wouldn't know the difference. My admiration for these six men driven by their vision for Cuba

Libre soared as I imagined them making landfall, tired, thirsty, beads of sweat stinging them temporarily blind. After living in exile for 16 years, Martí kissed the ground at Playita Cajobabo when they finally got ashore.

Given the gravitas of the event, I expected something epic at the site where Cuban independence was effectively launched. An eternal flame, maybe, or a couple of soldiers or color guard in period dress marking the spot. Instead, I rocked up to a rocky beach with aggressive, uninviting surf and discovered a simple marble monument marking the day and spot of the seminal event. When I expressed my disappointment to my friend Angelo, a Cuban who is a healthy mix of patriotic, revolutionary, mystical, and free thinking, he responded: "It is underwhelming, but there's some kind of supernatural energy going on at that beach, too." And he's right. It's hard to put a finger on. Maybe this queer vibe is related to the fact that Martí was shot and killed during the very first battle after the landing. Maybe it's because the monument was paid for and erected by Cuban Freemasons (the fraternal organization is still huge and active on the island; you'll see lodges in even small provincial towns). Or maybe it's just the sun, turning our brains to jelly. Cajobabo is right at the foot of La Farola, the preferred route to or from Baracoa and makes a simple side trip.

The other beachhead of historical import, of course, is where Fidel Castro and his disheveled band of guerrillas finally made landfall, sparking the Cuban Revolution. Except, they never actually landed. After a torturous sea crossing from Mexico, which threw one man overboard (later recovered) and sent them drifting toward their previously agreed upon meeting place two days late (resulting in missing their hookup with on-the-ground reinforcements), their forward progress was halted by the tangle of mangrove roots choking the southern shoreline. It was night, they were half-starved and exhausted but there was no choice: into the water they jumped for the long slog toward Playa Las Coloradas. By some accounts it took the guerrillas over six hours of swimming, sloshing and stumbling to finally gain *terra firma* that fateful December 2, 1956. Che Guevara is famously quoted as saying in retrospect, that "it wasn't a disembarkation; it was a shipwreck."

It's stunning that they even made it this far, considering the cabin cruiser in which they made the voyage, the *Granma*, was designed for 18 or so cocktail-swilling weekend warriors, not a week-long ocean-going voyage with 82 armed rebels. Nevertheless, X marks the spot at Playa Las Coloradas for the first step toward victory for the *barbudos* (the bearded ones, as the guerrillas were universally called). Even if you've grown weary of all the revolutionary history accompanying your Cuban travels, the Parque Nacional Desembarco de Granma, (a UNESCO World Heritage Site) is fascinating for its combination of endemic plants and animals, virgin forest, and stepped marine terraces that have eroded over millennia to create a staircase cliff looming more than 1500 feet above the shoreline. There are a couple of hiking trails, prime birdwatching possibilities and caves for exploring—likely used by the Taíno before Columbus and other Europeans showed up. The nearest settlement with facilities is the sugar mill town of Niquero, where the Cuban crank organ still wobbles out tunes at Saturday night street parties and you can munch on Cuba's best *polverones* (butter cookies) while people watching in the park.

68 Granjita Siboney

CUBA STILL SURPRISES ME, EVEN AFTER 16 years in residence—daily. There was the pair of elementary school children in Viñales who found a wallet with 3000 euros (a fortune in Cuba), and took it to their mom, who contacted the authorities, reuniting the gentleman with his money and wallet intact. And then we have a new national holiday, initiated in 2016 (which happens to be today, as I write this), where the entire country has the day off—for Good Friday. This is wholly unexpected in a theoretically communist country. Nowhere are these surprises thrown into starker relief than at tourist attractions, where expectations, high and low, can affect the experience.

The first time I visited Granjita Siboney, 9 miles southeast of Santiago de Cuba, it was out of professional obligation: I needed to include the little farmhouse of historical import in *Lonely Planet Cuba*. Sweating profusely under the Santiago sun, the sheaves of my notebook limp from the humidity, I hitched a ride on a truck and begrudgingly approached the *casita* where a sloe-eyed dog slept fitfully. The older fellow in charge of receiving the handful of visitors determined to glimpse where the Cuban revolution started seemed put out by my arrival—granted, it was lunch time. I wasn't much for social interaction either, so we agreed that I could wander from room to room at my leisure.

It was a revelatory 45 minutes. The modest red and white house is maintained as it was found on July 26, 1953, the day the attack was launched that would affect affairs in the western hemisphere for the next 65 years (and counting). On that historic Sunday, in the pre-dawn dark, 135 combatants squeezed into 26 vehicles and set out to take by force the Moncada Barracks, headquarters of Fulgencio Batista's troops. The attack was planned, equipped, and launched from this unassuming house. The well in the yard was used to stash weapons and the kitchen table converted into a command center, where each step of the operation was analyzed, debated, and coordinated. The attack was rather a disaster—six insurgents died in the attack, while another 55 were captured, tortured and killed by Batista's forces.

Similar disastrous circumstances befell the revolutionaries in 1956 when they made the trip from Mexico to Cuba aboard the 75-foot *Granma* (with typical Cuban hyperbole called a "yacht"); of the 82 would-be revolutionaries who made the trip, more than 70 perished upon making landfall. One of the most spine-shivering parts of the Granjita Siboney is the room which was occupied by the only two female combatants in the Moncada siege—Melba Hernández and Haydeé Santamaria (see Chapter 20). The flowered bed spread and curtains, the little night tables that likely contained architectural plans of the barracks and bullets instead of nail polish and hairbrushes, the faux roses: it feels like walking into any young Cuban woman's bedroom, then and now. Standing stock still between the single beds, imagining these two brave *cubanas* wrestling themselves to sleep the night before the fateful event and snapping awake long before the 5 A.M. departure the next day, is powerful. I stepped from the room, passed to the front door, bidding adieu to the somnolent docent/guard and stuck my hand out to hitch a ride to Playa Siboney, a passable beach a couple of miles down the road. The second time I returned to Granjita Siboney, it was born of desire, rather than obligation.

69

Museo Nacional de la Campaña de Alfabetización

ONE OF THE THINGS I love about Cuba and which has taught me a life lesson is that there is no problem too large that doesn't merit solving—or trying to solve. Examples abound: global shortage of primary care doctors? We'll establish a free, six-year medical school for smart kids from vulnerable communities. And in 1998, the Latin American Medical School was born; today more than 25,000 doctors from around the world are practicing in underserved areas from which they hail or similar (including 170 from the United States), free of med school debt. Lack of medicines in the national health system? Let's invest in biotechnology and make our own pharmaceuticals. And so Havana's Scientific Pole was created; today it provides more than 70 percent of the medicines used in Cuba's public health system and has developed unique, effective vaccines and therapies sold around the world (except in the United States). One of the first instances where Cuba showed the world—and importantly, its people—that it could punch above its weight and solve dogged, complex problems, was the 1961 Literacy Campaign. In the first months of that year, more than 260,000 volunteers—the overwhelming majority women and girls—fanned out across the island to teach every Cuban to read and write. As a result of this enormous effort, a total of 979,207 people in cities, towns, and villages throughout the country learned to read and write. On

December 22, 1961, the country was declared free of illiteracy,
a distinction confirmed by UNESCO.

It's an incredible story, for its magnitude and impact of
course, but also for its substance. The empowerment of Cuban
women is directly linked to universal health services and education, legal protections and rights such as generous maternity
leave and equal pay for equal work, and at the base of it all: literacy. In short, the Literacy Campaign was much more than the
sum of its parts. Many of the young teachers hailed from major
cities and well-off families who weren't keen on their daughters
and sisters, nieces and mothers venturing into the countryside
to live in dirt floor homes, most without electricity or running
water, to bring literacy to the masses during the year-long campaign. Not a few young women, unable to convince their parents
to let them participate, rebelled and went anyway. During the
day they worked in the fields and did household chores with host
families; at night the volunteers taught each family member to
read and write, often by lantern light. According to one *alfabet-
izadora* (literacy teacher), "I went to teach them, but...I think I
learned more from them than they did from me...I gave them
the light of learning, but they taught me how to be a person."

✳

Exclusive interviews and rare archival footage
make Maestra, a documentary about the Literacy
Campaign, a must-see. www.maestrathefilm.org

✳

Among the many astounding details of the campaign is the
fact that many of the girls who went to teach were between 12
and 15 years old. This was a transformative experience for the

young women and girls who participated: "We went to share what we knew...to work for the satisfaction of people learning to read and write. That gave us the values with which we've lived our lives ever since. It liberated us, because our entire generation of women gained a completely different view of life. The Literacy Campaign changed the meaning of life for Cuban women." Anyone interested in learning how this feat changed the lives and future of Cubans should head to the Museo Nacional de la Campaña de Alfabetización in Havana's Ciudad de Libertad. This is the only museum in the world solely dedicated to literacy.

70

Playa Girón

APRIL 15, 1961 WAS DESTINED to go down in infamy. It was also the day any doubts about the socialist direction of the new revolutionary government were squashed. That Saturday was violent, deadly, cruel, and woefully misguided. That day almost 60 years ago also set in motion events from which the United States and Cuba have yet to shake free—Donald Trump invoking the disaster in his June 2017 speech lambasting Obama's Cuba policy didn't help matters.

The Bay of Pigs invasion was, it's safe to say, a shit show. Known universally in Cuba as Playa Girón (the landing site which saw the most action), the failed invasion also laid bare the lengths to which Cubans would go to defend their sovereignty and their fearless tenacity in so doing, and revealed the depth of US misunderstanding of the Cuban character. It also exposed Fidel Castro and allies for the master strategists they were and provided hope and example for oppressed countries around the world, no matter how small or ragtag. It flipped a metaphoric middle finger to the United States and was the first example of "Yes we can!" in the hemisphere. As I type this, the once arch-enemies are locked in precisely the same pattern, with the United States impinging on Cuban sovereignty through the embargo and the naval base at Guantánamo Bay (a US military presence established and maintained on the island without interruption since 1902), while Cubans defend their priorities with the same doggedness that has allowed them to contend in the geo-political chess match all these years.

On that day way back when, CIA-trained Cubans, royally pissed off at the triumph of the bearded guerrillas who ousted US-backed Fulgencio Batista, bombed the Cuban Air Force. The attack failed but the fire was fueled. The following day, more than 1,400 of these irate émigrés landed at Playa Girón and Playa Larga. The Cubans responded, capturing nearly 1,200, killing 200, and shooting nearly a dozen B-26 bombers from the sky. Within 72 hours, the invading troops surrendered. It was, by any and all accounts, a rout. The losers blame President Kennedy, who cancelled air cover for the invasion at the last moment (conspiracy theorists link this decision to JFK's assassination; they may well turn out to be right), and the defeat has stuck in their craw since. Some of these same characters have been linked to deadly terrorist attacks on Cuban soil and the more than 600 attempts on Fidel Castro's life.

✳

The documentary *Fidel* (2001), by long-time Havana resident Estela Bravo, looks into the Comandante's life and times, including the hundreds of assassination attempts.

✳

While you may be, like me, lukewarm on museums dedicated to military invasions, the Museo Girón is surprisingly fascinating for the personal and strategic details it reveals. The town of Playa Girón, meanwhile, with its dun-colored beach and archetypical "Cuban-ness" (sleepy, friendly, hospitable despite crowing cocks at all hours) makes a good base for diving, snorkeling, and soaking up history and culture in one fell swoop. Caleta Buena, a protected scoop of turquoise sea teeming with fish located at the end of the road on the outskirts of town, is a destination in itself.

71 *Tombs of the Martyr & the Legend*

I'VE BEEN TO MY SHARE of funerals, wakes and burials in Cuba. I've even witnessed and accompanied friends during un-burials: limited grave space in Havana's Colón cemetery requires family members dig up their dead after two years and move them to a drawer in a mausoleum. It's a gruesome affair. Cremation is an obvious, sane alternative, but was the exception to the rule until heroine of the revolution Vilma Espín died in 2007 preferring her remains go into the oven rather than a box. Then El Comandante en Jefe Fidel Castro Ruz died in November 2016 and his remains were cremated, sealing the deal: cremation is now trending in Cuba and it's no longer the bureaucratic nightmare it once was to get the morgue to fire up the oven. As you can probably guess, I am decidedly pro-cremation—for environmental, financial, and real estate reasons (let's leave available land and building lots for the living, shall we?) and I am not restricted by any religious rites. Besides, who wants your hair and nails growing post-mortem, providing sustenance for the worms and bugs that make it into your coffin? This probably doesn't happen in the hermetically sealed caskets where you live (assuming you can afford one), but it sure does in Cuba, where the state assumes all costs for funeral arrangements, morgue, and interment, including the hearse and black plywood coffins in which all Cubans—save for children: theirs are white—are buried. Having attended so many death rites here and a few up north has made me loath to visit or tour any cemetery recreationally. But in Cuba, I make two exceptions: the veritable sculpture garden of the Necrópolis Cristobal Colón in Havana (see Chapter 13) and the Cementerio Santa Ifigenia in Santiago de Cuba, final resting place of Cuban apostle José Martí and Cuban revolutionary Fidel Castro.

There are more than 8,000 tombs at Santa Ifigenia, Cuba's second-largest cemetery, located in Santiago de Cuba. Although many notables are buried here, including heroes of the two independence wars, the guerrilla war against Batista's forces, some of the Bacardí family of rum fame, and past presidents, the two main reasons for traveling to this cemetery on the outskirts of Cuba's second-largest city are the mausoleum of José Martí and the tomb of Fidel Castro. Viewed from a raised gallery with balustrades, the hexagonal marble walls surrounding Martí's final resting place fairly glow from within—whether a trick of the burning hot Oriente sun or by architectural design, it feels almost holy. The effect is heightened at certain times of day when wide shafts of sunlight stream down to illuminate the Apostle's coffin, ceremoniously shrouded in a Cuban flag. If you time it right, the sun will be hitting the star on the flag like a spotlight. The mausoleum has two uniformed soldiers posted as sentries, who rotate duties every 30 minutes, lock-stepping to the loud beating of drums; no matter when you turn up here, it's worth it to hang around to see this formal bit of pomp and circumstance unfold.

Then there's Fidel. A respected Cuban intellectual and intimate friend of mine used to be asked all the time while on speaking tours of US campuses: "What's going to happen when Fidel dies?" His answer never varied: "A very long wake." Truth is, before the actual event, no one knew what would happen (except for a very long wake). And then the day arrived: November 25, 2016. The country went into official mourning for nine days; all cultural events and concerts were cancelled, all alcohol sales were suspended, parties called off, and quinceñeras postponed. People refused to even play music in their homes; those that dared were silenced by their neighbors and/or the cops. An eerie, disconcerting silence descended over the entire island— even the incessant barking of dogs seemed to stop. After a couple of days of lying in state at the Plaza de la Revolución, where Cubans and anyone else in Havana could pay their respects, Fidel's remains, with a full military cara- van, made their way slowly across the country, headed to Santiago de Cuba. The funeral cortege traversed more than 500 miles in three

days, the entire procession route lined with Cubans crying, hug- ging, silently mourning, disbelieving. Slogans professing unwav- ering faith to Cuba's most legendary figure were painted by the side of the road; you'll see them constantly driving along the Carretera Central—SOY FIDEL and FIDEL ENTRE NOSOTROS (I am Fidel; Fidel Is Among Us). What you won't see anywhere in your Cuba travels are statues or busts of Fidel Castro, nor will you see his visage on institutions or schools. In December 2016, the Cuban Parliament enacted one of his last wishes: that his name or likeness not be used in any public space after his death; the one exception is the wax re-creation of Fidel and Che emerging from the Sierra Maestra in Havana's Museo de la Revolución.

When the funeral caravan finally arrived at the gates of the Santa Ifigenia cemetery, his remains were interred in a two-ton granite rock brought down from the revolutionary battle-grounds of the Sierra Maestra mountain range for this purpose; it was a private ceremony attended only by family and his closest confidants—reporters were let in afterwards. The rock, rounded to look like a kernel of corn, was designed to invoke the famous verse of Martí's: "All the world's glory fits in a kernel of corn." I relate all this lest you visit and are reminded more of Fred Flintstone's man cave than Martí's immortal words. Today, anyone can pay their respects at Fidel Castro's tomb, which like Martí's nearby, has a color guard holding vigil that is rotated out every 30 minutes.

72 *Santiago de Cuba*

SANTIAGO DE CUBA, BOTH THE city and province, are like the bastard children of the country. This sounds harsh, I know, but closer to Haiti than Havana, hotter than hell, often crippled by drought and more economically challenged than other parts of Cuba, the eastern reaches of the island always seem to get the fuzzy end of the lollipop. Adding insult to injury is the fact that Santiago de Cuba was the country's first capital (1515-1607), and is recognized as the *"cuna de la Revolución"* (birthplace of the Revolution), which is to say, the Cuba we know and love (and sometimes hate), wouldn't be what it is today were it not for the events in this part of the country in the late 1950s.

Yet Santiago is finally getting its due and the respect it deserves. In 2015, the city of Santiago de Cuba celebrated its 500th anniversary causing a flurry of beautification and restoration projects, new hotel construction, and increased visibility for the cultural and historical attractions within the city and beyond. Things started looking better, but also working more efficiently and professionally in Santiago when Lázaro Expósito was transferred here from Bayamo (another revitalized city, see Chapter 64) to whip things into shape. A modest, committed fellow, he oversaw city improvement efforts using a creative approach like popping into state-run bread stores and cafeterias at 6 A.M. as a regular customer (he rarely acceded to

217

appearing on TV, maintaining his anonymity for the first part of his tenure, anyway). When he found bakeries without bread or cafeterias not serving coffee to early morning crowds, he assumed the ombudsman role to iron out wrinkles. This was followed by a public project to improve quality of life for santiagüeros called "Santiago Arte de Patriotismo" by increasing accessibility to healthy, affordable food, upgrading Internet access, and creating new media centers. The other factor contributing to Santiago's ascendant popularity is the recent interment of Fidel Castro's ashes in a two-ton rock brought from the Sierra Maestra in the Cementerio Santa Ifigenia. A veritable hall of Cuban fame, this cemetery holds the remains of many of the island's greatest historical figures including Emilio Bacardí (of rum fame), José Martí, known as the Apostle of Cuba, and the brothers País (Frank and Josué) who were key figures in the battle for Cuba's liberation from Batista.

I know many people who prefer Santiago over all other destinations and it's undeniable: there are many good reasons to visit "Cuba's second city" (though the second-largest city by Cuban population isn't Santiago, but Miami). The annual calendar is chock full of festivals unrivaled on the island including Caribe Fiesta del Fuego and Carnaval, multi-day parties held in July and August respectively with phenomenal live music, dancing 'til all hours, and rum a-plenty to keep the action well-lubricated and going strong. Take care with your valuables if you venture to Santiago for these events; the narrow streets get very crowded and pretty rowdy. If Cuban music is your passion, this is your place.

As befits Cuba's culture capital, there are many music festivals including one dedicated to *boleros* (Cuban ballads; June), another for choral music (November), and one for *trova*, the music that was born in the Santiago de Cuba mountains

(March). Compay Segundo, *trovador* and global ambassador for the genre since the *Buena Vista Social Club* achieved superstardom, hails from these parts; his paean to the area's fertility, "Frutas del Caney" captures the incredible variety and quality of fruit grown throughout the province: "Caney of the east, heavenly land, where blessings came from God's hand, who wants to buy my delicious fruits, *marañon* and *mamoncillo* from Caney." I'd always sung along with the catchy tune, but didn't realize the extent of the bounty until I saw little wooden roadside stands piled high with the cashew fruit (*marañon*) and lychee-like *mamoncillo* of song, half a dozen types of mangoes, mamey, bananas, pineapple, avocados, and bunches of sweet, purple grapes.

Fans of history won't want to miss the Cuartel Moncada (Moncada Barracks) where the attack that launched the Cuban Revolution took place on July 26, 1953; rummies should check out the Museo de Ron and the Museo Municipal Emilio Bacardí Moreau, which tell visitors everything they ever wanted to know about the rum industry and its place in Cuban history; and the Castillo de San Pedro del Morro, another of Cuba's nine UNESCO World Heritage Sites, with terrific littoral views, including over Cayo Granma, a quaint islet stacked with red-roofed houses and winding pathways.

VII

Best Beaches

73 *Playas del Este*

THERE'S NO BETTER EXAMPLE OF Cuba's lackadaisical approach to tourism than the Playas del Este. A short, straight shot east of Havana along a good highway, these powdery white sand beaches are home to only a few (mediocre) hotels and none of the beach kitsch and commerce you'd expect from a Caribbean idyll 30 minutes from the region's largest capital. This oversight won't last long and already the most overblown travel brochures refer to this 15-mile stretch as the "Havana Riviera." Spend an afternoon here and it fast becomes evident that this is a gross exaggeration: neither the services, nor restaurants—to say nothing of the lamentable fashion choices—come close to what you find in the French Riviera. Nevertheless, the soft sand, turquoise waves lapping at the shore, and coconut palms whispering in the breeze make the Playas del Este a choice escape from Havana's urban grit and graft. While these beaches are perfect day trip territory, modern, private houses with kitchens, several bedrooms, and air conditioning (some properties have pools, too) are rented in Tarará and Villa Los Pinos (near Playa Mégano) and the last beach on this stretch—Guanabo—is chock-a-block full of *casas particulares*, from cheap to chic.

Bacuranao, the beach closest to the city, is the least pretty of the lot, but the next stretch, Tarará, is simply lovely—even in summer Tarará, with houses for rent and scuba excursions, won't be crowded. The history of Tarará is fascinating: the US-style ranch houses were once popular among foreign residents—international correspondents and businesspeople mostly—while the big educational and health complex here has been treating and teaching victims of the Chernobyl nuclear accident, free, since 1986. Nowadays scores of Chinese students live out at Tarará, studying Spanish. MHAI Yoga, a Canadian-Cuban collaboration, holds retreats at Tarará; try to get in a class with the "father of Cuban yoga" and founder of the Cuban Yoga Association, Eduardo Pimentel.

Mégano, the next beach heading east, is wildly popular with Cubans and will be packed with glistening bodies and rum swilling families in the summer months. Playa Santa María is preferred by foreign visitors for the high-quality sea and sand and the cluster of beachside bars and restaurants. Head about half a mile east, however, and you come to my personal favorite: Mi Cayito. The last beach on the "Havana Riviera" is Guanabo, a proper beach town with restaurants, houses for rent, shops, even a disco. You can learn a lot about Cuban culture during a day at one of the Playas del Este beaches—locals don't swim between October and May (too cold); the best stretch, Mi Cayito, is the least visited, as it's known as a gay cruising spot and Cuba continues to harbor homophobic tendencies; garbage cans and public bathrooms are scant, so step/swim carefully; and it's not at all out of the ordinary to bring your bottle and lover into the surf for some rum and a romp.

74 Jibacoa

IF YOU ASK ME (and if you're reading this book, I guess you have), the best beach within striking distance of Havana isn't over-sold and hyped Varadero, but understated Cuban favorite, Jibacoa. This may sound like hyperbole, but as you wind down the road through a tree tunnel so dense it blocks the scorching sun, glance up toward the highest seaside cliffs. That gorgeous house overlooking this little slice of paradise? It was built to spec for none other than Silvio Rodríguez, the singer-songwriter who together with other *compañeros* (and *compañeras*) launched *nueva trova* (also known as the movement of protest songs) in Cuba, which caught fire and made its way around Latin America. For those south of the Río Grande, Sylvio is as big as the Beatles, packing stadiums with hundreds of thousands of screaming fans. Despite his catchy melodies, he's just passable as a guitar player, but is an accomplished poet and outspoken singer a la Phil Ochs. Many moons ago, the Cuban government reproached him, saying his music promoted "Elvis Presley-ism"; he was sent to work on a fishing boat to get on board and get in line. Now he's considered a national treasure and gives free concerts in poor Havana neighborhoods all the time. He can afford to: he long ago became rich and famous, allowing him to select any-where in Cuba for his vacation home. And he chose this enviable spot overlooking Jibacoa.

The beach achieved local notoriety for Silvio, but also for the three-day rave known as "La Rotilla," first held in 1998. A one-

of-a-kind festival in Cuba, thousands of young people descended upon Jibacoa armed with tents, tarps, booze, pills, and unlimited energy for a weekend of music, dancing, and debauchery. There were multiple stages, no bathrooms or washing facilities (totally gross, but no one seemed to care), and a freewheeling spirit rarely seen before or since. The party ran for a dozen years until it got too debased, too destructive to the beach, and too popular; authorities shut it down. A friend who attended religiously, says: "I loved Rotilla. But I don't miss it." It was that intense.

These days, Jibacoa is a great beach destination with an offshore reef featuring giant sponges and fans, spiny lobsters, eels, angel and trumpet fish, and plenty of coral. You'll want snorkel gear. There are caves worth exploring tucked in the limestone cliffs above the beach, and this area is emerging as another rock climbing hot spot (Viñales is another; see Chapter 49), with more than a dozen routes already mapped, including those at El Peñon and Peñon del Fraile. Horseback riding is another option, though in my experience the horses put to work on Cuban beaches are less than hale and hearty. This is one area where visitors can apply responsible travel principles and their conscience: if the horses are skinny, have saddle sores or other wounds, maybe skip that horseback ride. There are long stretches of soft white sand for beachcombing and romantic sunset walks, but my favorite scoop of beach (and I'm letting out a secret here) is Playa de las Artistas. Set out your chair or towel between October and April and you're likely to have it all to yourself. The hotel up the road rents the three-bedroom, three-bathroom beach houses right on this beach for absurdly low prices. Several other places in this book, including the Jardines de Hershey and Parque La Güira are easily accessed from Jibacoa.

75 _All-Inclusive Resorts_

CUBA HAS MORE THAN 400 beaches with all that beautiful white or golden sand for which the Caribbean is famous, just waiting for you to bliss out, a mojito never far from hand. Even if the aseptic resort scene isn't your typical cup of tea, the recuperative effects are measurable when the only decisions you need to take are what to eat at the buffet and whether to swim in the pool or sea. Let's face it, the beautiful eye candy (e.g., hot staff) doesn't hurt either.

In case you're wondering, I'm not an all-inclusive type of gal—in fact, the first time I stayed in one of these resorts was after I moved to Cuba and found myself craving a few creature comforts, like a proper toilet seat and firm mattress. Cuba can be a difficult travel destination—impossible to get public transportation information, the heat between April and October is positively cruel, and then you wake up one day and there's no toilet paper, cold beer, or running water. After two years in residence, when I couldn't face one more bucket shower or nosy neighbor, I popped my all-inclusive cherry and took a room in Varadero. When the traveling gets too tiring or you've arrived in Cuba already exhausted and need some hassle-free pampering, an all-inclusive resort is a fine alternative. Booking an all-inclusive with airfare included often works out to be extraordinarily economical—sometimes cheaper even than airfare alone. When there are deals like this, consider booking the package, whether you intend to stay at the resort or not.

Cuba's most popular resort area is Varadero—a 13-mile-long peninsula a couple of hours east of Havana almost entirely dedicated to all-inclusive hotels (though there are lovely homes for rent, as well). Varadero lacks soul but if powdery sand beaches and calm, azure seas fill your travel fantasies, this is the place. To attain complete isolation from reality, head to the resorts on the eastern end of the peninsula—the newer ones will be in better states of repair, with firm beds and all the promised amenities. Spend a little more time on the road to reach Cayo Santa María north of Santa Clara and you won't regret it. Reached via a causeway built over the sea—to great environmental detriment—the resorts here front endless stretches of white beach and enjoy a remoteness that's hard to come by so easily.

Farther afield, Cayo Coco and, better yet, Cayo Guillermo are other attractive options, especially if you're flying into the central or eastern provinces. The latter teems so wildly with marine life it inspired the setting for Hemingway's *Islands in the Stream* (he fished here often and patrolled for Nazi gunboats up this way during World War II with his trusty sidekick Gregorio Fuentes) and has fantastic scuba and snorkeling possibilities; a well-traveled friend who just returned says "this is the healthiest, most alive reef I've ever seen; better than anything in Mexico or Indonesia."

If money is no object, Cayo Largo, off the main island's southern coast, is only accessible by domestic flight and is as close to paradise as you can get without illicit substances or religious belief; its deserted white-sand beaches, where giant sea turtles trundle from the sea to lay their eggs between August and October, were voted among the World's Top Beaches by

National Geographic. Cayo Largo is also one of the very few locales in Cuba with a nude beach. No matter which resort you choose, once you're feeling recharged, venture off the manicured grounds and explore the real Cuba. As a whole, the island is safe and friendly and certain fun is to be had once you explore life beyond the resort.

76 *Cayo Levisa*

WHEN TRAVELERS COMING TO HAVANA ask me for beach recommendations other than Varadero with its canned entertainment and all-inclusive resorts, my first response is Playas del Este (see Chapter 73). Just over 30 minutes from the capital, the miles of white sand beaches and sparkling Caribbean Sea here are usually just what the doctor ordered for anyone wanting easy access to a picture-perfect *playa*. But their convenient location means they get crowded—like Jones- or Venice Beach-crowded when the weather's hot and right. Not everyone's cup of tea. My next suggestion is darling Jibacoa. Farther to the east, and a little less crowded, this beach attracts partying Cubans who frequent Jibacoa's trio of cheap campismos (cinderblock cabins located in naturally beautiful settings). Depending on where you are in your life cycle and the pressures and stress you're under, this may not appeal either. For those who are looking for real respite, a beach they can have all to themselves without the hassle of driving for miles on a dirt road and in relative proximity to Havana, I say: get thee to Cayo Levisa.

Measuring only two miles around—all of it the softest, finest white sand your toes will ever know—this offshore cay can easily be visited on a Havana to Viñales itinerary, providing an ideal combination of urban, mountain, and coastal adventure in seven days or fewer. Day-trippers are kept at a minimum since the only way to get here is by the once-a-day boat, and when they leave, you, the other overnight guests and staff will have the little island all to yourselves. There's only one low-key hotel on the island, with bungalow-style rooms right on the beach, ensuring the hypnotic lapping of the ocean is never out of earshot or eyesight. There's no disco, no shopping, and a single restaurant. The food can be bland and repetitive—they have a captive audience after all—but the tranquility and seclusion compensate. Kids tend to get bored out here, but randy couples certainly won't. Aside from circumnavigating the deserted beach, there are over a dozen offshore dive sites and a scuba outfitter here with all the gear. These waters are particularly rich in black coral—a signature marine resource in Cuba fashioned into fine jewelry and the first prize award in the Festival Internacional de Nuevo Cine Latinoamericano. Snorkeling along the shallow, well-protected reefs is another possibility with rental equipment available at the hotel. It takes just over 30 minutes to access Cayo Levisa from the coast guard station at Palma Rubia, from where the boat leaves once daily at 10 A.M. Don't be late!

77 Peninsula Guanahacabibes

EVOCATIVE AND EXOTIC: SIMPLY ROLLING "Guanahacabibes" around on your tongue is an exercise in tropical fantasy. From April to July, crab migrations so dense render the macadam a pungent red, threatening car and bike tires, while giant sea turtles trundle ashore from August to October, laying eggs in nests excavated from the sand under the cloak of night. This UNESCO Biosphere Reserve, once accessible only with written permission, now invites explorers to Cuba's western frontier to pick along the 56 miles of almost entirely virgin coastline, where cows ramble free, the world's smallest hummingbird (measuring the size of your thumb and light as a feather) flits between blossoms, and furry *jutias*—a ground rodent and tasty on the plate—rustle the undergrowth.

For those who just want to kick it in the sand, the Peninsula boasts 22 beaches, frequented only by local fishermen and like-minded adventurers like you. The off-shore barrier reef draws divers and snorkelers from around the world, but run for cover if you're caught here at dusk or dawn: the mosquitoes and *jejenes* (no-see-ums) are maddening, rivaled by the ubiquitous *guasasa*, defined as "a small, annoying fly (Cuba)" in Simon and Schuster's International English/Spanish

Dictionary. That's an understatement. Hurricanes striking Cuba often make landfall in and around Guanahacabibes—something to keep in mind if you're headed this way between June and November, official hurricane season.

The big draw here is María La Gorda ("Fat Mary"), a laid-back dive resort with individual cabins tucked in the woods and along the white sand beach offering a full array of scuba diving options, including certification (CMAS, SSI and PADI). Folks flock here to do one- or two-tank dives (snorkeling also available) to explore healthy reefs, underwater caves and coral gardens featuring all manner of marine wildlife including rays, barracuda, wrasses, grouper, whale sharks, and tarpon. There are 39 species of sponge and another 42 types of coral here alone, not to mention over 200 fish species and 1,000 types of mollusk. With such sea bounty at your doorstep, it's surprising how insipid the food can be, but the sundowner cocktails here on Cuba's western tip are strong and refreshing, arguing for a liquid diet after a day of romping in the sea. My honeymoon—including 11 of my closest family members from New York—was spent at María la Gorda and I promise you: for a completely unplugged vacation removed from the insanity and pace of our modern world, this is the place.

Every June, this hotel hosts the international underwater photography competition, IMASUB. This is a good opportunity to mingle with international divers of renown and top Cuban underwater photographers. Now for the bad news: in 2017, Cuba approved the construction of Latin America's largest golf course just to the north of the Peninsula, at Playa Colorado. Environmentalists around the island are up in arms about this project for the natural resources it will divert (and possibly contaminate) and travel agencies are confused as to how to market this resort at such a far-flung location. Stay tuned.

78 Cayo Saetía

CUBA REMINDS ME OF A tormented teenager: rife with anomaly and steeped in contradictions. Though blockaded by the United States for 57 years (and counting—lending credibility to the imperialist bully portrayal by Cuban press and decision makers), Koch Brothers chicken packs supermarket coolers, Hollywood fare dominates state TV, and antique cars from Motor City are the most precious coin in the realm, fast creating a class of Cuban nouveau riche. Democratic elections are held regularly for local, provincial, and national posts in which anyone is eligible to run, whether or not they are members of the Cuban Communist Party—the country's only political party. Once discriminated against and in some cases interred in labor camps for their religious beliefs, Muslims, Buddhists, Protestants, Catholics, Evangelical Christians, Jews, and even Jehovah's Witnesses have houses of worship where they openly, safely practice their faith. Across the country there are solar panel fields and wind farms generating renewable energy, but Cubans toss beer cans into the street and leave cars idling at the curb—the AC on full—without a second thought for the environment.

*

Democratic elections in Cuba?! It comes as a
surprise to most. The definitive book in English
explaining the complex process is Arnold August's
Cuba and Its Neighbors: Democracy in Motion.

*

Paradoxes such as these partly explain why Cuba is so intriguing and so damn frustrating at the same time. When I moved
here more than 15 years ago, Cuba still clung to a policy commonly called "tourism apartheid," under which Cubans were
prohibited from staying in hotels or resorts. My husband and I
experienced this first hand, getting turned away from lovely eco-
lodges and run-down city hotels because he was Cuban. Today
it's anecdote fodder; back then it stung with injustice—and contradiction—especially after I learned about a heavenly offshore
island called Cayo Saetía.

For decades, this cay about the size of the island of Manhattan
was for the exclusive use of Communist Party heavies who entertained Hemingway-esque fantasies hunting deer, zebra, buffalo,
and antelope by day, lounging on the white sands of the deserted
beach swilling rum cocktails at night. This hardly squared with
the social justice, environmental stewardship, and egalitarian
politics daily professed and alerted me to how glaring the contradictions here can be.

From these odd roots sprang the Cayo Saetía of today: a
beautiful islet ringed with long stretches of white, bright sand
and secret beach coves reached through wooded and grassy
expanses where wild game still roams. It's a slog to reach these
sapphire waters off Holguín's north coast, bumping over long

stretches of rugged secondary roads, but it will be worth the butt-aching effort—especially if you book a beachside cabin at the single hotel (bring your Cuban friends, now welcome!). The exotic animals still calling Cayo Saetía home can be seen by horseback or Jeep safari; thankfully, hunting is now prohibited, though big game trophies still hang morbidly in the restaurant.

For a remote getaway with enough amenities to be comfortable and a tropical beach you can call your own, Cayo Saetía is just the ticket. A word of warning however: this cay is a popular day trip from Guardalavaca resorts and gets besieged just before noon when scores of wristband-wearing tourists pour off catamarans for a beach-lunch package. Eat early or late and get far from the maddening crowd clustered in front of the restaurant with a 10-minute walk down the shifting sands.

VIII

Festivals, Fiestas, & Events

79 Annual Harley-Davidson Rally

CATCHING A GLIMPSE OF A 1956 Panhead, handlebar fringe flying, chrome gleaming, as it zooms along the Malecón is a thrill; beholding scores of majestic vintage Harley-Davidsons in one place, their riders astride their iron steeds with pride, is once-in-a-lifetime. Every year, hundreds of Cuban riders and their back-

seat Bettys (there's only one Cubana who actually drives a Harley—all hail Adriana!) gather in Varadero for three days of competitions, rock concerts, parties, and shop talk. These folks come from as far as Pinar del Río and Holguín to participate in this unique event now going into its eighth year. What an inspiration, to see antique Harley-Davidsons—all of which date from between 1936 (the oldest on the road here) to 1959—kept running by sheer Cuban ingenuity.

*

Want to ride to the annual Harley rally? Get in touch with the folks at Havana-based, Cuban-owned La Poderosa Tours. www.lapoderosatours.com

*

Thanks to the US embargo, there have been no parts available on the island, no Harley dealership where you can roll up and request service, since the revolution triumphed. This has elevated the mechanics, machinists, restorers and leather artisans who forge parts, fix motors, and fashion saddlebags that look like authentic Harley merch, to savior status. Among Cuba's Harley-Davidson community, there's one name repeatedly invoked: Pepe Milésima. The mechanical genius of this Harlista of Spanish descent revived many of the vintage bikes you see on the road today; by passing down his mechanical knowledge, taking novices under his wing, and rebuilding motorcycles previously abandoned in garages and vacant lots, he enabled countless Cubans to realize their dreams of owning a Harley-Davidson.

"Pepe was the old timer who helped young guys like us, just coming up. He taught us and shared his ideas—how to make and adapt our own parts, pistons, bolts, anything to keep our Harleys running!" says 67-year old Sergio Morales, recognized as one of Cuba's few mechanics who can get (and keep) these old bikes on the road. Each Father's Day, Milésima's memory is celebrated by a caravan of Harley-Davidsons making their way from Havana's Malecón to his final resting place in the Cementerio Colón's largest pantheon, where his remains are marked with a plaque bearing the emblematic Harley-Davidson trademark.

Cuba's tormented love affair with the all-American icon founded by William S. Harley and Arthur Davidson in 1903 is rich...and conflicted. For many decades preceding the revolution, Harley-Davidsons were the working motorcycles of choice. The latest film reels, just days after they premiered in Hollywood, were shuttled around Havana's movie theaters in sidecars, granny's medication was delivered to the door in

Harleys equipped with special hard cases soldered to the back (one of these, restored to its original 1946 glory, is still seen on the streets), and the entire national police force rode late-model Harley-Davidsons. These cops (known as "*caballitos*" then and now—little horsemen) even had an acrobatic team of great renown. They traveled around the country entertaining the masses with their amazing feats of derring-do, including The Pyramid of 13 men atop one motorcycle. It was their show-stopping denouement, leaving the crowds gasping in awe and wondering—when will they fall?! They didn't.

There were other death-defying tricks, including The Suicide and The Ladder. Antonio Miniet, an 80-something Cuban Harlista and co-founder of the Police Acrobatic Team, told me about the last time he performed The Ladder, for a high-level delegation headed by Fidel Castro: "I'd done this trick a million times—a 10-foot ladder is strapped to the bike, I put it in gear and let her roll at about 20 miles per hour, climb to the top of the ladder and ride along, arms open wide. That day, I was atop the ladder passing the grandstand and saluted Fidel. But when I went to grab the ladder, I couldn't find a hold and toppled off. The motorcycle sped head long, crashing into the crowd. No one died, but I was rushed to the hospital."

That was 1959 and the last time The Ladder was performed. Not long thereafter—around the time when Fidel and company declared the socialist bent of the revolution—Harley-Davidsons, a powerful American symbol representing rebellion, freedom, and maybe a little bit of larceny, were deemed inappropriate for the police force and the US bikes were swapped out for Italian models. Most of these Harleys were left to rust in garages, used for scrap or abandoned in backyards. But classic style always makes a comeback and by the late 1980s, Cubans were restoring these old bikes, machining parts and stuffing the tires full of hay when they couldn't get new ones—anything to keep them running.

Today, vintage Harley-Davidsons are all the rage, with gleaming, powerful 1950s Knuckleheads going for as much as $15,000. To see them all in one place and learn more lore than you can store, the Annual Harley Rally is for you. For the past several years, the international brother- (and sister-) hood has been well represented, with bikers coming from Germany, Finland, Panama, Mexico, the USA, Canada, and elsewhere. Most rent dinky mopeds for the event—anything to be on two wheels—since it's extraordinarily expensive and convoluted to import a bike temporarily. But if you ride and want to attend on a Harley, Che's son Ernesto, with his business partner Camilo, offer full on tour packages, including accommodation, English-speaking guides and motorcycle with La Poderosa Tours; these trips are made on modern Harleys since the antique ones are a bitch to kick start and drive (suicide shift, anyone?!). Whether you ride or not or have never given a second thought to Harley-Davidsons, this event is fun, free, and a great opportunity to ogle a slice of Cuban (and American) history.

*

Official rally site: www.harlistascubanosrally.com

*

80 *Feria Internacional del Libro*

ONE OF THE SIDE EFFECTS of having nearly 100 percent literacy is that Cubans love to read. You wouldn't necessarily know it looking around Havana where people stand in interminable lines, no reading material at hand (Cubans prefer to gossip while waiting). Meanwhile, bus stops are packed with folks not looking down at books, but rather down the street to see if transport is coming. Nevertheless, the country has a robust book and magazine publishing industry—print and digital—and bookstores and newsstands dot even the smallest towns and neighborhoods. Nor is it a question of money, necessarily: heavy government subsidies for publishers combined with too small advances for authors, short print runs on low quality paper, and no marketing of new titles whatsoever means the average new book here costs less than 50 cents. Says Minister of Culture Abel Prieto: "That Cuban families, no matter how poor, have a space in their house for books—a small library—is unique in the world and gives you an idea how important books are in Cuba." This emphasis on reading is nothing new: Cuba debuted its first printing press in 1723 and its first monograph that same year; the first public library, meanwhile, opened its doors in 1797. Nowhere is this passion for reading more evident than at the Feria Internacional del Libro (International Book Fair).

Each February, Cubans embrace their hunger for the written word at the International Book Fair when tens of thousands descend upon the Parque Histórico Militar Morro-Cabaña in Havana to get their fix (it's not uncommon for 10,000 people to walk through the gates on opening day). In addition to book sales, there are poetry readings, book launches, concerts, and lots of activities for kids. Each year is dedicated to a different country, where star authors and major publishers come to share their wares and craft and Cubans grab at the chance to get affordable books and meet their favorite authors. The 2017 edition, dedicated to Canada, featured writing all-stars like Margaret Atwood and Graeme Gibson.

The Fair has come under fire in recent years for prioritizing space for sales of all kinds of tchotchkes and kitsch like Messi jerseys and Frozen towels—i.e., nothing to do with literacy or reading—and the venue is a rabbit warren of small, dark rooms typical of a construction dating to 1763, but somehow it works. The Morro-Cabaña is a destination in itself and this is a great opportunity to kill two birds with one stone. Highlights here include the museum at the Comandancia del Che—where the guerrilla forces set up headquarters after their victorious arrival in Havana—and the Cañonazo, a historical re-enactment (with soldiers in 19th-century costume) of the cannon shots that signaled to the citizenry that the gates of the city were closed and the gigantic chain slung across Havana Bay; it happens every evening at 9 on the dot. From here you can also walk to the Cristo de la Habana, a 60-foot tall statue of Christ sculpted by Cuban artist Jilma Madera. From any of these points, the views of the Malecón and the city beyond are Havana's best.

81 International Day Against Homo/Trans/ Biphobia (IDAHOT)

CUBAN SOCIETY HAS COME A long way since the days of "re-education camps" for homosexuals (and others) once considered anti-revolutionary. These UMAPs (Unidades Militares de Apoyo a la Producción) were cooked up to work gay Cubans straight, square the hippies, and convert the religious to atheists. Forcing these folks to work in the fields to instill revolutionary values was an abject failure (not to mention a violation of civil rights, for which Fidel Castro issued a public apology) and now the country has gyrated 180 degrees away from this intolerance; Cuba is no longer an atheist state (in fact, there's now a church in Matanzas headed by LGBT pastors), long hair—even the man bun!—is totally in style, and same-sex couples now enjoy a freedom unimaginable just a decade ago. The last is thanks, by and large, to the National Center for Sex Education (CENESEX) directed by Mariela Castro, a multi-service center dedicated to anything and everything under the sun related to sexual diversity. They run sensitivity workshops for police and health professionals, provide legal counseling for LGBT folks, publish queer lit and academic studies, host queer galas with safe sex messaging, convene Cuban and international experts for conferences, consult on movie and soap opera scripts tackling sexual diversity issues, and more.

Since 2007, Cuba has celebrated International Day Against Homo/Transphobia, an initiative spearheaded by CENESEX;

around the world, this is observed every May 17 and the first couple of years, Cuba faithfully celebrated the day with a gay parade (called a conga here for the abundant drums and dancing involved), academic presentations and panels, symbolic weddings, concerts, and galas. I remember seeing the first rainbow flags draped over balconies and flapping in the Malecón breeze around May 2009 or so; the weeks leading up to the actual date became a time to rejoice, bond, and build community. It was absolutely fabulous! Until Cuban farmers got wind of it. Before IDAHOT, May 17th was reserved for celebrating country life and industries, when farmers around the nation took the day to get drunk, dance and slap each other on the backs, for May 17th is also Día del Campesino (Campesino Day) on the island. There ensued one of the hush-hush, all-too-common turmoils that happens behind closed doors in Cuba but to which everyone is somehow privy: farmers had their knickers in a twist over sharing "their" day, which had been sacrosanct for decades.

*

Everything you need to know about this
international event: www.dayagainsthomophobia.org

*

But rather than abandon IDAHOT, adjustments were made (Cubans are very savvy this way, finding resolution out of very tight spots—witness the Bay of Pigs, the Missile Crisis, the entire Cold War): the actual parade was held a few days before or after May 17, TV coverage was limited until after that date, events were scheduled for a week-long period following IDAHOT, and Día de Campesino was afforded more press and visibility. Additionally, one province was selected each year to accompany

Havana in the festivities and educational efforts. After 10 years, the results are impressive and each year around May 17, Havana (and one province; in 2017 it was Villa Clara, in 2018 it was Pinar del Río) converts into a rainbow coalition of LGBTQI activists and allies from around the country and around the world. There are panels, concerts, drag galas, parades, art exhibits, symbolic weddings, and rapid HIV testing (free).

The annual IDAHOT parade in Havana has become a destination event in and of itself, with a giant float shimmying up Calle 23 from the Hotel Nacional to Pabellón Cuba, the live band and tranny dancers whipping the crowd into a joyous frenzy. Meanwhile, classic convertible cars packed with beautifully proud gay and transgendered folks trundle along flanked by thousands of men in dresses or leather chaps, women marching hand-in-hand, children in rainbow wigs, and dogs on pink leashes. In 2017, the international contingent was huge, with queer Puerto Ricans waving their tri-color alongside the rainbow flag, a bear contingent from the USA, Brazilian queens of admirable elegance and sass, and many tourist allies coming out to show support. The campaign to sensitize the country to sexual diversity is working: in Santa Clara in 2017, I stood behind three women to await my blessing from a queer pastor when my Cuban companion said: "But you're not gay, why are you getting blessed?" Before I could answer about the need for all people to pull together when it's a question of human rights, one of the women in front of us turned around, tears in her eyes, saying: "I'm not gay either, but I'm here supporting my sister (motioning to the tallest, biggest boned of the trio), who has lived in a man's body her entire life. I love her, I want her to be happy, to be who she is. Thanks to Mariela, now she can." Now we all had tears in our eyes, waiting under the hot sun for our blessing.

82

Día de San Lázaro at el Rincón

EVERY DECEMBER 17TH, THE ROADS heading south out of Havana are choked with pilgrims making their way to the church at El Rincón—dragging cinderblocks and chains, dressed in burlap sacks, or on bloodied hands and knees—as they fulfill promises to San Lázaro, patron saint of the sick. Popular petitions include health, travel, or clemency for incarcerated loved ones, among others (wealth is always a popular plea). It's a dramatic, sometimes traumatic sight but evidently, San Lázaro works in mysterious ways: Cubans inexplicably cured of cancer, paralyzed children who can suddenly walk, and procuring a coveted visa to the United States have all been credited to this saint. In local argot, San Lázaro is known as *milagro*—the miracle maker. In syncretic Afro-Cuban religions that are observed clear across the island, known generically as Santería or more specifically as Regla de Ocha, the *orisha* or saint overlaying Saint Lazarus (as he's known in the Catholic canon) is Babalú Ayé—Desi Arnaz crooned his praises in his homage *Babalú*. Disciples of this popular *orisha* are easy to identify by their white, brown, blue, and black beaded necklaces.

*

Afro-Cuban religions are parsed in *Cuban Santería*
by santero and author Raul J. Canizares.

*

The pilgrimage to the Santuario de San Lázaro is an all-day, all-night affair providing an indelible glimpse into the guts of Cuban spirituality. This isn't an event for the faint of heart or stomach since some promises can be downright brutal. I once saw a man drag himself for miles along the ground, backwards, a toddler on his stomach and a rock chained to his ankle as he made his way painfully, slowly to El Rincón. Often these pilgrims haul along a wooden box for dropping coins à la San Lázaro himself who is represented as a hunched, hobbled man with a staff looking for alms and always accompanied by a pair of dogs. You will see people leading up to December 17th carting around totems of the saint and collecting coins for their pilgrimage. Giving to someone fulfilling a promise is supposed to provide some protection for the donor.

Crowds are dense and slow-moving leading up the long path to the church and hundreds of people sit on the grassy expanse to smoke a cigarette or swig some rum. Inside, where pilgrims pray in front of the saint's altar, lighting candles and leaving bundles of flowers, can be very hot and claustrophobic. El Rincón is about 14 miles due south of the Malecón in the suburb of Santiago de Las Vegas; Cuba's leprosy sanatorium (now dedicated to treating dermatological conditions) was located behind the church—ironic, considering the effigy of San Lázaro is covered in sores.

83 *International Women's Day*

AS I WALKED MY DOG Toby around the park today at 7 A.M., before my morning espresso, before I swept the sleep grit from my eyes, neighbors and strangers were wishing me *"felicidades."* It took me a moment, concerned as I was with the consistency of my dog's stools, to realize why they should congratulate me. Then the synapses clicked: today is March 8, International Women's Day. Along with Mother's Day and Valentine's Day (giving you an idea of the underlying matriarchy and romance that drives this place), Día Internacional de la Mujer is one of the biggest dates on the Cuban calendar. If you happen to be here on this day, you'll hear *felicidades* wherever you go and you'll see women of all ages toting gladiolas, sunflowers, and roses, given to them by friends, family, co-workers, and lovers. The Cuban Women's Federation (FMC) holds special events every March 8th; you're sure to happen upon some since more than 90 percent of females 14 and over (that's more than 4 million *cubanas*) are members of this, one of the island's largest organizations. The FMC has a slew of national programs like the network of 1,078 free nursery schools around the country, social service centers for women's development, and other initiatives dedicated specifically to women and girls.

In my hometown of New York, March 8th is just another day, which is ironic, considering New York is also headquarters to the United Nations, which asked member states to declare

March 8 Day for Women's Rights and World Peace. Cuba, on the other hand, has a wholly different take on the role of women in society and the history of humanity, and while many female travelers focus on the machismo and unrelenting and/or unwanted attention of men in the Cuban context, it's important to attune your cross-cultural antennae to how empowered Cuban women are, too.

✽

A good literary entrée into the world of Cuban women is the collection *Cubana: Contemporary Fiction by Cuban Women* edited by Mirta Yáñez.

✽

The impact of universal education and healthcare on the development of Cuban women and girls cannot be overstated. In 1970, Cuba established the Program for Maternal-Child Health, guaranteeing all care and services across the country before, during, and after pregnancy, including a minimum of 13 pre-natal exams, vaccination against 13 childhood diseases, family planning and birth control, and abortion free and on demand. A full 99 percent of births are in hospitals, compared to 40 percent before universal care was implemented in 1960.

Around the world, 1 of 4 children is born and lives undocumented, outside the formal system and without a birth certificate, an indispensable document no matter the country or context—in Cuba, all newborns are issued a birth certificate before leaving the hospital. According to UNICEF, Cuba is the only country in Latin America and the Caribbean without severe malnutrition in children under the age of five and was certified by the World Health Organization in 2015 as the first country to have eradicated mother-to-child transmission of HIV. Cuban women enjoy gender parity with their male colleagues and are entitled to robust maternity leave of up to one year at their full salary or salaries if they hold more than one job. Paternity leave is also available and in 2017, Cuba instituted similar benefits for grandparents who care for newborns when both parents opt to continue working.

Cuba's universal education system, which the World Bank heralded as the best in Latin America, has similarly supported the development of women and girls. According to an article in *Nature*, more than 51 percent of Cuban professionals working in science and technology are women and the United Nations' Global Women in Politics data show that Cuba has the third largest percentage of female parliamentarians of any country—a point shy of 50 percent. Might a female president be next?

84 *Festival Internacional del Nuevo Cine Latinoamericano*

"WHAT'S THE CUBAN OBSESSION WITH CHARLIE CHAPLIN?" a visitor asked me recently, supposing that the cinema great had spent some time on the island. This isn't a bad deduction given that Havana's premiere movie theater—with good air conditioning, Dolby surround sound, and a lobby gift shop—is named after the actor, and there are works of art, posters, graffiti, and businesses sporting the actor's name and visage all over Cuba. According to historical record and local account, Charlie Chaplin never set foot on Cuban soil, but no matter: he is beloved and revered here by a population that, on the whole, are rabid *cinéastes*. This isn't surprising given that Cuba was among the first countries in the hemisphere to inaugurate a movie theater, in 1897, and to film moving images—a one-minute simulation of a fire and the firefighters response. From that moment on, Cubans have dedicated resources disproportionate to the country's size making and consuming films.

Of course, movies and theaters were largely limited to the cities until the triumph of the revolution, when art and culture in all forms were extended to every nook and cranny of the country. One of the great cinematic moments in Cuban history is captured in the documentary *Por Primera Vez* (1968; *For the First Time*), when a team armed with a projector and screen set up outdoor theaters in the most remote mountains of the country, bringing moving images to rural populations for *la primera vez.* They captured the awe and joy of the crowd as they watched the first movie of their lives—a Charlie Chaplin film.

*

Por Primera Vez is available on YouTube; no matter that it's in Spanish—the faces of the Cubans watching their first movie tells the whole story.

*

The Cuban mania for movies coalesces in Havana every December for what is officially called the Festival Internacional del Nuevo Cine Latinoamericano but is known more familiarly as the Havana Film Festival. Going on its 40th year, this festival screens hundreds of films in theaters throughout Havana during a week packed with star-studded galas, parties, and schmoozing. Although only those films made in the Americas can compete in the juried categories, movies from all over the world are shown during this prestigious festival. Heavyweights from Hollywood, New York and other filmmaking centers descend on the city and take cocktails and broker deals in the gardens of the Hotel Nacional, unofficial headquarters of the festival; slip into a wicker chair on the hotel's terrace and you might spot Stephen Spielberg, Werner Herzog, Benicio del Toro, Gael García Bernal or Pedro Almodóvar—all participants in past festivals.

Many of cinema's superstars take advantage of their stay on the island to visit and give classes at Cuba's world-renowned film school La Escuela Internacional de Cine y Televisión (EICT) in San Antonio de los Baños. Co-founded by Colombian prize-winning writer Gabriel García Márquez, the EICT has been training filmmakers, cinematographers, and screenwriters since 1985. Lines can be very long to get into festival showings in high demand (a couple of hours isn't uncommon); to avoid this fate, you can buy a partial- or all-access credential at the Hotel Nacional. Dedicated Cuban moviegoers are known to take their annual vacation during the film festival to get their proper fill of foreign and domestic films. I've witnessed Cuban crowds literally break down the doors of movie theaters in their desperation to get into certain showings. But that was years ago (during a showing of *The Minority Report*) and organization has become safer and more efficient since then.

85 *Bienal de la Habana*

JUST LIKE CERTAIN LIFE EVENTS can transform a person—a near-death experience, writing a best-seller, marriage, divorce—so too, can certain events transform a city; New York after 9/11 comes to mind, as well as Río after hosting the World Cup and the Olympic games. Havana hasn't been victim of overt, fatal attacks for a while now and is too cash-strapped to dream of hosting a major athletic competition, but the city does crackle toward change at certain moments. Every building on official parade routes is freshly painted when a Pope or President comes to town, for example, creating its fair share of cynicism and grumbling since the state only pays to paint the facades; that perky paint job beautifying the local high school or multi-family apartment building? It ends around the corner, precisely beyond your line of vision. Cubans are masters of putting a good face on a bad situation, epitomized by the popular saying: "*mal tiempo, buena cara*" and for finding negatives in a free, albeit partial, paint job. But there is one event when the city undergoes an authentic metamorphosis, like passing from a homely chrysalis to a spectacular butterfly: when the renowned international art opening known as the Bienal de la Habana rolls into town, even the jaded and apathetic are smiling spontaneously and the downtrodden forget their woes.

If you have any doubt that Cuba is an illogical place (try and apply logic and your adventures are doomed), consider that the Bienal de la Habana is held not every two years as the name indicates, but every three—and sometimes four—years for reasons unknown. But it's worth the wait for the epic public art, incisive performance pieces, and contemporary, international energy the hundreds of artists from dozens of countries inject into Havana for the month-long event. A herd of elephants lingers in a plaza, a jumble of giant pickup sticks painted like the US and Cuban flags litter the Malecón, and an oversized, Facebook-blue "thumbs up" sculpture frames the Morro lighthouse if you look at it from the right angle.

✳ www.biennialfoundation.org/biennials/havana-biennale

The Bienal de la Habana is a fun, family affair with surprises at every turn. Two of the biggest draws during the 2015 Bienal were the faux beach, with its palm-thatched umbrellas and chaise longues, erected on the Malecón, and the temporary ice rink that provided innumerable Cubans the first skating experience of their lives. The public art is just a part of the action, however, with some fine, thought-provoking installations and exhibits hosted at official Bienal headquarters, including the Centro de Arte Contemporáneo Wilfredo Lam, as well as at the Museo de Bellas Artes, and the Morro-Cabaña across the bay. The biggest collection is shown at this colonial fortress, the ultra-modern and conceptual pieces contrasting beautifully with the 18th century ramparts and sprawling views of the Havana skyline.

The Bienal brings its share of whimsy to the city, but there's a deeper, darker side bubbling with political commentary and controversy as well. At the last edition, Cubans were buzzing about the jibes implicit in a collage of political phrases used in official rhetoric; a cityscape constructed entirely of soda cans, Coca-Cola and Cuba's version, Tu Kola, included; and an enormous, empty soup pot stabbed through with forks.

The Bienal is not immune to agit-prop art either. Cuban-American Tania Bruguera always manages to get her name in the international press with her inflammatory performance art—whether or not she actually performs—and authorities were not at all amused by El Sexto's attempt to parade two live pigs painted with "Fidel" and "Raul" through the heavily trafficked street fronting the Capitolio. Sometimes dying, or in El Sexto's case, landing in jail, makes a career. Fallout from the 2015 Bienal was far-reaching, with a series of high-level resignations from the Bronx Museum after works from that museum were exhibited at Havana's Museo de Bellas Artes sparking accusations of mission drift and financial funny business. No one can guess what the 2019 edition of the Bienal de la Habana has in store, but I guarantee it won't be dull.

IX

Uncommon Adventures

86 Camping Canasí

I'VE CAMPED THE LENGTH AND breadth of Cuba, but few locations rival Canasí for its (relatively) easy access and natural beauty. Located on a small protected bay fed by the Río Canasí, the shoreline here is composed of dramatic cliffs that taper down to hug the coast then rise up again the farther from the river mouth you venture. Not appearing on any map that I've ever found, Canasí has yet to be discovered by tourists, but chat up any Cuban between the ages of 20 and 40 and they've likely had adventures here—it's a legendary spot for a quick weekend break from Havana's hustle. Nevertheless, getting here takes a certain amount of pluck and determination, since the only practical access is by crossing the shoulder-deep river and hiking a mile to the makeshift campsites, which are basically flat, cleared areas with rock ring fire pits. But with scenery so grand, what more do you need? A friendly gent from the collection of Canasí's shoreline dwellings is usually around to shuttle people across the river on a large Styrofoam raft for a couple of CUCs; simple food and fresh yogurt can also be had here before setting off.

Once you're safely on the other side, a steep, short path leads up to the first cliff and a large clearing, from where you get excellent ocean views. Continue on the path through secondary forest for a bit and you come to several tidy campsites overlooking a small crescent beach facing a turquoise sea. For my money, this is the best place to set up. About a half mile farther along, there are more heavily used sites at La Cazuela (The Stewpot), popular for its direct access to prime cliff jumping and good snorkeling. But the accumulated garbage is a turnoff and since it's so close to the other, cleaner campsites with a sandy beach to boot, I see no charm in sleeping next to empty beer cans and discarded tins of tuna.

A trip to Canasí is wild camping: you have to bring all your gear, food and potable water, though in good weather, Cubans make do with a hammock or sleep directly on the ground. There are no snakes or threatening animals in this part of the world (if you don't count the mosquitoes—though they aren't terribly annoying here), so this is a practical solution if you're not carrying a tent. There is plenty of downed wood for cooking fires as well. Canasí is accessed from the small town of the same name, 40 miles from Havana via Villa Blanca toward Matanzas (turn off just before the bridge to Canasí)—if you hit Puerto Escondido, you've gone too far. A couple words of warning: Canasí is so captivating, you will want more days here than you originally planned and tourism authorities already have the hotel and development plans drawn up for this pristine spot—go here *now*. If you can't camp out, make a day trip of it, getting there early and leaving before dark.

87
The Train to Chocolate Town

IF YOU HAVE ANY DOUBTS about the deep, historic roots between Cuba and the USA, just check out the history of Hershey's chocolate on the island. In 1921, Milton Hershey, the famous confectioner whose sweets are enjoyed the world over, built an electric railway running from Havana to Matanzas in order to shuttle workers, materials and most importantly, sugar between his giant mill and the country's two main ports. He built a "model town" to house Cuban mill workers in barrack-style dwellings, while the US managers of his lucrative operation were set up in elaborate wooden plantation homes.

For two decades, the town of Hershey (pronounced heir-see by Cubans) boomed, with the American bosses enjoying Cuba's high tropical lifestyle, sipping cool rum drinks on their screened-in porches and strolling among the sensual fruit orchards in their spacious backyards. Meanwhile, local workers were paid in coupons and bought their supplies and food in the town store—all owned by Milton Hershey. When he sold the enterprise in the mid-1940s and departed Cuba for greener pastures, the workers were left with worthless coupons, a store laid bare, and no jobs; the boom town went bust. When the revolution triumphed, the Hershey sugar mill was nationalized and the town's name changed to Camilo Cienfuegos—the label which appears on all road maps and signs, though I've yet to meet a Cuban who calls this quaint town anything but "Heirsee."

✳

Model Town (2007) is a moving documentary
about life in Hershey, as told by retired workers
as they look back on the good old days.

✳

The Hershey Electric Railway, Cuba's first (and only) electric train, still runs today and is proof positive that slowing down to get where you're going has its benefits. This milk train rumbles from Casablanca, just across the bay from Havana, poking through every village and burg on its 75-mile trajectory to Matanzas. It's a cheap, fascinating way to see Cuban country life and take in some gorgeous scenery through the emerald fields of the Valle de Yumurí (see Chapter 47). Hopping off at Hershey, the once-thriving sugar town built by the US chocolate magnate, is like stepping into a sepia-toned photograph of a bygone age—even the wooden train depot still has a rough-hewn shingle emblazoned with the original name.

In its heyday, the mill here was the main sugar producer for all Hershey chocolate. Although the sugar mill was shuttered for good in 2002, its chimneys loom over the town, its neat streets, wooden "chalets," and yards reminiscent of a Midwestern suburb. Now many of these houses, listing and patched, are for sale and are hot properties for people of certain means. Some old timers in these parts still remember the days when Americans ran and owned the town—though few lips here have ever tasted a Hershey Kiss (few American products have been sold here since the triumph of the revolution in 1959). Since the mill closed, jobs are scarce and Camilo Cienfuegos, nee Hershey, limps along in typical Cuban style. A mile downhill from the train station is Jardines de Hershey; once a playground for the capitalist upper crust, today it's a verdant oasis with short nature walks, natural swimming holes and one of the tastiest $2 meals around. In 2016, plans were announced to upgrade the electric train service and extend the line to Varadero with funds provided by a Russian firm.

88 San Diego de Los Baños

THE LANDSCAPE WEST OF HAVANA begins to get interesting around the Sierra del Rosario Biosphere Reserve, where the ubiquitous *marabú* (a spiky invasive bush that is running roughshod over much of the island's arable land; think Cuban kudzu) gives way to waving fields of tobacco, pine trees, and the limestone hills known as *mogotes* for which Viñales is famous (see Chapter 49). The fecund air is laced with gardenia and cow shit, loam and burning charcoal—a major local industry in this region, and Cuba has even started exporting all-natural charcoal made from *marabú*. But it's the smell of sulphur that permeates the small town of San Diego de los Baños, famous for the healing properties of its thermal waters.

These are the oldest medicinal baths on the islands, used by Spanish settlers in the 17th century who discovered the wonders of soaking in the waters rich in sulphur, of course, but also calcium, sodium, magnesium, fluoride, and other minerals; today Cubans are remitted here by their doctors to treat psoriasis, respiratory illness, cerebrovascular disease, and rheumatologic conditions, stress, and for healing wounds. Cuba's universal health system incorporates natural and traditional medicine whenever possible and patients come to San Diego de los Baños for treatments of 7, 15 or 21 days.

The Balneario (thermal waters and treatment center) is open to foreigners year round and offers a variety of different treatments including soaks, massage, hydrotherapy, mud therapy, and steam baths. There are private changing rooms and areas to lie out and relax after enjoying the thermal waters, which maintain a temperature of between 97° and 100° Fahrenheit. The recommended soak cycle is 20 minutes, followed by an equal amount of rest before re-immersion. The specialists staffing the center suggest a full body massage after a session in the thermal waters. The group pool costs $2CUC for a 20-minute soak, but my advice is to splurge on a private pool for $4CUC—unless getting intimate with Cubans undergoing medical treatment is your idea of a good time. The river right below the Balneario is clean and beckons, whether or not you come for a hot soak. There's a lovely little park facing the Balneario and a couple of decent *casa particulares* that rent rooms nearby; for something more formal and private, the Hotel El Mirador, with a pool and a view, is a good alternative. If you're out this way, don't miss the opportunity to visit Parque Güira (see Chapter 48).

89 Get Lost in Las Tunas

THERE ARE SOME PARTS OF Cuba you never hear about. Las Tunas, wedged between colonial Camagüey to the west and artistic Holguín and historic Granma to the east, is one of those provinces that gets lost in the shuffle. I can understand why: natural beauty is scant, national monuments few, and while Cuba is a wonderfully welcoming place, "*los tuneros*" (those from Las Tunas) tend toward gruff and standoffish. When I asked Lázaro from nearby Holguín what gives, he didn't hesitate: "They've got a reputation for being unfriendly and arrogant to boot. It's funny really, because they have no reason to throw down a superior attitude." Maybe it's overcompensation for an inferiority complex or maybe it's conditioned by the judgments from neighboring provinces along the lines of Lázaro's observation, but Las Tunas feels less inviting than the rest of the country somehow. Nevertheless, I've made wonderful memories in this forgotten corner of Cuba, like jostling along a dirt road to what seemed like the end of the island to discover four couples roasting a pig on the shore of a deserted beach. It was the first *puerco en púa* to pass my lips and I will never forget it.

Unbridled adventure and unique experiences: this is what Las Tunas has to offer, and if you're willing to make the effort to get there and break the ice with the locals, you will surely be compensated by travel memories that will stick with you like

that pig on the spit sticks with me. That day was also a learning experience, and if there's one thing I love about Cuba it's
that it teaches me something new every day. That day of my first
roasted pig, after we'd licked our fingers clean watching the sun
go down, bellies full and hearts happy (that's another classic saying here: *barriga llena, corazón contento*), I asked for a mailing address
so I could send prints of the pictures I took to each couple. The
men's eyes grew big, despite having been at half-mast after several bottles of rum: "Oh no. Don't do that! We'll get in a lot of
trouble with our wives." And I thought the lovelies we'd been
hanging out with all afternoon *were* their wives; how terribly
naïve of me.

My first Las Tunas experience also reinforced a travel principle worth underscoring: if there's a dirt road leading to the coast
on the map, take it. This is how I found Playa La Boca, north
of the sleepy little town of Manatí (apparently manatees inhabit
the waters here, though no local I talked to had ever seen one).
Remnants of Manatí's long-gone glory days are still in evidence,
like the extravagant iron entrance gate decorated with artistic
flourishes and the words "Argelia Libre"—the name of the now
defunct sugar mill casting its shadow over town. Fuel up here
before hitting the road to Playa la Boca, which isn't a fun, "Oh,
look at the nice scenery" kind of drive. Rather, it's 10.5 miles of
dirt and rocks, hemmed in by a hellish scourge known as *marabú*—
a thorny type of Cuban kudzu. You'll be lucky to see another
car, truck or horse—but once you arrive, the road opens on to a
white sand beach with only a few souls braving out this way, and
maybe a pig or two nosing the sand around the pizza shack.

There's not much to do out here but walk the beach and
choose the prettiest of the palm-sized conch shells that roll in
by the half dozen with each wave. There is a campismo here,

with cabins for rent to foreigners (meaning they have AC)—a cheaper beach vacay you'll be hard pressed to find. While the road is equally rough (and more than twice as long) to Playa Covarrubias, you need not rough it to deposit yourself on a deserted Cuban beach. After bumping and weaving to this beach on the other side of Bahía Manatí from Playa la Boca, the washboard road suddenly ends at a pristine white-sand beach dotted with palm trees, the turquoise Atlantic winking seductively beyond; the lookout tower provides a panoramic view. The great surprise, however, is the all-inclusive resort here, easily Cuba's most remote. Forget Varadero—what Cubans call "our little Cancún"—and give Las Tunas a try.

90 *Surf's Up! (Sort of)*

BY LANDMASS, CUBA IS THE 17th-largest island in the world (bigger than Iceland) and the largest island in the Caribbean by far. Taken together, the archipelago has more than 4,000 islands, cays, and coral reefs, many of them uninhabited and strung with virgin beach. It's the rare Cuban who doesn't know how to swim, and scuba diving—particularly off the little-explored southern coast—can be spectacular. Logic follows, therefore, that there should be some damn good surfing off the island's 1,500 miles of coastline.

*

Good advice, videos, and more are available at
www.havanasurf-cuba.com. There's even a section
dedicated to Cuban women surfers.

*

Rule #1 with anything having to do with Cuba: logic does not necessarily apply. If you're coming here, board in tow, looking for small bohemian beach towns boasting killer breaks and the surf shops and fried fish shacks to outfit and fuel local and visiting surfers, you've come to the wrong place; you really wanted to be in Rincón, Puerto Rico, a couple of islands over. Nevertheless, there are some places to catch decent waves—especially in the

June through November tropical storm/hurricane season when Cuban surfers monitor the weather closely, hustling to paddle out once (or even before) the immediate danger has passed. Aside from the waves brought by big storms, surf is up on the north shore from December to March and in the Oriente south's shore from August to November. If you've surfed in Brazil or Hawai'i or southern California, on the whole you'll probably find Cuban waves lame, mushy, or for amateurs. But surfing in Cuba

offers something rare and coveted in this over-explored, globalized world: an opportunity to pioneer a passion with locals who are still discovering where and how to surf in their own backyard. So blaze a trail down here with your board and some extra wax and you'll find instant community and camaraderie with like-minded folks who are just starting to feed their addiction.

"It's catching on, big time," my friend Javier tells me, one of the first to start surfing in Havana. "I'm meeting new young surfers all the time." Diagnosed with chronic asthma as a child, his doctors prescribed inhalers and medicine, but also as much time as possible seaside; he took up surfing and now has been surfing in Havana more than half his life. According to Javier and other surfing friends, the most reliable Havana surfing spot is near Calles 70 and 1ra in Miramar, very near the blue-mirrored, hideous-as-hell Panorama Hotel. It's a bit of a paddle to get clear of the spiky *diente de perro* (dog's tooth) rock and reef that blankets the Havana coast, but there are usually some bumps worth catching. Trade winds from December to March ratchet things up a notch and locals hit the water the two days before and after hurricanes—keep an eye on weather reports during hurricane season for the biggest swells; even when the surf is roiling, you'll still only share the water with half a dozen people at most.

Many of the young Cuban trainers working with the dolphins and sea lions at the National Aquarium a couple of blocks away are heavy into the surf scene and can be a good source of local information. I knew surfing had become a real thing when my neighbor Victor, one of the trainers at the Aquarium, stopped me one night with a gleam in his eye.

"We're flying to Santiago tomorrow to go surfing!"

"When are you coming back?" I asked.

"Tomorrow night!"

A one day cross-country trip to catch waves? This is more than just a hobby; he was hooked.

Victor came back with tales of a reliable left-hand point break at Mar Verde, a pretty recreational beach popular with locals from Santiago de Cuba—a quick 10 miles away on good roads with public transportation. The next time I saw Victor, I was the one with a gleam in my eye. "I'm going to Santiago," I told him. "I can't wait to check out Mar Verde." He raised an eyebrow. "Forget Mar Verde. You have to go to Onda Media. The paddle out to the break is long, a quarter mile or so, but it's the real deal." Medium Wavelength ("Onda Media") is so-called because the on-shore spot marking the break is a giant radio tower transmitting at—you guessed it, medium wavelength. It's located a few miles before Chivirico—a terrific home base for a surfing adventure (see Chapter 39). You can hire a driver there (make sure the car is in good repair and that your GPS is working) because the access to the coast is a little tricky, with a short forge of river required to get there. I guarantee you'll be trailblazing.

91 La Farola

"YOU'RE GOING TO DRIVE LA Farola? On a 1946 Harley-Davidson?!" Friends in Havana expressed concern as plans were laid for a visit to the Oriente and specifically Baracoa—arguably the jewel in Cuba's crown for its one-of-a-kind combination of history, culture, and natural landscapes (see Chapter 38). "La Farola is awesome. Pure engineering genius," said Denis, one of my most adventurous Cuban friends who is always game for a backcountry hike or pedal to a remote beach. No matter that Denis has never set foot in Guantánamo, let alone Baracoa: all Cubans know La Farola, the 24-mile road of tight successive switchbacks which finally provided a road connection between Baracoa and the rest of the country in 1965. Climbing through the majestic Sierra de Purial mountain range, where palms transition to pines and back to palms again, the road winds down and then back up, repeating the pattern during dizzying changes in elevation before leveling out at the coast.

"Drive carefully," locals told us. "If there has been a lot of rain, don't go," veterans of the road warned.

Too many people to quote voiced doubts that a 71-year-old motorcycle, for which factory parts haven't been available here for almost as long, could make the trip. The cautionary tales wormed their way into our collective unconscious and trepidation now mixed with high expectations for our adventure along this visually arresting road. Of one thing we were sure: after climbing the rough, rocky, straight-to-the-top road leading to Cuba's Highest Waterfall and hazarding the rain-slicked, precipitous incline to El Nicho (see Chapters 59 and 57), not to mention various forays directly on the beach, the antique Harley wouldn't have a problem on La Farola.

Indeed, the only problem was caused by my trusty driver letting his eyes stray from the road to take in the sublime views— luckily, the route is dotted with pull-outs perfect for snapping photos and breathing deep the pine-perfumed air. In between beholding the mountains beyond mountains rippling into the distance and pondering the substance of the lives unfolding beneath the thatched roofs of the humble wooden homes lining the road, listen closely: yes, that's pure mountain spring water you hear, trickling down from the peaks and spilling on to La Farola. Keep an eye peeled for high-flowing springs equipped with small black hoses where travelers and inhabitants alike fill water bottles, rinse the road grit from their hands and splash the cool, natural water on tired, sweaty faces.

The domestic tableau is as intriguing as the natural one along La Farola, as families emerge from shady bends in the road to sell fresh-cut pineapple and bananas, balls of 100 percent pure cacao and shredded coconut laced with orange or papaya wrapped in palm frond cones—the famous *cucurucho* of the area. Parked jauntily in front of each home you'll see an odd contraption on four wheels, with a rectangular base and upright steering mechanism constructed of cobbled-together wood. These are known as *chivichanas*, a wholly Cuban invention and the main means of conveyance along La Farola's twisting, diving length—sacks of cement and rice, produce going to market, and children going to school are zoomed downhill piled on these gravity-powered platforms. Making their way back up is more of a chore.

At the highest point along La Farola, more than 1,500 feet above sea level, you come to Alto de Cotilla, with coldish Hatuey beer for sale at the cafeteria and hawkers of all products locally-produced and harvested swarming around newcomers. Shop to your delight, but responsible travelers refrain from buying trinkets and jewelry fashioned from polymita snails—their shells of trippy colors and swirls are so eye-catching and income generating, they're now an endangered species. No matter how hot and tired you are, make the trek up the scores of stairs to the lookout point here for 360-degree mountain and sea views; "The only spot in Cuba where you can see the Atlantic and the Caribbean at the same time," a strapping young fellow offers as we catch our breath at the top.

Though we found the road conditions tame compared to some we'd traversed (La Farola is very well-designed after all), a couple words of warning: rock slides are a very real possibility, as the graphic signs with rocks crashing down on passing cars and the random boulders in the road attest; take particular care during the rainy season. Also be sure you set out with enough gas—there are no services on this road. And prepare yourself for what comes *after* La Farola: the dry river beds and throat-closing heat that epitomizes Guantánamo is a hot, depressing drive—especially after experiencing one of Cuba's most enchanting roads. Going the other way toward Moa, headquarters of Cuba's nickel mining industry, is even worse.

92

Get Inked

A YOUNG PROFESSOR OF PHILOSOPHY at the University of Havana, who may be the smartest Cuban I know, likes to say, "In Cuba, a lot is totally legitimate, but not exactly legal." Things like pirated US shows (*Friends, Big Bang Theory*) broadcast daily on state TV, door-to-door sales of "diverted" goods, and the gamer intranet laced across the island are a few examples of this maxim at work. Tattoo studios also fall under this rubric—there is no legal license for operating a tattoo parlor, which is hard to believe given the amount of ink Cubans are sporting these days. It's also hard to understand why Cuban health authorities haven't regulated this ferociously popular trade given the emphasis on and resources dedicated to prevention and public health here.

All the tattoo artists I know agree: legalizing this service would benefit everyone. With proper licensing, all studios would have to adhere to proper health and hygiene standards, the state could collect taxes, the artists could pursue marketing strategies and enact formal business plans, and clients would be assured a safer, more professional service. Legitimate but not exactly legal, Cubans have been creating tattoos for decades—some good, others bad, many terrible, and a few real works of art—to clients with little interference from the authorities. That all changed in 2015 with the opening of the high-profile La Marca tattoo studio in the heart of Habana Vieja. Officially a gallery—and they do show art—their real bread and butter comes from inking tourists. Other tattoo artists around town were encouraged, yet puzzled. Was there a change in policy, suddenly? Was tattooing finally legalized? Then authorities started making the rounds, issuing cease and desist orders to tattoo artists all over Havana (save those at La Marca). Were things getting worse for those in the trade instead of better? But as often happens in Cuba, after a month or two—the questions still unanswered—things settled down, the heat subsided, and the artists got back to work. None of the tattoo artists I know with established studios have had a problem since.

The advantages of getting inked in Cuba are many. First, the best studios are well-equipped, using only ink and machines made in the USA (rather than China, for example) and observe scrupulous rules of health and hygiene born of their experience with cradle to grave free healthcare. Second, many Cubans doing tattoos are formally trained artists, having graduated from the Instituto Superior de Diseño Industrial (ISDI; School of Industrial Design) or the Instituto de Arte Superior (ISA; see Chapter 25), so their designs are original and well-drafted. Last, but certainly not least is the cost: for a fraction of what you would pay almost anywhere else on earth, you can get a professional, expertly executed tattoo and a one-of-a-kind souvenir of your trip in the bargain.

There are three Havana studios I recommend without reservation. Zenit Tattoo, led by the incredibly talented Ana Lyem, is legendary in Havana and you're guaranteed a great tat—whether it's created by her, or Mr. Black the other artist here. What's more, hanging out at Zenit, with its gregarious cast of characters in lovely seaside Sante Fe, makes for a fun afternoon. While you're out this way, you can get a fabulous, affordable lunch at La

China before touring the shell house—a home decorated floor-to-ceiling, inside and out, with seashells (the owner is going for the Guinness Book of World Records, literally). Meanwhile, Asol Perera got her medical degree, worked as a chef, and then decided to pursue her passion for tattoos professionally, opening Matrioshka Tattoo Studio a few years ago. She speaks fluent English and is easy to work with, ensuring your dream design translates beautifully into reality. And then there's Pepe Alonso, an extraordinary sculptor and wicked talented with the needle who prides himself on his original designs. Says repeat client Alfredo Carmenate, "These are works of art on skin instead of canvas." Pepe's World Map Tattoo Studio is centrally located and he also speaks English.

✳

My favorite Havana parlors:
Zenit Tattoo: www.facebook.com/zenittattoostudio
Perrera: www.facebook.com/assol.pereravechjaizer
World Map Tattoo: www.facebook.com
/World-Map-Tattoo-Studio

✳

93 Wi-Fi Parks

ONE OF THE MOST PERVASIVE myths about this island is that Cubans are without internet connections, that they're cut off from world developments, and stuck in time. Anyone who has watched a gaggle of Cuban teens re-hashing the latest *Game of Thrones* episode or is drawn into a discussion about Brexit or Putin's ties to the US Presidency knows this is pure folly. Sure, internet works differently down here—technically Wi-Fi is only available in public parks (though people bootleg off these connections in a number of ways) and most in-home connections are via frustratingly slow dial-up, the speed of which precludes streaming but allows access to almost everything else. To save time and money, we compose our emails offline, then connect and send them in batches. The fastest and most reliable connections, meanwhile, are in state offices and enterprises, one reason why some people hold on to jobs that pay a miserable $29CUC a month on average: the job is mind-numbing and poorly compensated, but there's Facebook and Twitter and YouTube all day long. There's also a vast, sophisticated intranet constructed by gamers so they can play "shooters" (Battlefield is huge) and multi-player survival games (Rust is now all the rage) with other geeks connected throughout cities across the island. SNet (short for Street Net) has news portals, gossip, and chat rooms, hook-up sites—the works. Cuba even has its own Craig's List, Revolico, where you can contract a plumber or buy anything from a house to antique pocket watches. And though much of this activity is not altogether legal, let alone authorized, the government lets it all flow. Hell, policymakers are glued to *Game of Thrones* too, anxious to see who will win the Great War—the living or the dead?

The point is, while Cubans are not connected 24-7 (due to limited bandwidth and severely limited finances) like most of the world, they find workarounds. Nowhere is this more evident and lively than in the 600-plus parks and public spaces across the island with Wi-Fi access. From the Isla de la Juventud to the remote southern coast, tiny towns like Caimito to bustling cities like Trinidad, parks are packed day and night with Cubans surfing the 'Net—often for the first time.

At some point in your Cuban travels, you'll probably want to check in with your job or family (reason enough to rock up to a park to connect), giving you the chance to observe the fascinating anthropological phenomenon of an educated, curious, and gossip-driven population getting connected en masse to the World Wide Web. You'll notice at once that this is an inter-generational affair: to your left there's a pierced, tattooed teen helping his grandmother enter her password, while across the way a baby opens and closes her fist, waving to her aunt in Miami during a video chat. The application of choice here for real time video chats is Imo; overhearing (and seeing) what Cubans do publicly on Imo is hilarious. You'll hear about visa paperwork and prison sentences, wives cheating on their husbands and husbands wooing a foreigner so they can ditch their wives and move to "la Yuma" (the good 'ole USA in

Cuban-speak). People show off new manicures, sandals, haircuts, and plastic surgery procedures on Imo and talk about their most personal issues.

✳

A full, searchable list of public spaces across the
island with Wi-Fi is available at www.etecsa.cu.

✳

Cubans are an open and immodest bunch by nature, taken to new heights when they're chatting in real time with faraway friends and family. Even for some, locals it borders on over-sharing and TMI (Too Much Information).

"I get so annoyed sometimes. I'll be talking to a client and the girl next to me is squealing about her new jeans," my friend Fahd laments. "Last week a lady was going on and on about her recent surgery and lifted her shirt toward her phone to show the scar! It was gross. I can't wait until we have Wi-Fi at home."

That day is coming—indeed, an ongoing pilot project launched in 2016 has installed high-speed, expensive, connections in thousands of Habana Vieja homes. But until these connections are extended to everyone, we've got Wi-Fi in parks, accessible using $2CUC cards sold by guys hanging out at the park good for an hour of internet. In other travel destinations you might go to the park to score weed and get high; in Cuba you go to the park to get connected.

94 *Agropecuarios*

IN 2015 THE CHANGE IN travel policies for US citizens sparked a tourist boom the likes of which Cuba has never experienced and is a topic of heated, daily debate both on the island and off. The effects are mixed and some (like gentrification and a shortage of housing, classified as Cuba's most serious and chronic problem) won't reveal themselves for a long time to come. But initial visitor figures are in and are nothing short of spectacular: in 2016, US arrivals to Cuba were up 74 percent from the year before and up a staggering 191 percent in 2017. Cubans working with (and over) tourists were quick to take advantage of the waves of Americans pouring into Havana, treating them as if they'd just fallen off the proverbial turnip truck. And some have, unfortunately. I've met many people who've come here for a long weekend without doing any pre-trip research or even looking at a map, and young Americans who spent their Spring Break in Havana getting shit-faced. Then there are cruise ship passengers who have only 36 hours in port—at the pace with which this island moves, time enough for a couple of cocktails and snapshots, if you're lucky!

My favorite conversation was with a millennial from San Diego who responded to my top recommendations about what to see and do by asking: "What's the Malecón?" That's like going to Paris and asking "What's the Louvre?" Being unprepared, uninformed, misinformed, or just plain naïve has revealed one of the immediate effects of the tourism spike: it has caused a commensurate increase in hustling and what Cubans call "folklore." Often uttered with lament or an outright sneer, anything harkening back to pre-1960 Cuba including convertible car tours and Sloppy Joe's, qualifies as folklore, as do most musical performances mentioning the Buena Vista Social Club or trios cranking out yet another version of "Lágrimas Negras" (or "Guantanamera," *por dios*). This rejection of cliché kitsch designed to hook tourists and part them from their CUCs has created a niche for "authentic" travel experiences, which can have its own patina of folklore and grift, but there are some real educational and participatory opportunities to get to know Cuba.

One of the easiest and most instructive activities even short-stay tourists can have is visiting the local *agropecuario*. These fruit and vegetable markets are the only place where fresh produce is sold (aside from people's porches and patios) and are part of the weekly—if not daily—Cuban grind. You can also buy beans and rice, plus meat and sometimes flowers at any "agro." Pro travel tip: nothing brightens up your hotel or casa particular room like a bouquet of mariposas. Known as white ginger lilies, these fragrant beauties are Cuba's national flower and were used during the revolution by Celia Sánchez to smuggle notes of tactical import from the Sierra Maestra mountains to rebels fighting in the cities. All prices in agros are displayed in *pesos cubanos* (CUP), one of which is equivalent to about four cents CUC. So when you see the price of a mango or avocado is five, it means you can buy four with $1CUC—and should get some change. Herein lies the first lesson in Cuban reality: appreciating what this currency can buy, keeping in mind that over 60 percent of the population earns their salary in *pesos cubanos*, to the tune of 600 a month.

Both currencies are accepted at agros, but for the full, local experience, jump on the end of the line at the CADECA (*casa de cambio*), sweat under the blistering sun, change some CUCs into CUPs, and go shopping.

Another pervasive myth here is that there is one currency for foreigners, another for Cubans. Wrong: anyone can use either currency. The second lesson an agro visit provides is that the produce hawkers at these markets are notorious for ripping off everyone—Cubans, foreigners, pensioners, children—they don't discriminate with their shortchanging and fixed scales. The butchers are the worst. You probably won't be cooking up any pork ribs during your visit, but take a turn through the blood-stained granite slabs staffed by jocular men in surgical scrubs and chainmail gloves to get a full sensory Cuban meat experience. The liquid-filled bags hanging over the meat are supposed to keep the flies at bay but don't, and you'll see every pig part for sale, including feet, heads, organs, even entrails and bones, which are used for dog food; kibble is not sold in Cuba and anyone with a canine pet has to cook for their four-legged friends. Notice the lines—especially at the markets where the state caps prices or anywhere when potatoes are in season. And don't miss Cubans' fanaticism for plastic bags; sold for 1 CUP at agros, they're stolen from state stores and though people wash (and rewash) them, Cubans are creating a lot of plastic waste with these bags known as a "fifth limb" because everyone carries one at all times in case they come upon bread, fried pork rinds, or lard-laced pastries while making their daily rounds. Or for when they shop in a state store, which won't have any plastic bags because they've all been stolen for resale.

95 *Finca Tungasuk*

YOU'LL REALIZE QUICKLY AFTER ARRIVAL that you can't believe everything you read about Cuba (besides this book, of course!). Seriously, though: myths abound about this island. One of the most pervasive? Cuba is an organic paradise. Like most myths, there's a grain of truth to this, but in reality, farmers who can grow pest-resistant crops faster, using chemicals, are more than willing. Debate around this issue is hot and heavy in Cuba, a country where the government guarantees every citizen a minimum amount of food via the ration card (known as the *libreta de abastecimientos*). They're meant to last a month, but hard economic times mean that the ration of oil, rice, beans, coffee, legumes, chicken, and other staples only provide 10 days, at most, of sustenance. Other government subsidies support local fruit and vegetable markets with capped prices—and long lines—to offset the cost of produce (much more expensive markets, known as "supply and demand," charge whatever the market will bear). These steps are necessary to ensure that none of the 11.2 million Cubans living on the island go hungry.

As in other parts of the developing world experiencing food insecurity, pesticides and genetically modified organisms (GMOs) offer an attractive, short-term solution for policymakers responsible for keeping the country fed. Cuba imports up to 80 percent of its food, sparking an aggressive effort to attain food sovereignty and sustainability, including the development of domestically produced GMOs, which has Cuban organic farmers and permaculture specialists up in arms—to the point that they submitted a petition to Parliament with 10,000 signatures requesting the brakes be slammed on GMO cultivation. It was only partly successful (or a total failure, depending on how you look at it): Cuba currently has small test fields of GMO corn and soybeans. And the debate rages.

In recent years Cuban has taken other steps to increase the possibilities of achieving food sovereignty, including allowing the formation of cooperatives. Several agricultural cooperatives within striking distance of Havana have taken up the challenge and are pursuing organic farming with admirable passion and dedication. Finca Tungasuk, part of the Jesús Menéndez Cooperative 20 miles west of Havana, is a family-run farm leading the sustainable, organic charge. Bordering the picturesque Coronela Reservoir, the Wilson-Cantarero family grows everything from cauliflower to passion fruit, yucca to bok choy, using organic, sustainable techniques and materials. Additionally, they dedicate part of their land to the propagation of medicinal herbs, from which they make tinctures, and to crops that are difficult or impossible to find in Cuba, like daikon, recommended by doctors for patients with chronic disease.

Intrinsic to their social mission is recapturing traditional fruit and vegetables that other farmers have abandoned in favor of more lucrative crops; the first time I and several of my Cuban friends tasted *mamey santo domingo* (looks like a fuzzy brown softball, tastes like a cross between an apricot and a mango) and *melon de castilla*, a type of cantaloupe to which Yemayá, the Santería goddess of the sea is partial, it was at Finca Tungasuk. They keep their prices low to make their produce as accessible as possible to as many as possible—a 100 percent organic head of broccoli from this farm costs a fifth of what Havana's (non-organic) supply and demand markets charge. Finca Tungasuk has also started an organic seed bank which they share with other farmers in their cooperative, fueling an enviable barter system: neighboring farmer Remache brings over his oxen team when Finca Tungasuk's fields need tilling and in return they give him seeds, vegetables, and share knowledge about organic farming, for example.

❄ www.tungasuk.wordpress.com

With advance notice, Finca Tungasuk provides volunteer opportunities for travelers wishing to learn about organic techniques and trends in Cuba—and who aren't afraid to get dirty! After you return from the fields, lunch is created from the harvested crops, prepared by Annabelle Cantarero who before becoming an organic farmer, apprenticed with a Parisian Michelin-starred chef. French, English and Spanish are spoken here.

96 *Bicycle Tours*

THERE'S NO BETTER WAY TO connect with the landscape, people, and currents of Cuba than pedaling about on a bike. Despite Cubans' prejudice—a hangover from the 1990s economic crash known as the Special Period when 1 million bicycles were imported as transport of last resort—cycle culture here runs deep. You'll see guys slowly pedaling with their girlfriends riding sidesaddle on the crossbar, a pastel-colored cake balanced in

a perfectly manicured hand and dads dropping their kids off at school, the little ones sitting on specially made wooden seats. There are bike parking lots everywhere and Cubans have made an art out of fixing flats, patching inner tubes with condoms and sewing burst tires with thick needles and thread. Cuba being Cuba, there are challenges to cycling here, including poor night lighting, the heat, air pollution, and of course, giant potholes in the middle of the street—or streets that are more holes than blacktop as my friend Santi liked to say. On the upside, the Special Period experience taught many drivers how to properly share the road with cyclists and the lack of motorized transport in general means traffic is lighter on Cuban roads and city streets than what you're probably used to.

*

The documentary *Rodando en la Habana* (subtitled
in English) by Cuban cyclist Jaime Santos
explores Havana's bike culture.

*

Known as a *"chivo"* (goat) or "faster" (because you get around faster!), bikes can be rented by the day/week for independent adventures. While there is no city bike rental system like you find in other popular tourist destinations (yet—I have it on good authority that it's coming), several outfits in Havana rent bikes with helmet and locks for as little as $10CUC a day. A couple of highly recommended places are Vélo Cuba, a women-owned and -operated business, and Cuba Ruta Bikes; both are pioneers in bike activism and tourism in Havana.

With either of these outfits you can rent bikes or sign on for a city tour led by cool, multi-lingual guides. Cuba Ruta Bikes also hosts a free city tour the first Sunday of every month, which makes a great way to get the lay of the land and meet like-minded travelers. For longer cross-country tours emphasizing Cuba's cultural and ecological heritage, WowCuba is the oldest, most experienced agency with medal-winning Cuban cyclists in their employ. On these tours you adventure to off-the-beaten track destinations—their promotional photo of a farmer peddling through the countryside, a goat slung across his back, is not Photoshopped!—with full road support and creature comforts at the end of the day. This agency, run by experienced cyclists and divers, is a good option for booking a Cuban scuba adventure, as well. Even if you're not up for one of their tours, their bar in Habana Vieja, Ciclo Cuba, is a great people watching spot and chock full of bicycle and motorcycle ephemera old and new.

*

Get on your bike and ride:
www.veloencuba.com
www.rutabikes.com
www.wowcuba.com

*

97 Paying Respect at El Cobre

THERE ARE SOME SURE-FIRE WAYS to bring a smile to a Cuban's face—a marriage proposal from a foreigner, a weekend at the beach, or an ice cold beer on a sweltering summer day. Invoking one of the perennial favorites of Cuban literature, culture, or sport is another: toss out a mention of José Martí, Teófilo Stevenson, or Pánfilo (the most popular comic in the country today, his prime time show keeps Cubans glued to their sets each Monday night), and watch the smiles erupt. But bust out some knowledge of La Virgen de la Caridad, the patron saint of Cuba, and you are going to make fast friends. Call her by her local term of endearment, "La Cachita," and drinks will likely be on them.

According to the story known to every Cuban, three fishermen were out on the Bahía Nipe on a tempestuous night in 1606, their humble vessel in danger of capsizing when a wooden statue floated by. The trio scooped her up and returned safely to shore, attributing their fortuitous voyage to the wooden virgin who wore a sign that said: "*Soy la Virgen de la Caridad*" (I'm the Virgin of Charity). It's a wonderful tale of divine intervention and salvation which is as powerful today as it was more than 400 years ago. But little is sacrosanct in Cuba, even the Virgen: as Fernando Martínez Heredia, Cuba's historian of singular renown and respect once told me, "Conner. Do you really think the fishermen who found her centuries ago could read that sign around her neck?"

Apocryphal or not, Cubans don't care (when I relate Martínez Heredia's comment to friends, they laugh and nod their heads in agreement), and a pilgrimage to her sanctuary in the church built high on a hill is as much a rite of passage as summiting Cuba's highest peak (see Chapter 98). La Virgen moved a couple times before setting down roots at her current home, the Basílica de Nuestra Señora del Cobre (built in 1927, it was declared a basilica 50 years later), 13 miles from Santiago de Cuba. Sitting amongst the emerald hills ringing the nearby defunct copper mine, the bright yellow church with terra cotta-tiled tower is an ethereal vision bringing Cubans in droves to pay their respects and plead for miracles—for a loved one's safe passage across the Florida Straits, for a paraplegic's ability to walk, for good results on upcoming university exams.

On Pope John Paul II's historic visit to Cuba in 1998—the first Catholic Pope to land in Cuba since the revolution—he made a pilgrimage to the Virgen, as has Fidel and Ernest Hemingway; the last donated his Nobel Prize for Literature medal to the Cuban people and it's kept here along with all the crutches, war medals, family photos, baby shoes, and other thousands of offerings made over the years. There are so many offerings here they occupy an entire room and there are surely more in storage.

The Virgen, dressed in yellow satin finery and dripping with beads, is kept in a glass case behind a small altar. All this emphasis on the color yellow is by design: the Virgen is associated with Ochún, a powerful deity (known as an *orisha*) in the Afro-Cuban religious canon, known for her dancing prowess and powers of love. Santería, Ifá, Yoruba and other syncretic religions overlaying Catholic saints with African deities and beliefs transported here by slaves are widely practiced in Cuba and there's absolutely no contradiction between having an Afro-Cuban *orisha* kept in a Catholic basilica. If you're inclined to get in her good graces, purchase some flowers—preferably yellow—in El Cobre, a town that depends economically on the pilgrims making their way to the Basilica, and lay them at her altar. Every September 8, the Virgen is taken from behind her altar and paraded around El Cobre, a perfect time to visit.

98 *Summiting Cuba's Highest Mountain*

EVERY CUBAN CONSIDERS CLIMBING PICO Turquino, the island's highest peak, a rite of passage. Given my addiction to nature, hiking, and iconic experiences, it was among the top items on my bucket list when I first moved here in 2002. I imagined a challenging, all-day trek through the towering trees of the Sierra Maestra, drop dead views, a bit of wildlife perhaps, and a sense of accomplishment as I reached the top.

As I mentioned earlier, travel expectations can compromise the actual experience. If I needed more convincing of the dangers of expectations, Turquino, as it's known colloquially, was it. First off, the summit is just a bit over 6,000 feet and a cake walk for anyone with hiking experience—and all visitors must be accompanied by a guide who is as disgruntled to be with you as you are with him (I did not meet any female guides, which is a feature of Cuba's machismo, I'm convinced: there are professions which women are actively discouraged from pursuing, like metalworking). What's more, the actual trek isn't a challenge, except for some very short ascents here and there and the views, while nice, aren't nearly as impressive as those from below, where the Sierra Maestra meets the sea (see Chapter 99, Cuba's Most Beautiful Road).

Attaining the summit is also a bit of an anti-climax since it's nothing more than a flat grass plateau surrounded by trees. The bust of Cuban apostle José Martí atop a huge marble base provides some compensation if only to contemplate how the hell they got it up there. Interestingly, Celia Sánchez Manduley, the first woman incorporated into the guerrilla forces in the Sierra Maestra, and her father lugged the titanic bust to the top on the centennial of Martí's birth. She was one tough cookie and according to Fidel Castro, the most important figure in the revolution. Though summiting Turquino is a national rite of passage, it always surprises me how many Cubans haven't climbed the country's highest mountain, usually because they don't have the money or the transport to make the trip. This trek can be a whole lot of fun if you're in good company—make some Cuban friends and invite them to accompany you.

Celia (2004, in Spanish) is the definitive book about
this Cuban heroine; in English, check out *One Day in
December: Celia Sánchez and the Cuban Revolution* (2013).

*

There are two routes to the summit, both of which have their advantages and pass through thick cloud forest festooned with orchids, ferns, multi-colored lichen, and the odd pig or two. One route originates from the Santiago de Cuba side, the other is from the province of Granma; link the two routes and you have a decent multi-day loop hike. The first route is steeper, but if you get an early morning start, you can reach the summit and descend in a day (plan on about 10 hours roundtrip). Sleeping over at the shelter atop Pico Cuba (3280 feet from the summit) is a good alternative if you want to enjoy the landscape and not go up and down in a day. The trailhead, where you contract a guide, is at Las Cuevas on Santiago de Cuba's southern coast;

sometimes they let hikers overnight here before ascending, but there are no facilities. The other camping option is at the La Mula *campismo*, 7.5 miles to the east of Las Cuevas.

The second route begins at Villa Santo Domingo in Granma (which is best reached using private transport) where you contract guides; the actual trailhead is at Alto de Naranjo. The eight-mile hike from here has better views and can be done over a couple of days, overnighting at the Pico Joachín shelter, before making an early morning summit of Turquino. The added value to this hike is that you can visit the Comandancia de la Plata, two hard miles from the trailhead, before setting out on the hike. This is where Fidel Castro and company directed troop movements, selected battle sites, and developed their strategy for the revolution. Radio Rebelde, the station which broadcast clandestinely across Cuba during the three years of fighting, first went on the air here; you can still tune in today, at 710 AM or 96.7 FM on your radio dial. There's a museum, field hospital and various war ephemera here—a visit to the Comandancia provides in-depth historical context for the hike. The options for sleeping the night before hitting the trailhead include the La Sierrita *campismo* (with basic cement cabins, single beds, and a fan), or the slightly more upscale Villa Santo Domingo, which is a hotel with individual cabins equipped with private bathrooms and nearby, a river for cooling off.

Whichever route you choose for summiting Turquino, you must bring all your food and bedding. And don't slack on the latter: I summited in August and was pelted by hail the size of walnuts during a nighttime storm. There is water along the trails, but it must be purified. Bringing some extra food and snacks for the guards at Pico Cuba and/or Joachín is a great way to make new friends.

99 Cuba's Most Beautiful Road

No, IT'S NOT HAVANA'S PICTURESQUE seaside drive, nor the famous engineering feat "La Farola" connecting Baracoa to the rest of the island. No, you have to work harder (and travel farther) than that to glimpse Cuba's most jaw-dropping landscape. And unlike those other cinematic routes, you'll need your own transport since taxis are reluctant to head so far afield and will charge an arm and a leg, so to speak. Besides, you'll want to stop often—to swim at a secluded beach or put your GoPro to good use.

Even in jaded, seen-that-done-that Havana, people's eyes grow wide and dewy at the mention of the coastal road connecting Chivirico to points west in Santiago de Cuba province. This is where Cuba's highest mountain range, that of revolutionary legend, the Sierra Maestra, plunges down to the batik blues of the Caribbean Sea with a skirt of palm trees framing the tableau. For more than 62 miles, your entire field of vision will be dominated by the variegated greens of the mountains, rivaling the undulating blue of the sea, which seems close enough at times to touch. It's enough to cause whiplash and you'll be hard pressed to just stay on the road, the view is that distracting. Luckily, you'll have the road to yourself since hardly anyone heads out this way and there is nearly nothing to speak of in the way of public transport. Drivers should still be on their toes, however, because horses and bicycles are how people make their way around in rural Cuba and the odd cow or goat (or chicken or pig) can always wander onto the road at a moment's notice. Rockslides are also a very real danger here, especially during the May–October rainy season.

Although I definitely tend toward the "fly by the seat of your pants" travel doctrine, this road is remote and lonely enough to argue for some preparation. The landscapes between Chivirico and Pilón (the first opportunity to head north, once the Sierra Maestra is in the rearview) are the most awe-inspiring, but there are zero services; if you're lucky you'll happen upon a limp ham and cheese sandwich or glass of yogurt sold from roadside stalls along the way. The last chance for provisions including water, snacks, gas, and toilet paper (at some point you'll be peeing—or something more dramatic—roadside) is in Chivirico going west, Pilón going east. Pack a picnic and get an early start to allow for the best photography opportunities and to beat the legendary Oriente heat.

Whatever your itinerary and pace, try to reach Chivirico (see Chapter 39) or Pilón before nightfall as there are very few accommodations along this stretch; the all-inclusive hotels around Marea del Portillo are, in my humble opinion, places to stay of last resort. Though beautifully situated and with decent snorkeling and diving, they are expensive and I've received first-hand reports of unsavory (and illegal) activities centered around here.

Seeing as this route hugs and bends along the base of the Sierra Maestra mountains, where Fidel and comrades hid out and fought for three years surviving on land crabs and other foraged food, slept in hammocks under tropical downpours, and nursed festering sores while trying to defeat Batista's well-armed troops, there are several sites of revolutionary import along the way. Heading west from Chivirico is palm-flanked El

Uvero, where outnumbered, ill-equipped rebel troops scored their first major victory against government soldiers on May 28, 1957. This marks the spot where the rebel army, numbering only a paltry 50 or so souls at this point, realized that triumph was possible—*sí, se puede*, as Cubans have been saying for decades ("yes, you can"). Further west, travelers come to Las Cuevas, trailhead for hiking to Cuba's highest peak, Pico Turquino, which is about as deep as you can get into the Sierra Maestra without getting into trouble—the entire range is considered a military defense zone.

✳

New York Times reporter Herbert Matthews hiked
into the Sierra Maestra in 1957 and published
The Cuban Story in 1961, rallying international
support for revolutionary forces.

✳

Hardy hikers can do a through-trek from Las Cuevas to the rebel headquarters, "Comandancia de la Plata," established by Fidel Castro in 1958. From this proper HQ, rebel forces consolidated their support and strategy, which led to victory later that year. A few miles after Las Cuevas is La Plata, site of another rebel victory, marked with a roadside monument. And beyond La Plata? Nothing for miles but mountains, crashing surf, and a visceral sense of trailblazing adventure.

✳

Once rebel HQ was established, they began broadcasting on Radio Rebelde. The station still exists;
turn your dial to 710 AM or 96.7 FM for the ride.

✳

100 La Isla de la Juventud

THIS IS A PLACE WHERE legends are made and thrive. Rebels caught during the attack on the Moncada Barracks (including the Castro brothers) were imprisoned here; famous Cubans hailing from La Isla include renowned artist Kcho (Fidel's favorite) and pop star Kelvis Ochoa, who hit it big by melding modern phrasing and riffs with traditional *sucu-suco* rhythms native to the Isla de la Juventud; it has one of Cuba's only English-speaking Caribbean settlements; and the entire southern chunk of its 1,895 square miles are set aside as a naturally protected area. Other distinguishing characteristics of La Isla de la Juventud include the diverse population, which has moved here from the length and breadth of the main island of Cuba, giving it a rich mix and vibe unlike anywhere else, plus some of the country's best scuba diving, off the island's western coast. This is also one of the top places to enjoy some slow travel and get to know Cubans—with only one traffic light, the preferred mode of travel is horse or bicycle, locals are genuinely friendly and helpful, prices are much lower than on the main island, and you'll likely not see another foreigner during your stay (you will, however, see and hear tons of parrots, endemic to this island).

Now for the bad part: getting here can be headache and frustration rolled into one. Options are limited to a bus/boat combo that may or may not be running when you show up (at the time of writing, four of the five boats composing the fleet that make this trip from Batabanó were out of commission), or plane. While the latter sounds faster and saner, the one plane making this trip is often re-routed to other domestic destinations when there are equipment failures. But quality experiences rarely come easy; persevere and you'll be rewarded with travel memories of a lifetime.

For total relaxation, the spacious beachfront bungalows at Hotel Colony on the island's western coast are just what the therapist ordered. The Colony, fronting a golden beach where starfish bigger than my head linger in the shallows, was inaugurated on December 31, 1958 with US dignitaries and dictator Fulgencio Batista himself taking the waters and feasting on local fish. It makes for a wild kind of vision, bobbing in the ocean, imagining the elite at the over-the-top inauguration celebration fleeing with suitcases full of jewels and cash just days later when the rebels entered Havana, changing Cuban history forever. These days, The Colony is the place to arrange dive trips with certified dive masters; these are boat dives with a minimum one-hour travel time to sites. Few divers make it out this way, which is a bonus because there's a good chance you'll have the boat and underwater scenery to yourself. The downside is with such low demand, the skipper and dive masters are sometimes slow to get on the water. Book at least a night longer than you might, in a beachside bungalow, not the drab rooms, to enjoy a long soak in the deep tub.

The southern part of the island is a protected area for which you need a special day pass, easily obtainable in the capital at Nueva Gerona, and private transport. It's not cheap, but very few foreigners make it down this way to the Sea Turtle Breeding Center, the Cueva de Punta del Este, with the largest collection of pre-Columbian indigenous cave paintings in the Caribbean, and the tiny town of Cocodrilo, settled by Cayman Islanders in the 1800s.

No visit to La Isla would be complete without visiting the cell blocks of the massive Presidio Modelo, a penitentiary complex with half a dozen round cellblocks that at its height held 5,000 prisoners. Built between 1926 and 1931, the most famous inmates were those who attacked the Moncada Barracks to launch the Cuban revolution. Walking around here, stepping into the cells, deciphering the graffiti and beholding the massive mess hall, vine and plants pushing through the floor, is a creepy experience. Meanwhile, the capital, Nueva Gerona, is dotted with pocket parks and is so chill, you don't even have to wait in line for ice cream at Coppelia. In Nueva Gerona I ate the most delicious fish sandwich, seasoned with garlic and parsley, to ever pass my lips in Cuba—all for five pesos Cubanos (that's 25 cents!).

Appendix 1
Cuba: A Necessary Primer

This island of 11 million souls is as slippery as a watermelon seed: it's hard to get a grasp on precisely what makes this place tick and how to navigate even the simplest travel tasks like procuring potable water or figuring out transportation. There's the double currency system (no small source of confusion for visitors), the language barrier, the dearth of cultural calendars, and Cubans themselves, who often take advantage of all the complexities to fleece the unsuspecting or uninformed. So this doesn't happen to you (too often, anyway!), I've devised this cheat sheet of tips, crafted over 15 years of being schooled in the ways of Cuba:

❋ Limit headaches and money scams by learning beforehand the exchange rate, terminology, and uses of the two currencies. Anyone, Cuban or not, can use either—it's when to use which where the confusion lies. Hard currency, known as CUC ("kooks"), convertible pesos, and *divisa*, is used for everything save local transport, fresh produce, and street food. While you can pay in CUC for these goods and services, prices will be quoted in CUP, also known as *moneda nacional* (MN) and *pesos cubanos*. The official rate is 24CUP to 1CUC (one kook is equivalent to $0.88USD). If you see a street pizza costs $10, that's 10MN or about 35 cents. You can tell the bills apart easily: CUCs are multi-colored and CUPs are monochrome.

❀ Money exchange bureaus are known as CADECAs (Casas de Cambio) and after hotels, are the most efficient places to change money; skip the banks, which have notoriously long lines. To procure CUP, you must first change your currency into convertible pesos and then change those into *pesos cubanos*.

❀ Learning a few words of Spanish will endear you to locals and smooth your travel path. *Permiso* means "excuse me" and is useful when squeezing through a crowd or interrupting someone to ask a question. *¿Último?* means "Who is last?" and should be employed on each and every line you join. This is a mechanism devised over decades of tedious line-waiting: you ascertain who is last in line, take your place, and then "pass the *'último"* to the next arrival. This way you know precisely who comes before and after you, allowing you to slip away for a beer or to sit in the shade while the line progresses, however slowly!

❀ Buying groceries in Cuba can be an adventure unto itself. Staples like beer, water, pasta, cheese, butter, chicken, etc. are sold in *tiendas* (literally "stores"), also known as *la shopping*. Save for a few exceptions these are poorly signed, but anyone on the street can direct you to the closest one. All fresh produce is sold in markets—either *agropecuarios* or *organopónicos* (at least some of the fruits and vegetables sold at the latter are organic). Eggs and all cuts of pork, from the feet to the organs and everything in between are available at *agropecuarios*. All prices in these produce markets are in *pesos cubanos*.

❀ Local transport comes in many varieties and price ranges; none of it is intuitive and takes a bit of practice. Crowded buses (*guaguas*, pronounced wawas) with pushy folks anxious to get where they're going, cost one *peso cubano* (pay as you board); no route maps exist and be on guard for pickpockets. Black and yellow *ruteros* are air-conditioned mini-buses with guaranteed seating. You flag these down and can disembark anywhere on their route (5 *pesos cubanos*). Fixed-route collective taxis known as *almendrones* or *maquinas* cost a minimum of 10 *pesos cubanos*, maximum 20, depending on the length of the route; most often these are pre-1960 Detroit hulks that you'll share with a gaggle of Cubans. Door-to-door taxis have meters but rarely use them. These are strictly in CUC.

* Scams abound in Cuba—from padding a restaurant bill to the long-play grift (bewitching a foreigner into marriage for a visa abroad is extraordinarily common, for instance). Many scams revolve around the double currency. Learning to distinguish between CUC and CUP bills and pricing is fundamental for not getting ripped off or short-changed. Another widespread scam is women pleading for milk, babes in arms—you buy the powdered milk in the store and they re-sell it on the black market. Just FYI: the government provides milk via the ration card for all Cuban children under age seven, diabetics, and others prescribed a special diet by their family doctor. Selling fake cigars or sealed boxes filled with sand or the 1 peso cheroots smoked domestically (people will approach you constantly, especially in Habana Vieja) is another bait and switch occurring with frequency in these parts. Not every Cuban is out to trick visitors, and it's important to remain open to serendipity and genuine solidarity; a good rule of thumb is to be wary of anyone who just sidles up to you on the street with some sort of charming (or not so) opening line. Regular Cubans don't have time or energy to approach strangers out of the blue.

* There's a saying around here (Cubans do love their *dichos*): "Real men don't eat soup. When they do, they eat it with a fork," which pretty much encapsulates the macho attitudes

of many across the island. This machismo comes in many veneers, including verbal come-ons known as *piropos*. Ask a Cuban, male or female, and most won't characterize it as harassment. The best approach is to take it like a *Cubana*: ignore them completely, make the dismissive sucking sound, very common here, known as "frying an egg" (you'll hear it everywhere), or throw down your own "get lost" response. Another time while I was walking my dog Toby, a man said "Beautiful dog for a beautiful lady. Does he bite?" To which I responded: "He doesn't, but I do." The guy beat a hasty retreat. If it gets too much, you can resort to wearing head-phones and listening to your preferred music, another strategy employed by Cuban women to positive effect. Just yesterday I saw a beautiful young *Cubana* walking down the street (wearing headphones) brandishing her middle finger with a smirk at two young men grabbing their crotches in her general direc-tion. All my male Cuban friends who saw it agreed it was base, gross, and highly disrespectful. Meanwhile, I applauded the woman for her confidence and counter-attack.

 ❀ Given that Cuba is such a safe, fun place to explore (kissy-kissy come-ons notwithstanding), travelers should consider ditch-ing the guidebook, grabbing a map, and heading out to lands unknown. There are some terrific off-line maps using GPS that can track and plot your route and have all the functional-ity you're used to back home (except Yelp!). In research for this book, I used and highly recommend Maps.Me. But when we hit a huge dip in the road on the 1946 Harley which served as transport during research, the smartphone went flying and I was glad I'm old school and had a copy of International Travel Maps Cuba—water resistant, highly detailed, and sur-prisingly current. This is the best hard copy map I've found.

Appendix 2
Online Resources

Travel Agencies & Info

- Regulations for US travelers to Cuba: www.treasury.gov /resource-center/sanctions/Programs/pages/cuba.aspx
- WoWCuba bike and scuba trips: www.wowcuba.com
- Harley-Davidson Tours: www.lapoderosatours.com
- Adventures in Good Company (all-women tours): www.adventuresingoodcompany.com
- Internet connectivity/cell phone in Cuba: www.etecsa.cu
- Avalon fishing and diving trips: cubanfishingcenters.com
- Windward sailboat charters: www.windward-islands.net/en /yacht-charter-caribbean/cuba
- Veló Cuba bike tours and rentals: www.veloencuba.com
- Cuba Ruta Bikes tours and rentals: www.rutabikes.com
- Caribbean Conservation Trust birding tours: www.cubirds.org
- Center for Cuban Studies & Art Space: centerforcubanstudies.org
- Topes de Collantes: cubatopesdecollantes.com

Sports, Fitness & Well-Being

- Surfing in Cuba: www.havanasurf-cuba.com/index.html
- National baseball schedule and info: www.beisbolencuba.com
- O2 Club: www.O2habana.com
- MHAI Yoga retreats: mhaiyoga.com
- Rock climbing in Cuba: www.cubaclimbing.com
- Scuba and snorkeling: www.cubadiving.org

For Culture Vultures

- Monthly cultural listings for Havana: www.lahabana.com /content/events-listings
- Artbooks by Ediciones Vigía: vigia.missouri.edu
- Fábrica de Arte Cubano (F.A.C.): www.fac.cu
- Mabel Poblet, Emerging Artist: www.mabelpobletstudio.com
- Instituto Superior de Arte (ISA): www.unfinishedspaces.com
- Carlos Acosta Dance Company: www.acostadanza.com
- Yissy García: www.yissygarcia.com/en
- Havana Curve Ball documentary: www.havanacurveball.info
- Literacy Campaign documentary: www.maestrathefilm.org

Festivals & Events

- Gibara Budget Film Festival: www.cinepobre.com
- Festival Internacional de Nuevo Cine Latinoamericano (Havana Film Festival): www.habanafilmfestival.com
- International Day Against Homo & Transphobia: www.dayagainsthomophobia.org
- International Women's Day: www.internationalwomensday .com

- Feria Internacional del Libro: www.filcuba.cult.cu
- Bienal de la Habana: www.biennialfoundation.org
  /biennials/havana-biennale
- Holguín's Romerías de Mayo: www.romeriasdemayo.cult.cu
- Annual Harley-Davidson Rally: www.harlistascubanosrally
  .com

Quirky & Queer

- Finca Tungasuk organic farm: www.tungasuk.wordpress.com
- National Center for Sex Education: www.cenesex.org
- Paquito's Blog (LGBTQI): www.paquitoeldecuba.com
- Zenit Tattoo Studio: www.facebook.com/zenittattoostudio
- World Map Tattoo Studio: worldmap@nauta.cu
- Matrioshka Tattoo Studio: www.facebook.com/assol
  .pereravechjaizer
- Havana's most luxe hotel: www.kempinski.com/en/havana
  /gran-hotel-kempinski-la-habana

Index

Acknowledgments

This book would have been impossible without my indefatigable support system which kept me fed (including spiritually), lent me places to lay my head and an ear for honing my off-the-wall ideas, made valuable suggestions, and accompanied me on many of the excursions described in these pages. My family stateside, including Sandra Gorry and Carolyn Gorry, whose contributions are too numerous to elaborate here, deserve medals: they helped me to the finish line holed up in a little cabin in the Maine woods, eating everything I dream of during Cuba's long, hot days (trust me: there will be a moment in your trip where you think "not one more pizza or ham sandwich!"). Any good writing I do is thanks in part to the unflagging feedback and encouragement I receive from fellow author and confidant Alexandra D'Italia—I'm so grateful I joined your writing group all those years ago, amiga.

What can I say about the team at Traveler's Tales? Each time I publish with this outfit reaffirms my faith in the industry; it's telling that I enjoy their titles equally as writer *and* reader. A special thanks to Larry Habegger for recognizing my expertise—16 years in the making and I thank him and his colleagues for providing me the opportunity to broaden my knowledge of Cuba through researching and writing this book. Were all publishers and editors like them.

I owe the deepest gratitude to *mi central* in Cuba, those people who allow me to do what I do and keep loving what I do. The Cuba Libro Team withstood my little spasms of author panic, keeping me well-caffeinated and our café/bookstore/oasis running with aplomb as I explored and wrote. To Douglas, Gaby, Angelo, Alfredo, Takeshi, and Yenlis: you are proof that small endeavors can create greatness and that family is made, not born. You are the future; live your dreams! Dear friends who provided input and catharsis (not to mention Toby care) during the research and writing include Iliam Suárez, Gail Reed, Chris Mills, and Rose Ana Berbeo—adventurous women all. Sorely needed intellectual stimulation, plus the occasional package of *jamón serrano*, was provided by my brother from another mother Pere Soler; thanks *hermano*. Kristen MacQueen and Abel Pez provided a transformative experience by introducing me to the Cuban Harley family so many moons ago; who knew how life-changing it would turn out to be! Thanks also to the entire MEDICC Review crew who endured several down-to-the-wire filings of my articles, improving them with their fine editing. Finally, José Salgado and I shared over 2,000 miles on the intrepid Kundingo, his 1946 Harley-Davidson, (re)discovering the beauty of Cuba during the writing of this book. The laughter and fun, peace and tranquility provided by him—not to mention gallons of good, strong espresso—helped me pull this off amid the craziness of Cuban life. *Mil gracias.*

About The Author

Conner Gorry is a New York writer and journalist who has called Havana home since 2002, where she works as Senior Editor for *MEDICC Review*, the only peer-reviewed journal in English dedicated to Cuban health and medicine. In addition to contributing to many newspapers, magazines, and anthologies, *The Best Women's Travel Writing* and *The Best Travel Writing* among them, her recent books include *Cuban Harlistas: Mi Amor* and *Havana Street Style*. Her blog Here is Havana has been called the "best writing that's available about day-to-day Cuba." In 2018, she published TWATC, a collection of poetry and prose, available at Cuba Libro, the English-language bookstore and café she founded in 2013. To celebrate the publishing of this book, she got a tattoo of Cuban Independence hero and native New Yorker, Henry Reeve.